Boy Soldiers of the American Revolution

Boy Soldiers
of the American Revolution

Caroline Cox

With a foreword by Robert Middlekauff

The University of North Carolina Press CHAPEL HILL

Published with the assistance of a gift from Eric R. Papenfuse and Catherine A. Lawrence

© 2016 The University of North Carolina Press
All rights reserved
Set in Espinosa Nova by codeMantra
Manufactured in the United States of America

Cover illustration: Detail from a picture of Washington reviewing the troops
at Valley Forge, made by John Andrew and published in 1856; reprinted in *The
American Revolution: A Picture Sourcebook* (New York: Dover Publications, 1975)

Library of Congress Cataloging-in-Publication Data
Names: Cox, Caroline, 1954–2014, author. | Middlekauff, Robert, writer of foreword.
Title: Boy soldiers of the American Revolution /
Caroline Cox; with a foreword by Robert Middlekauff.
Description: Chapel Hill : The University of North Carolina Press, [2016] |
Includes bibliographical references and index.
Identifiers: LCCN 2015039985|
ISBN 9781469627533 (cloth: alk. paper) |
ISBN 9781469627540 (ebook)
Subjects: LCSH: Child soldiers—United States—History—18th century. |
United States—History—Revolution, 1775–1783—Participation, Juvenile. |
Children—United States—Social life and customs—18th century.
Classification: LCC UB418.C45 C69 2016 | DDC 973.3/4083—dc23
LC record available at http://lccn.loc.gov/2015039985

To Victor Ninov

Contents

Foreword

In the years following the American Revolution, there has been a broad range of perspectives, sources, and subjects included in the books telling its history. The Revolution has been described as a forecast of the French Revolution with radical beginnings and a conservative ending, a work of God in this world or a sinful triumph of the Antichrist, a rising of the people or the work of a wealthy elite. These broad strokes of its champions and its enemies have not discouraged moderate interpreters. Several of such historians have even denied that what took place in America between 1775 and 1783 constituted a revolution. There has also been a multitude of interpreters who focused on the Revolution's ideas; some have concentrated on what they took to be its origins in economic grievances—and not surprisingly analyzed its politics in terms of a conflict of social classes. Others build their versions on actions of British officials and describe the whole affair as a crisis of the empire, an interpretation that can be made to accommodate the popular ideology and discontent of the "people," as well as the policies of imperial officials.

Just about every group that had a part in the Revolution has been studied and written about many times. Soldiers, Indians, blacks, women, merchants, lawyers, religious ministers, to list a few, have had their historians. And broader studies have tied together a number of these groups. In the last fifty years scholarly attention has shifted somewhat from a political emphasis to the social character of such groups and peoples. How the people involved actually lived—that is, acted in the Revolutionary crisis or were affected by it—has seemed as important as what they actually did.

This brief sketch of interpretations and their creators is only a sample of the immense variety and number of attempts to come to terms with the Revolution. Whatever one thinks of such efforts, historians' resourcefulness in finding "original" sources on which to base their arguments has been impressive. But as Caroline Cox's study demonstrates, there still remains opportunity for fresh questions and original work in untapped sources of the American Revolution.

To be sure there are aspects of it that seem so remote or elusive as to resist systematic study. One example of such elusiveness has been the experience of boys in the Revolutionary War. Scholars for many years have assumed that such experience could not be recovered, primarily because the sources—military records as well as other kinds of documents—did not exist. What boys in the Continental army and state militias actually did in the years 1775–1783, they assumed, must remain unknown. The sources for reconstructing their lives as soldiers in these years could not be found, if they even existed.

Caroline Cox did not agree and, before her death, wrote this book that proves these scholars wrong. Undermining other people's theories did not constitute an activity that she favored, but before writing this book her curiosity had sometimes carried her into unknown country. In fact, she had explored a number of questions that others had not taken on, or had delivered unsatisfactory answers to. In her first book, *A Proper Sense of Honor: Service and Sacrifice in George Washington's Army* (2004), she reconstructed the making of the culture of the Continental army through study of such matters as the differences between officers and men, an analysis of both class and status. This was a crucial question and essential to the character of one of the important institutions called into being by the Revolution. She uncovered materials in her research on class differences that had not been considered before—extending for example to burial practices, a finding that helped define the culture of both officers and enlisted men. In her second book, *The Fight to Survive: A Young Girl, Diabetes, and the Discovery of Insulin* (2009), Professor Cox opened up a new field in social and medical history. The book brought together the discovery of insulin treatment of diabetes and the experience of one of the first patients to receive the hormone. Perhaps the book's most fascinating feature is its telling of the life of this patient, Elizabeth Evans Hughes, who faced death with bravery and spirit. Professor Cox's book also provided an example of an extraordinary historian's imagination at work in a spectrum of sources that included medical records, technical analysis, embracing the thoughts and actions of medical researchers, and the resourcefulness of a young girl tormented by illness.

Writing about a girl with diabetes and the culture of officers and men in the Continental army calls for a broad range of talents and resolve. Caroline Cox certainly had such an array, especially of imagination and empathy. These qualities are on display in this book about boys in the Revolutionary War.

The most taxing problem Cox faced in writing this book lay in recovering evidence. The eighteenth century was not one in which written records were absent, and compared to centuries preceding it, documents and unprinted materials abound. If you want to learn something about the churches of New England in the seventeenth and eighteenth centuries, there are many church records available; or something about ministers of almost any of the colonies, there are hundreds of sermons still in existence. A similar abundance of written sources reveal much about politics and governance, the economy, slavery, Indians, schools, and colonial colleges. In fact, most subjects of interest and importance to the history of early Americans can be studied in the sources. This statement applies to the officers and adult soldiers of the Continental army. There are problems of interest to historians of the army for which the sources are thin or nonexistent. But much on these problems has been discovered, and much has been written about the army.

But information on boy soldiers—that is, soldiers younger than sixteen—is difficult to find. We know that compared to adults, few boys up to sixteen actually served, and of those who actually joined the army, or colonial militias, little has been known—little, that is—until Professor Cox undertook the task of finding the sources and composing an account of the boys' history. She proved to be an assiduous and resourceful searcher. She scoured collections of letters written by soldiers and others, memoirs and diaries, court records, statutes, local histories, among other materials bearing on the war.

Pension applications by veterans probably yielded more information than any of the other sources she used. Her search, she said, sometimes yielded rich returns, but often ended in failure. The pension records, and occasionally discharge certificates, gave up the most revealing information among all that she surveyed. These accounts had been closely scrutinized when they were first made in applications to a government official whose duty it was to judge their authenticity. This official, James Edwards, a marine in the War of 1812, from Virginia, judged applications for over thirty years. He doubted the truthfulness of many of the applicants, sometimes justifiably so, sometimes not, but he did provide continuity to the process of review. Caroline used the cases carefully and on occasion found Edwards's decisions lacking. In several ways, she had an advantage over Edwards, for she often had sources that he did not, and she examined the applications as a group; he looked at them over a long period and occasionally may have lost a consistent perspective because of the scattered presentation of the lot.

Although establishing the authenticity of an appeal for a pension required much of Edwards, it did not compel him to examine all aspects of the life of the applicant. In contrast, Caroline looked at everything present in an application—after all, her purposes were different from Edwards's. She wanted to know how and why a boy joined the army, or, in many cases, how he was forced to join. She wanted, after that matter was made clear, to reconstruct what the boy had done. Thus a boy's experience from joining up to the aftermath of his life in the war became her focus. Edwards did not need to conduct such exploration after he established the initial claim of the petitioner.

It is not surprising, given Edwards's methods and purposes, that the pension records were not always as useful as they might have been in establishing an account of a boy's experience in the army. Edwards's single-minded interest was in determining whether youthful applicants had served. He was skeptical of many of the appeals that came to his office. Once he answered questions about whether a boy had served, he had only to learn how long the service had been. When Edwards felt doubtful about the veracity of an applicant, he asked for more information; the responses he received might contain details valuable in fleshing out a picture of a boy's full military service.

Of all the sources available to Caroline in her work, these pension records were the most important to her research, slim or fat as they might be. Had they been her only source, she could not have written the book; fortunately she could call on other sources, and did to good effect. What troubled her most in putting her story together was the difficulty in creating a rounded account of boys' lives in the army, an account that provided a breadth of understanding that transcends the truncated experience of an individual soldier.

To establish what might be this sort of understanding of boy soldiers, she resorted to a technique found in books by other historians writing about questions for which empirical data was lacking. She used the sources available—pension records, letters, memorials, newspapers, and the like—to imagine soldiers' lives, or elusive parts of them. Readers of this book will discover that she did so tentatively, in such a way as to engage them in an attempt to establish a more complete reconstruction of the boys' experiences.

What was the process, she asks, that made soldiers of boys in the war? The process is reconstructed in several vignettes she sketched, each beginning with the sentence "Perhaps it was like this." There are six of these word-portraits in the book, fascinating pieces presented simply and honestly. She makes no special plea for these imaginative trials—her "perhaps" is to be understood that she is recounting possibilities. She might have made much of the fact that other historians trusted their imaginations to form such links. This practice, carefully explained and qualified as it is in her book, leads to broader understanding, and each case can be trusted; each is enlightening as it is here, offered by a historian who values evidence. Writing a book about boys in the Revolution required resourcefulness and sensitive imagination. Caroline Cox had both.

Robert Middlekauff

Preface and Acknowledgments

In this book Caroline Cox, who died in July 2014, sought to discover why American boys joined the army and what happened to them after they joined. Those questions about the experiences of boys brought her to other questions. Several deal with the war experiences of boys in America and elsewhere in the world. The experience of European boys in particular, in earlier times and different places, thus became a part of Caroline's account. She turned to such experience to make the history of the young in America clearer. A similar interest led her to explore the circumstances of such lives—the muskets some carried, the drums they played, for example, plus varieties of motives and feelings that are on display throughout their lives and service. These matters all have their complicated sides, all considered in this book with clarity and grace.

Caroline had help that scholars and friends provide. If Caroline still lived, she would wish to cite all who gave her assistance. I cannot list them all, and offer the following with the hope that those who came to her aid, but are not listed here, will understand.

Near the end of her life two scholars, Holly Brewer and Cori Field, gave her manuscript especially incisive readings. I know that Caroline would wish to have them singled out for their extraordinarily perceptive reviews. There are others who gave assistance, including several who gave criticism and advice almost from the beginning of the project. Diane Hill stands at the top of this list, along with Jacqueline Carr and Michelle Krowl. Patricia Lin was of great assistance to Caroline. The following may have given as much help as those just listed: Daniel Krebs, Stephen Hick, Holly Mayer, Judith Van Buskirk, Larry Cebula, Justin Clement, Lisa Trivedi, Kevin Grant, Jenny Hale Pulsipher, and Mary V. Thompson.

Caroline would have thanked again libraries and other holders of records for their assistance: Doe Memorial Library and Bancroft Library at the University of California, Berkeley; Huntington Library; John Carter Brown Library; Library of Congress; and the Mount Vernon Ladies Association. Her home institution, The University of the Pacific and especially the Department of History, had her gratitude, affection, and loyalty.

She would have acknowledged with much gratitude the [San Francisco] Bay Area Colonialists, an informal organization that she served with high concern and efficiency. Her co-leaders in the group, Dee Andrews and Mark Peterson in particular, earned her esteem.

RM

Boy Soldiers of the American Revolution

Introduction

As Well As I Can Recollect

Bergen Common Pleas
State of New Jersey
Bergen County

On the 21st day of October 1832 personally appeared in open
court before the judges now sitting being a court of record
so constituted by the laws of the State of New Jersey John D.
Piatt a resident of Piquan[n]ock, Morris County and State of
New Jersey aged sixty six years 17th March last who being
sworn in according to law, doth on his oath make the following
declaration in order to obtain the benefit of the act of Congress
passed the 4th June 1832.

So began the court record of John Piatt's application for a pension from
the United States government for his Revolutionary War military service.[1]
As soon as I read this paragraph, I knew that Piatt might have been a boy
soldier, one who had begun his service when he was nine, well under sixteen years of age, the cutoff I was using for this study.[2] He stated that his
memory was not sharp and that he was recounting events "as well as I can
recollect." The 1830s pension acts of Congress bade Piatt, like other former boy soldiers, to search his memories of events of a half century earlier.

The pension application process demanded from applicants a narrative of their service that emphasized battles and military leaders.
Courts wanted to know where a soldier had enlisted, under whom he
had served, where he had gone, and any notable events he had experienced or witnessed that might locate him in place and time. That way a
veteran's testimony could be checked against other surviving regimental
records when it was passed on to the pension office. A few veterans
offered vivid accounts of their service that provide details of day-to-day
life. Most offered only basic information.

Alas, John Piatt was among the latter. In December 1775, he had
enlisted with his father, Captain Daniel Piatt, in the First New Jersey

1

Regiment of the recently formed Continental army, the new regular army of the patriot cause. After their enlistment, his father having almost certainly signed any necessary papers on his son's behalf, Captain Piatt marched John and other local recruits to Elizabethtown to join the rest of the regiment. They then went to New York where they stayed until early spring. In court, more than fifty years later, John Piatt briefly recounted the events that then unfolded: "[They were] ordered to march to Long Island and from thence to Canada (the Regiment at this time commanded by Col[onel]. Winds) and proceeded toward Quebeck [sic] as far as Three Rivers, there had an engagement with the British, and retreated to Ticonderoga and lay there till late in the fall, or beginning of winter, and then returned to the State of New Jersey."[3] This was all he offered about the grueling journey to Canada, his first battle, the arduous retreat, the spring and summer of 1776 when sickness and death swept through the encamped troops, and his return to familiar terrain.

Missing from his testimony, of course, is any context for his experiences. And he had no reason to offer it. The people he was addressing, probably men a generation younger than he was, knew—or thought they did—something of his world. They did not need information they would have seen as superfluous; nor did they seek it. The facts they wanted were those that confirmed an applicant was indeed a veteran and entitled to a pension. Piatt gave them what they needed; he was granted his pension and his file contains little additional information.

If we venture into a broader knowledge of the multifaceted world encountered by boy soldiers of the Revolution—the demographic with which this book concerns itself—we must draw on a range of sources in addition to government pension records, the core database used. To vivify the lives of the boy soldiers, imagined—but carefully constructed— accounts of their circumstances are presented in each chapter, coupled with often tersely described experiences found in the historical documentation that anchor the pages that follow. The reconstructions are guided by a comprehensive knowledge of the period and setting, thus enabling the reader to gain a historically informed context for the boys' experiences. Some personal records from the era have survived by luck or accident: a letter tucked into the pages of a book, a receipt in the back of a ledger, a notebook or diary stored in a chest of old clothes. Others were carefully placed in boxes or tied with ribbon and handed down from generation to generation. All involve the decision by someone to make the document available to libraries or museums. Public documents, such as court records or pension applications, were often kept by the government bodies that created them. But in all these public or private records, few people felt inclined or saw a need to offer long explanations of the nature of their daily lives. Rather, each offers a piece of a jigsaw puzzle. Together, they create a picture of life in the era. As historian John Demos observed, "Some things we have to imagine."[4]

Although soldiers younger than sixteen are the smallest demographic of campaigners, does that make an attempt to collect their dispersed stories of little meaning? I think not. Foregrounding the voices of patriot boy soldiers for whom documentation exists is a worthwhile pursuit to widen the historical record, however slenderly, for individuals mostly overlooked and dismissed as peripheral to the larger story of the war. Their accounts still provide a window into the varied experience of childhood, work, and war in Revolutionary America.

Guided always by the supremacy of the primary documents, we can provide a reasonable, contextual sketch of some of these youngest soldiers' experiences, such as John Piatt's first year in the army. The sources that survive from him and his relatives are few. However, there is a broad range of other historical sources, genealogical records, other pension applications, memoirs, letters, and regimental records that survive from the era that provide information about military life generally and this campaign in particular. By piecing together other evidence, we can imagine his first year in the army.

Perhaps it was like this:

In early December 1775, John Piatt enlisted as a fifer in the First New Jersey Regiment. Or rather his father, Captain Daniel Piatt, enlisted him. His father probably thought service would be an interesting and useful experience for the boy and decided to bring him along. Back on the family farm, his mother and grandmother would manage with help from relatives, including John's older brother William. William was a staunch supporter of the patriot cause but he was waiting on the sidelines. He hoped he could secure a lieutenant's commission and so bided his time.

His father quickly took John and the other local recruits to join the full regiment gathering at Elizabethtown. Once there, no one seemed to pay any attention to him; the boy wandered around, looking at the scene with amazement. He had never seen so many people in one place before. It was a hive of activity. A few people were huddled around fires but most went about their duties quickly in order to keep warm. There were hundreds of soldiers and officers, horses and supplies. Men loaded carts with baggage. Sutlers, traders licensed to sell goods to the soldiers, were hawking their wares. Some families had come to say farewell to their menfolk. A few women and children arrived to travel with their husbands and fathers who were in the army. Officers and their sergeants were barking out orders. Men moved about, gathering everything they needed, shouting to the wagoners to move their carts. Some people seemed to know each other, calling out greetings to friends and acquaintances. Others worked silently or talked quietly, preparing cartridge packets containing musket balls and gunpowder, calming horses, attending to the business of setting the army in motion.

Although Piatt may have been a bit overwhelmed by the strangeness of it all, he was also restless with anticipation. All he knew about war and armies came from songs, adventure stories he had read, and games he had played. He had heard news of the war from his parents and uncles and listened to their raised voices as they talked about the political issues of the day. He heard them sharing the summer news that the Continental Congress had organized an army, and that the Virginian, George Washington, had been appointed commander in chief. He knew the patriot forces were besieging the British who were holed up in the city of Boston, but this was not much of a guide as to what he would actually be doing. Still, whatever it was, it would be different from his usual farm chores and schoolwork.

Piatt stood watching the bustle and recognized some of the men from his neighborhood. He caught sight of his father and his Uncle Jacob, also an officer in the regiment, but both were now too busy to pay much attention to him. The boy looked around to see what he should do and who might become his companions. He did not have to wait long to find out. The fife major called all his fifers together, and the boy found himself with the other musicians. They all had to learn to play their fifes. He was not worried about that. He had seen others play and was sure he could pick it up quickly. He discovered he would get to know the other musicians well. They would not only spend hours practicing; they would also mess together, sleeping and eating in the same tents or cabins. With luck, they would become his friends. He had traveled with his father to the muster unsure what to expect, but as the days passed he grew excited about the adventures that might lie ahead.

Little did he know he was in for a long, hard year. The regiment traveled from Elizabethtown to New York and from there to Long Island. Then, in late spring, they set off for Three Rivers in Quebec, on the St. Lawrence River in Canada. Most of the 500-mile journey was on foot, although on rivers and lakes there were bateaux, flat-bottomed boats, to transport them. Sometimes, when tired, he might have thought of sneaking onto a cart, hiding himself amid the baggage to ride a few miles. But that was risky as his father or some other officer was likely to give him a few sharp blows if he were caught, so it was hardly worth the trouble. They trudged along for miles on trails that became almost impassable with mud when it had rained.

When they arrived at Three Rivers in early June 1776, they found themselves almost immediately in action. They met a sizable British force and the regiment was compelled to retreat to Ticonderoga, more than two hundred miles away at the southern end of Lake Champlain. They stayed there as the warm summer set in, but it was a frightening time. Many around him fell ill with fever, including some of the other musicians. It was a deadly couple of months, but Piatt stayed healthy and tended to the needs of his messmates. In late fall, the regiment made its way back to New Jersey, mostly on foot, to join Washington's army.

In December 1776, as they all crossed the Delaware River into the safety of Pennsylvania, it may have felt to Piatt he had tramped over the length and breadth of the country. Not quite, but he had certainly covered more than a thousand miles.[5]

BUT JOHN PIATT'S military service was not over. Although his deposition offered scant details of the next few months, we know that his father, now promoted to major, was sent to raise recruits in Pennsylvania. He took young Piatt and a few other musicians with him to attract potential candidates. Meanwhile Washington and his troops made a successful, surprise attack on Hessian troops at Trenton on Christmas Day 1776. Piatt's recruiting party rushed back but missed the excitement. They marched onto Princeton a few days later, but if Piatt witnessed or participated in that battle on January 3, 1777, young John did not comment on it. It was the sight of the "dead and wounded in the college," the College of New Jersey, now Princeton University, being used as a hospital after the battle, that stayed in his mind over the intervening decades.[6]

After this hectic activity, the regiment went into winter quarters and Piatt finally had a chance to rest and probably play. But in spring, he was badly hurt when the colonel's horse kicked him. He suffered no permanent damage, but he was sent home to recover from his injuries. The regiment, and the war, moved on without him. It was shortly after his eleventh birthday—and his career as a Revolutionary War soldier was over.

THE PRESENCE OF boy soldiers in a European army in the late eighteenth century was not unusual. The British, French, and Hessian forces that fought in the Revolutionary War also had boys among them who usually served with their fathers or other male relatives, but they were proportionally fewer than their patriot counterparts.

However, military service by boys was a new phenomenon for the colonists of British North America. In earlier colonial wars, no more than a handful of boys are identifiable. Soldiering was seen as a hard life for hard men. Even though boys everywhere worked on farms and in workshops and merchant houses, adults did not consider a military campaign suitable employment for them. Even steady army pay and the bounty, a cash bonus for signing up, had not sufficed to attract boys or their families. The presence of boys in the ranks of the patriot forces during the Revolution may be a sign of the army's desperate need for manpower as the war dragged on as well as the desperate economic calculations of boys' families. The fact that boys (and their families on their behalf) began to see the army as an acceptable and valuable source of employment is an important part of the story of childhood in this era.

Boys were in the ranks from the beginning of the conflict and their numbers increased as the years passed regardless of where they lived in relation to the military campaigns. Bounty payments were an attractive lure to boys and their families, especially as the wartime economic crisis deepened. But more importantly the great variety of short- and long-term service options gave boy soldiers the opportunity to revisit any decision. In the militia, service could be from a few days to two months. Even in the Continental army, terms ranged widely from a few months to lengths of service well short of the maximum of three years. Also, over time, strong community networks crossed from civilian to army life, allowing military service to be viewed as another work option. Boys rarely served without being near someone they knew. The substitution system, which allowed any male to serve in the place of a drafted man in either the militia or Continental troops, also drew boys into the military. Young sons and other relatives did not need to be paid to go in a father's, uncle's, or neighbor's place. In other words, army service became enmeshed in the same patterns by which boys had often entered the civilian world of work. Many families considered any boy old enough to work to be old enough for military service and were guided more by a boy's physical maturity than any prescribed minimum age in making their decision.

A variety of other factors drew boys into military service in the American Revolution. Some were enlisted to fight by their fathers. Others made their own decisions to serve and were eager to earn money to give to their families, or to get away from a boring job, a new stepparent, a strict father or mother, or a harsh guardian. Some were inspired by the rhetoric they heard around them in political songs, speeches, and sermons. And they were drawn to service through their community networks, enlisting alongside relatives or neighbors. Some, like Piatt, trailed their fathers into the service the same way they followed them into other work activities on the farm or workshop.

Whatever drew boys to volunteer, the army did not actively discourage them. They were more useful than they had been in previous centuries. New, lighter weight, and easier-to-use muskets did not require the great physical strength to carry that had been necessary in the early days of gunpowder weapons or in the era of the pike. The eighteenth century also saw the widespread adoption of the snare drum as the critical instrument of military communication; drummers could now split the beat and play a range of readily distinguished patterns. Boys could easily carry and play this small drum. The fife, a small, side-blown, wind instrument, was also a new instrument to army life and playing it a task the young could do. With these changes, boys joined the lines of battle rather than remaining servants in camp.

It is impossible now to know the age profile of the patriot troops during the American Revolution. Too much information is missing. During the war, not all officers were diligent in their record keeping, as the commander in chief, George Washington, frequently lamented. Fewer still saw the need to retain muster rolls or other administrative records after the war. The total number of men who served remains elusive, and a number of about two hundred thousand for all who served in all branches of the military for any length of time is the midpoint of the range of estimates. Historians in recent years have only been able to reconstruct the age distribution of small groups of soldiers for brief moments in time and place. Most of the soldiers in these groups were between thirteen and fifteen, but some, like John Piatt, were as young as nine or ten.[7]

Piatt's story survives because, when he was over sixty years old, he applied for a government pension. To do this, he had to go to court and give a deposition about his experiences. His friends or family or former officers who would provide testimony to support his claim had also to go to court with him to be deposed. Some future questions from the pension office could be resolved by mail, but many claimants who had to provide additional testimony made several trips to court to provide their answers. Piatt's surviving pension file, and those from hundreds of others from war veterans who served when they were very young, help elucidate military life and provide additional context regarding childhood in colonial and Revolutionary America.

Boys were legally under their fathers' control but that played out in a variety of ways. Some sons showed their fathers deference. Others found their parents willing to accommodate their interests. A few fled the constraints of home. Whatever the family ties, all children could be buffeted by death and loss; working was central to their lives from a very young age; and the journey to adulthood varied greatly. By studying these boys and their lives, we can expand what little firsthand knowledge we have about childhood in this period. Through the pension records, we can glean information about roles they played in the army, cultural forces that encouraged them to enlist, dynamics between generations, their work options, tensions surrounding their financial dependence, and the part military service away from parental supervision may have played in accelerating boys' desires to be masters of their own fates.[8]

BASED ON A general examination of the colonial views of youth, this study uses age sixteen as a cutoff between boy soldiers and their older comrades in arms. But in any era, the age categories of boyhood or childhood are hard to pin down. Consider present contradictions in the United States. An eighteen-year-old can vote and serve in the military but cannot buy an alcoholic drink. In Illinois, thirteen-year-olds are too young to drive cars or buy cigarettes, but they may be tried as adults if they commit serious or violent crimes. Under federal law, girls under eighteen do not need parental consent for an abortion, but in many states they need it to get a tattoo. Legislatures and courts have wrestled with the issue of the age at which children can make responsible decisions, and as these examples indicate, they have not been able to establish a general rule. Context is everything.

Eighteenth-century society was equally inconsistent. The words "boy" or "girl" were then commonly used to refer to a wide range of ages, having been applied to those in their twenties who were immature or simply unmarried, to someone of slight build even if not young, and even to someone much older but of low social status, such as a servant or slave. Legal history guided some usage. In ancient Roman and medieval canon law, infancy was defined as between birth and six years old; childhood was from seven to fourteen; youth from fifteen to twenty (or twenty-eight in some aspects of canon law); and adulthood followed. In English common law, by the late eighteenth century, anyone under twenty-one was a minor. But in many social settings, these categories were not hard and fast. Schools and colleges did not force children into age categories until later in the nineteenth century. In any teaching setting, whether school or private home, children of all ages were together in one room. In college, students ranged in age from about fourteen to late twenties. In applying the label boy or girl, people cared more about physical stature, social status, or economic dependence or independence.[9]

Census takers were equally inconsistent in their categorizations of children, and the categories they chose often reflected local needs and interests. In French Canada in the 1730s, an administrator at Fort de Chartres in present-day Illinois did not record the ages of those classified as children at all. But he did note how many white children in each town were "legitimate" and how many were "Orphans and Bastards," reflecting both moral and material concerns. In the same decade in New York, the census used age ten as a demarcation between children and adults. That may have been the age at which local children were confirmed in the Church of England, to which most of the ruling English elite belonged, or the age at which more productive labor commenced. Whatever the reasoning, the age division did not survive long. In the census of 1746 taken during the emergencies of King George's War (1744–1748), public officials wanted information that met the community's immediate needs. The population was now broken down into those under sixteen, those sixteen to sixty, and those over sixty. This grouping matched the age requirements to serve in the colony's militia. The militia was a force within each colony used for local defense, and, in New York, the law required males between the ages of sixteen and sixty to serve.[10]

Colonial people showed more consistency about the age at which children could take on the responsibilities of paid work. Many families thought twelve was about the right age for children to enter formal apprenticeships. Benjamin Russell, for example, was thirteen when his father apprenticed him to the Massachusetts printer Isaiah Thomas. But children could be bound out to work at much younger ages either by parents unable to cope with the number of mouths to feed or by the courts. Samuel Dewees's impoverished father bound his son out at age five to a local farmer to work in exchange for his keep. Town officials in Middletown, Connecticut, seeking a home and employment for an impoverished seven-year-old, Rebecca Baxter, bound her out to a tailor so she could learn that trade.[11]

Even very young children, such as Dewees and Baxter, were expected to contribute to their own keep if circumstances required it. Courts and municipal authorities wanted to protect vulnerable children but they also wanted to be relieved of the cost of support as quickly as possible. While there were local variations, all expected children to work in exchange for the food and shelter offered no matter how young they were. Magistrates often had other social imperatives. They wanted to be sure poor children were inculcated with good work habits so they would grow up able to support themselves. Also, courts sometimes took children from families they saw as unsuitable, because they were very poor or fatherless, for example, and placed them in more economically successful families with a father or father figure at their head. While children bound in early childhood would have had limited economic value, they would soon grow and be able to take on more demanding labor.[12]

But the limited abilities of the very young caused some to set a higher age for children's usefulness. Some slave traders used age ten as a cutoff because their human commodities below that age did not fetch so much at market. Potential buyers saw a slight child as not capable of heavy labor. Still, children as young as ten could be valuable. At the beginning of the eighteenth century, slave traders on the West African coast purchased "small boys & girls of 10 years of age and upwards." This was because, as the administrators for the Royal Africa Company told the agents at the company's trading fort, Cape Coast Castle, they were useful to fill up spaces on ships. However, near the end of the century, in one of the first accomplishments of the nascent abolition movement, the British parliament passed a law that used a different definition of childhood. The "Act to Regulate the Carrying of Slaves" assigned a fixed amount of space for all slaves on ships. In it, children were defined as those who "shall not exceed four feet, four inches in height."[13]

While slave traders were concerned with physical maturity, some people were reconsidering emotional maturity. Enlightenment thinkers such as John Locke in his *Essay concerning Human Understanding* and Jean-Jacques Rousseau in his book *Emile* emphasized that the young did not have the ability to reason as adults. Rather, reasoning was a skill learned as children matured, and acquiring it was a long and individual journey. Influenced by this thinking, adults reconsidered the ages at which children should take on critical religious, social, and civic responsibilities.[14]

These ideas percolated unevenly through western society. However, as historian Holly Brewer has shown, the age at which society considered that a child might make a mature, reasoned decision rose in Britain and its colonies during the eighteenth century. For example, at the beginning of the century, fourteen had been the minimum age for jury service in most colonies and was usually linked to the ownership of a minimum amount of property, but by the end of the century it was largely restricted to men over twenty-one, often still with a property requirement. Many ministers similarly felt that children could not make informed decisions about their faith. In the seventeenth century, Puritans in New England believed that children under five had the necessary understanding to enter into covenants with the church. But over time religious leaders questioned whether children so young could really understand that commitment. By the mid-eighteenth century, few children under fourteen covenanted.

The age for militia obligations had risen similarly. In the Elizabethan era, English militia laws required any "man childe" over seven to train for service. However, by the time of the Revolution, there was no obligation for boys to train and the minimum age for militia service was sixteen in all North American colonies except Pennsylvania and Delaware where it was eighteen. Society was grappling with new thinking about child development and the resulting realization that the journey to adult maturity was a long and variable one.[15]

If eighteenth-century society reflected varied understandings of who was a child, then Revolutionary legislators and commanders of the patriot forces had only slightly greater clarity. They knew they needed youths or men who were up to the physical demands of soldiering. They held firm to the minimum age of sixteen for militia obligations, although substitutes could be younger. But in the Continental army, there was no legal minimum age. There was a moment in January 1776 when the Continental Congress was not even sure that anyone under twenty-one could be trusted with an enlistment decision. It resolved that such a soldier could, "within 24 hours after such inlistment [sic], obtain his discharge," but only if he immediately returned the bounty and any equipment he had been given. Later in the year, as the war went badly for the patriots and military enthusiasm waned, it abandoned this grace period. In November 1776, the Continental Congress set broader guidelines and directed recruiting parties to enlist "able-bodied men, not under sixteen years of age," and senior officers agreed. Thereafter, the demarcation of who constituted a "boy" soldier was guided by the militia regulations and recruiting orders and, with a few exceptions, focuses on the lives of boys who began their service when they were fifteen or younger.[16]

IN RECENT DECADES, historians have made great strides in exploring the different strands of children's experience: the fluid yet rising age of consent, the options available to young children and those who controlled their lives, the opportunities to acquire skills, and the impact on young lives of familial death and illness. But scholars have been hampered by the lack of sources. Historians have uncovered little firsthand information about children's lives for any century prior to the twentieth. Letters, diaries, or journals written by children before the modern era are rare, and those that do exist are mostly from elite families. In the eighteenth century, diary keeping was not yet common. Most were kept by merchants or prosperous adults as they traveled or underwent a religious transformation. A few craftspeople and traders kept them as a brief daily record, but if a young child created one, it has not survived.[17]

The difficulties and cost of procuring paper, making a quill pen, buying ink or making it, all created barriers to writing for most eighteenth-century American children, even if they knew how to write. And letters were difficult to send. Using the colonial post office was expensive and useful only when sending letters to towns along the few well-traveled post roads. Otherwise letters were most easily transmitted through friends and neighborhood connections. Even if all these difficulties could be overcome, children and their parents, guardians, siblings, or friends needed to be some distance away from each other to create the need for letter writing. All this meant that the few letters from children of this period were not only mostly from prosperous families but were also written in late teenage years.[18]

This does not mean we know nothing about what colonial children were doing. The population of British North America was young—about 50 percent of the population was under sixteen—and references to them litter the historical record. Apprentices and other young indentured workers and slave children crisscross the account books and diaries kept by merchants, shopkeepers, and craftsmen. Court or poorhouse records also offer rudimentary information on the community's most unfortunate children. For example, the court in Talbot County, Maryland, paid a widow to care for Mary Cartwright, "a poor, decrepit girl," and after their father's death, dispersed and bound out the Macway children, Patrick, Elizabeth, and Anne, to homes among his friends and neighbors. But in these sources, writers noted only what was being done by children or for them.[19]

Some adults wrote about what children should be doing. In the seventeenth century, some colonial legislatures weighed in. The Massachusetts General Court lamented "the great neglect in many parents & masters in training up their children in learning, & labor, & other imployments" and recommended that "boyes & girles bee not suffered to converse together" lest it lead to "wanton, dishonest, or immodest behavior." By the eighteenth century, colonial governments had given up on attempts to legislate children's behavior, and instead books such as William Buchan's *Domestic Medicine*, William Cadogan's *Essay upon Nursing and the Management of Children*, and others offered advice about how children should be raised and educated. But while these sources offer us some guidance about what adults hoped for the children around them, they also indicate that others perhaps thought some children were not living up to social standards.[20]

We have further detail about children's lives in this period from adult observers, typically parents or tutors. For example, Elizabeth Drinker, a prosperous Philadelphia Quaker, recorded the daily activities of her children, even noting when their sleep was interrupted by the light of a "fier in Elfriths Alley." Philip Vickers Fithian from New Jersey lived for a year on Robert Carter's substantial Virginia plantation teaching Carter's children and other young relatives. In letters to friends and in his journal, he spelled out the daily routine of their lives marked by a ringing bell ("which may be heard some miles") and the accomplishments, or failings, of his charges.[21]

We do have a few records created by colonial children themselves, but these are usually from those who were elite, educated, and older, such as seventeen-year-old Eliza Lucas. Her wealthy father had moved his family from the island of Antigua to South Carolina and then returned alone to the Caribbean. Her mother was sickly, and Eliza shouldered responsibility for the management of the mainland plantations. Because of this role (and fortunately for historians), she did what many planters and merchants did—she kept a letter book in which she kept copies of all her correspondence. She wrote to her father "on business of various sorts," and about the joys of her "Musick and the Garden," and her pleasure in her father's "little library." Another young South Carolinian about the same age, John Laurens, also wrote to his father when separated from him. John and his two much younger brothers were taken by their father to England and Switzerland for their education, and John reported on his activities after his father returned home. But letters like these are scarce.[22]

Adults' reminiscences of their childhoods are by far the most important source of information about the lives of children in colonial America. However, these memoirs, whether written for family or published, usually did not focus on childhood but on some noteworthy accomplishment of the authors' later lives. The events of their childhoods were incidental. The most famous reflection on childhood from this era is the autobiography of Benjamin Franklin. His rags to riches story, beginning with his days as a hungry runaway apprentice roaming the streets of Philadelphia has become iconic. Like many memoirs, his is that of a man who went on to great achievement, acquiring both fame and fortune.[23]

There are a few memoirs from ordinary men and women, but childhood moments are usually only mentioned in passing. The former slave, Venture Smith, remembered being purchased for "four gallons of rum and a piece of calico [cloth]" before being transported to Barbados and then Rhode Island. Morgan Lewis of New York remembered his delight in going to school and finding a piece of sausage in his lunchtime basket, which he then cooked "on the shovel in the kitchen of [the] school house." These sources are scarce, and, like the recollections of more famous authors, they are shaped—or misshaped—by the distortions of memory, a desire to celebrate or condemn some person, choice, or event, by the personal experiences of the intervening years, and the interests of the intended readers.[24]

THIS BOOK DRAWS on all these, the few letters, court records, civilian and military memoirs, and one other vital source—veterans' pension applications. Servicemen who were permanently disabled and the widows of men killed in the war received pensions shortly after the conflict ended. In 1818, Congress granted pensions to long-serving Continental army and navy veterans who could demonstrate pressing financial hardship. Over the next decade, eligibility steadily expanded. In 1832, pensions were awarded for service to any man (and later his widow) who had been in any branch of the military for any length of time, without regard for his or her need for support. Pension applications are often overlooked by historians because they are difficult to work with. The records are organized strictly alphabetically, a system of great service to the pension office at the time and to later genealogists. However, finding a particular group of veterans, in this case those who served when they were boys, is like looking for a needle in a haystack, necessitating diligence and perseverance. The records, held in the National Archives in Washington, D.C., were microfilmed in the 1970s and digitized forty years later, but names and the states in which soldiers enlisted remain the only means of sifting through them. Applicants sometimes provided their exact dates or years of birth. More commonly, they only offered their ages at the time of their pension applications. Finding even a few hundred of the applications from men who served when they were boys required some creativity, and about one hundred or so of these provide meaningful information about the veteran's experience in the Revolution and insights into perceptions of childhood during this time of transition. Small as this sample is, it increases significantly the number and diversity of sources about childhood; pensions were available to all men who could prove their service without regard to race, ethnicity, age, or social status.[25]

But pension applications have their limitations. Pension applications oblige focus on patriot boy soldiers and their lives. They do not illuminate the lives of all children or even all children in war. Women and girls are largely absent. Only one woman, Deborah Sampson, wrote a military memoir and received a pension on her own merit. She was in her twenties when she served, masquerading successfully as a man for about a year and a half. Widows, when they applied for pensions through their husbands' service, began the accounts of their own lives at the time of their marriages and are silent on their childhood stories. Sometimes a sister or female cousin offered an important childhood reminiscence in her deposition to support an applicant, but she rarely dwelt on her own story. In these, she might present a family scene she had observed while she was at work or play.[26] Court records occasionally offered darker tales of girls' vulnerability to the ravages and dislocations of war. Two young New Jersey girls, Elizabeth Cain, age fifteen, and Abigail Palmer, about thirteen, gave depositions in which they testified that British soldiers "had ravished them both." But the soldiers were not present to face trial. The girls' depositions were simply passed to the Continental Congress and nothing more is known of them. Firsthand accounts of girls' experiences are difficult to come by but they make only scanty appearances in the pension records.[27]

Neither do the pension records tell us the experience of all boy soldiers. Those, free or slave, who served with the loyalists, fighting alongside or supporting the British army, received no pensions from either side and therefore their stories are not known. It is possible that a few boys were among the slaves who, early in the war, fought with and supported the British after the British offered freedom to slaves who came to their lines. But the British position quickly became inconsistent as the war progressed. Southern slaves followed the possibilities for freedom and weighed their options carefully. The British edict did rob patriot sympathizers of a valuable resource. However, loyalists were slave owners too, and while some slaves indeed found freedom and left with the British at the end of the war, the British seized others as part of the spoils of war, gave them to loyal plantation owners, or sold them for profit. Loyalist regiments, those organized and led by colonists to fight alongside the British, came to exclude slaves from serving, and few presented themselves to try to do so. Blacks of any age became a rare sight in their ranks.[28]

Among white loyalists, some boys enlisted alongside their fathers. John Peters, who served as a lieutenant colonel in the Queen's Loyal Rangers, wrote to a friend after the war and referred to his eldest son, at fourteen, having been with him in the Rangers in 1777. Peters was recounting his own hardships and only mentioned in passing those of the rest of his family. Earlier in the year, after harassment by patriot sympathizers, he had led his wife and eight children from their home in New Hampshire to Canada in a harrowing journey in which his eldest son had carried his toddler brother for prolonged periods. From Canada, Peters led his new military command alongside a British force under General John Burgoyne as it marched south into New York toward Saratoga, where they were defeated by the Continental army and patriot militia. Peters, wounded, was given permission to return to Canada with what was left of his Rangers before the surrender was signed, as it was unclear what the status would be of loyalist prisoners of war. His eldest son now had to aid and support Peters through the woods on the long and arduous journey back to the rest of the family in Montreal. Peters's letter indicated that two more of his sons later served (each beginning his service around twelve or thirteen) as the war dragged on, but he never names them, and there are no records from the boys themselves of these experiences. The stories of boys who fought on the losing side are lost.[29]

Nor do the records include all patriot boys. The majority of them did not serve in the military. Among the boys who did serve, some died either during the war or in the decades between the war when pensions became available. Their stories too are lost. Also missing are the stories of many of the patriot boys who went to sea. They were only eligible for pensions if they had served in the Continental navy. Some did, but the navy was small, only about sixty vessels, and boys on board were proportionally few. A greater number served on privateers, ships authorized to prey on enemy shipping in the hope of earning prize money. More than sixteen hundred such vessels were licensed. Service on these ships was specifically excluded from pension benefits as these were private enterprises, not state military service. However, some boys moved between the militia or army and work on-board a privateer. They made pension applications on the basis of their land service but sometimes included information about their sailing days. Thus, there were a few boys in the Continental navy and others who were sailors and soldiers who recorded something of their choices or experiences at sea, but information about most boys on privateers is not available in the pension files.

The pension records provide us with a concentration of boys' stories as no other set of sources can. Some applicants provided additional information at the behest of a fraud-sensitive pension office, which was eager to verify that the men were telling the truth. In those cases, the pension commissioner, James Edwards, asked pressing questions. He wanted to know how and why they came to enter the service as boys when "no law required it." In response, the veterans told their stories.[30]

Edwards, a former marine from Virginia who ran the pension office for over thirty years (1818–1850), was probably born shortly after the Revolution. As noted above, during the eighteenth century, attitudes toward children and childhood responsibilities had shifted, and those changes continued in the beginning of the nineteenth century. Edwards's decisions in the pension office were inconsistent and reflected both the shifting political and legal world around him and his own experience. Sometimes he accepted a very unlikely story from an applicant that could be corroborated by muster rolls and all other available evidence and, on other occasions, he challenged seemingly pedestrian tales as impossible. For example, Edwards questioned Ebenezer Couch's straightforward account of his enlistment at thirteen to serve as a soldier and waiter under his officer father. Couch was surprised that the pension commissioner doubted that he had served at such a young age. After all, when Couch had been posted to West Point in 1781, where both militia and regular troops were encamped, there were a number of soldiers "who from their appearance were not older if as old as I was." These boys, Couch argued, "could not perform the duties of a soldier better than I could." Couch convinced Edwards of his truthfulness and received his pension.[31]

But other pension applications Edwards dismissed quickly, particularly those from men who claimed to have held positions of authority when they were under sixteen. No boys that young were appointed as officers by state legislatures or the Continental Congress. There were a number of officers in their late teens, most famously the French nobleman, the Marquis de Lafayette. But any application for an officer's pension by someone who said he had been appointed when he was under sixteen was rejected. One of these was from John Updike of Rhode Island who claimed to have been an adjutant, the administrative aide to the captain of a company or colonel of a regiment, when he was fifteen. The pension commissioner had no doubt the boy had served and awarded him a soldier's pension—but not an adjutant's. That position, after all, was usually held by a junior officer, and Edwards did not believe the boy could have held that post. Updike and his defenders made a strong case that indeed he had. He served initially out of military necessity. From the earliest days of the war, the British were committing all kinds of depredations on the shores of Narragansett Bay, burning buildings and stealing cattle, and the militia was repeatedly called out. Updike served as a substitute for his father when he was fourteen. But, in addition to his willingness to serve, the lad had two other important assets. Young Updike, according to those who knew him, was an "extremely active and useful" youth "of good education." More importantly, he was from "one of the most respectable families in Rhode Island" and a "wealthy and influential one." For these reasons, he claimed, he had been appointed adjutant. But the pension commissioner was having none of it. Edwards wrote that at age fifteen Updike's orders would not have been respected, "recognized and obeyed."[32]

Edwards's views represented shifting attitudes toward age and power. In the European world and in much of the colonial period, less wealthy neighbors would have deferred to a young boy from a powerful family. By the beginning of the nineteenth century, as Holly Brewer observed, the limits on children's rights and abilities to offer informed consent meant that they could not "exercise authority over themselves or others" in a broad range of legal and political matters. It is possible that young John Updike was indeed deferred to by those who knew his abilities. But, by the time Edwards was reviewing the pension records decades later, he considered it "not very probable."[33]

During the decades Edwards spent in the pension office, he was never completely at home with the fact that boys had served in the Revolution. An applicant such as Rufus Beckwith, who applied in 1832 and who had served when he was about eleven, was as puzzling to him as Benjamin Peck, who joined the army as a ten-year-old and who had applied for a pension more than twenty years earlier than Beckwith. In 1818, applying on the basis of financial need, Peck had to prove his poverty, which was easily done. Despite a few possessions that hinted at a more prosperous past, a "turning lathe" and "looking glass" for example, he had recently been in a debtor's prison, and it was probably only being eligible for a pension that allowed him to get out so he could apply and begin to pay his creditors. Not only his youthful service and age at application (forty-eight) made him stand out; it was his dependent, who was not a young child or spouse but his eighty-eight-year-old mother. To support her, he noted, was his "legal as well as moral obligation," but he needed to receive a pension to be able to do it. Despite this early experience with this former boy soldier and many others at the time and over the years, in 1832 Edwards was surprised to receive an application from Beckwith who had served at age eleven. He had been a waiter to a captain who, although not his father, had raised him for many years. In denying Beckwith's claim, Edwards wrote that eleven was simply "too young for him to have been a soldier as no persons of an age less than 16 years were liable to be drafted" and neither would he "have been allowed to volunteer." Yet the many applications he had seen and approved indicated that while the first point may be true, the second was not.[34]

There were probably four reasons why Edwards was suspicious about applications from boy soldiers. The first was the practical one that he simply lacked the necessary muster rolls and other regimental records to corroborate a veteran's service. Secondly, he could draw on his own military experience as an officer during the War of 1812, and then he had seen hardly any children in camp or in the lines. Historians of that war, with much better data at their disposal, confirm that boys were a rarity. Between the outbreak of war in June 1812 until it ended in February 1815, about sixty-two thousand men served. They were a mature group, with an average age of just below twenty-seven, and more than half of them were over twenty-five when they enlisted. Most joined for only short terms in what turned out to be a brief war. When recruiting soldiers for this war, officers accepted very few below the minimum age of sixteen. And for the militia, the minimum age everywhere was now eighteen, making it harder for very young substitutes to slip into that branch of the service. A handful of boy soldiers appeared in the ranks: John Hallmick, a nine-year-old from Virginia, enlisted in 1813; and Amasa Holden, an eleven-year-old from Massachusetts, was assigned to "learning music" when he enlisted in 1812. But they would have been lost in the adult crowd.[35]

A third reason why Edwards did not expect to see boys in the lines was that, since the Revolution, public debate increasingly connected citizenship and soldiering. Citizenship had come to be associated with having an informed, reasoned understanding of issues and problems. Thus children were explicitly excluded from a range of civic and social responsibilities, such as jury service and testifying in court as credible witnesses. Early in the eighteenth century, children as young as four could testify in court, but by the beginning of the nineteenth century, fourteen was, in most states, the youngest at which adults believed a child could fully understand what it meant to give evidence under oath. The guiding question was always who could make reasoned decisions on a subject. The Militia Act of 1792, in which Congress set up uniform standards for all state militias, set age eighteen as a minimum for this important civic obligation, and states adjusted their militia laws accordingly. The new federal constitution allowed only men over twenty-five to sit in the House of Representatives. According to James Madison, this decision was easily reached because there was a broad consensus by the drafters of the document that younger men were simply not mature enough. Summarizing the discussion in his notes, Madison quoted George Mason, who noted that even young men of twenty-one held opinions "too crude and erroneous to merit an influence on public measures." It was not surprising then that Edwards was sometimes puzzled that young boys had served. Citizenship, its rights and responsibilities, was associated with mature adults.[36]

Lastly, part of Edwards's suspicions had nothing to do with the former boy soldiers at all. When, in 1818, the federal government introduced pensions for Continental army and navy veterans who could demonstrate financial need, the office had been overwhelmed with applications, a number of which were fraudulent. A scandal ensued and Edwards, working at first under Secretary of War John C. Calhoun, brought order to the system, stamped out abuse, and restored the integrity of the program. As the pension system expanded, Edwards remained vigilant about fraud.

Over the decades, there were more than eighty thousand applications from veterans or their widows. Edwards, who became the nation's first pension commissioner, zealously protected the integrity of his office—even if it meant challenging that of those applying. Thus, many applicants had friends and neighbors who came forward to testify that the applicant was a man of "good moral character" and had a reputation for "truth and veracity."[37]

If his name was not on a muster roll, a veteran could produce one piece of unimpeachable evidence of his service—a discharge certificate. Palfry Downing, who had enlisted in Massachusetts shortly before his sixteenth birthday, had one signed by George Washington, no less. But many soldiers did not get such certificates and those who received them did not see them as important or potentially valuable. Some kept them for a few years; many lost them long before pensions were granted. Without a name on a muster roll or a discharge certificate, most men could only offer detailed information about their service and the testimony of friends to support their claims. As the veterans reminisced, they revealed details of their lives, and both family tensions and childhood adventures came to light.[38]

WHILE REMINISCENCES FROM veterans and others are vital tools, they are, of course, burdened by the problems of the fallibility of human memory. It is hard for any of us to retain clear images of particular events and our emotional and practical responses to them. Many of the veterans' applications began, as John Piatt's did, noting that he was relating events "as well as I can recollect." The joys and travails of later life shape the way we remember and even what we remember. Individual memories become blurred with those of family or friends. Shifting cultural and political attitudes toward an era or new ideas also alter people's recollections. And personal memories of key events, such as those experienced by soldiers in wartime, become intertwined with larger national memories of the same occasions, such as parades and speeches on July 4 or the anniversaries of battles. For example, a man who participated in the great patriot victory at Saratoga in October 1777, would, at the time, only have been aware of his small corner of the battlefield, and even right after the victory would not have known that the defeat of the British would alter the course of the war. But as the years passed it became clear that the victory was critical in turning the tide of the war, prompting the French to enter on the American side with its military and financial resources, and also drawing in the Dutch and Spanish as allies. Later still, victory parades and annual celebrations, speeches of commemoration, and books on the subject, would infuse people's recollections.[39]

Sometimes memories are subject to contradictory forces. Memories fade as the years pass, yet memories of intensely emotional events such as wars may be more vivid and lasting. Distance of both years and miles may allow people to view some experiences more objectively. But sometimes memories are colored by values, ideas, or attitudes acquired later in life, making the recollection more subjective. People may celebrate, and perhaps even aggrandize, their youthful accomplishments or sufferings. They may have an image or legacy to protect. But the elderly may also be less concerned with what others think of them and lose inhibitions when revealing certain aspects of their lives that are less than noble.[40]

And there are more problems. Going to court and giving a deposition in itself put the veteran in a stressful situation, especially in an era when most Americans had no contact with the federal government beyond going to the post office. All writers, whether writing for family, publishing their reminiscences, or applying for a pension, may have reasons to be less than completely honest. Published memoirs can be especially problematic. After all, writers are creating public identities and may want to present themselves in a particular way to their audience. Veterans' memoirs had an audience of at least family, neighbors, business associates, and fellow church members among many others. Perhaps the writer had a reputation to maintain or enhance. Pension applicants wanted to receive a pension. Their testimony had an audience of a local jurist, the pension commissioner, and sometimes family and friends. It is easy to imagine others, awestruck or nervous, carefully editing their reminiscences. All these problems have to be borne in mind when reading these records.[41]

However, there were some practical aspects of the pension application process and the conventions of memoir writing that make the family information reliable. Military service was the focus of applicants' testimonies, and any discussion of the journey toward enlistment and other details of family life were incidental and less subject to exaggeration or alteration. In the application process, local officials taking depositions tried to elicit dates, locations, names of officers served, and battles fought. For memoir writers too, their audience was primarily interested in their military exploits, and the information about their family circumstances that brought them to enlistment was given only to get the hero to the real meat of his book, his wartime adventures. For both, information about family life was tangential to the real narrative.

But sometimes it was the family circumstances that were, in fact, the more enduring memory for the veteran. That was the case for Samuel Younglove, recalling his service as a fourteen-year-old militiaman. He experienced combat for the first time at the Battle of Bennington on the New York–Vermont border in August 1777. It was an important patriot victory as it undermined the advance of British General John Burgoyne and his army as they traveled south from Canada. Burgoyne's defeat at Saratoga followed almost two months later. However, in neither his pension application nor his short memoir written for family members did Younglove give significant details of his enlistment. He simply noted that he "took a very active part in the battle." As an old man, it was the death of his beloved mother at the end of the war, a blow from which it took him many years to recover, on which Younglove focused. Similarly, when Jonathan Brooks of Connecticut wrote his account of the fateful day when the British stormed the fort at Groton Heights in Connecticut in September 1781, the day's military events had equal time in his account with a drama on the home front. Jonathan and his father left to join the fort's defenders, but before they rode away, his father gave instructions for the rest of the family to go to a safe place, a farm "two and a half miles distant." He directed Jonathan's seven-year-old and five-year-old brothers to herd the family cow to the farm and advised his mother and sister to pack up other necessities and make their way there too. Later that day, Jonathan arrived at the safe farm only to find his mother frantic with worry. The two little boys had never arrived— and neither had the cow. Jonathan's mother told him to "get up on the horse and go look for them." Jonathan remembered that, exhausted, he "did go and rode and rode" for hours but found "no tidings of the boys." The children (and the cow) finally turned up, and, years later, the hours of frantic searching figured significantly in his recollections of the day. This shifting terrain of memory and the tension between objective and subjective memories are things to keep in mind as we read the recollections of the Revolution's youngest warriors.[42]

The experiences of Revolutionary War veterans who served when they were boys deepen our understanding of military life and offer a window into society's changing and sometimes contradictory ideas about who had the capacity, physical and intellectual, to serve, and who had the responsibility to do so. Boy soldiers' experiences help us grasp the nuances of family life that are otherwise hidden and allow us to explore a range of individual journeys from boyhood to manhood, from dependence to independence. They focus our attention on a brief period—the 1760s (the decade most of them were born) until the end of the war in 1783. The veterans' accounts show the halting, changing, and incomplete nature of ideas about maturity. And their stories confirm, despite a legal system giving fathers control over their children, that the vagaries of daily life, strong personalities, and the shifting events of war sometimes gave boys room to take an active role in shaping their own lives.

Each chapter in this book begins with an actual pension record and a reconstruction of that pension applicant's experience as a boy at the time of the Revolution. While these reconstructions required some historical imagination, they are grounded deeply in verifiable historical sources.

CHAPTER ONE

Answer the Purpose

The State of Alabama
County of Blount

On this 7th day of September in the year of our Lord one thousand eight hundred and thirty three personally appeared in open Court before the Court of Blount County now sitting George Hoffstaler, [*sic*] a resident of Gurleys settlement in the County of Blount in the State of Alabama aged seventy years who being first duly sworn according to law doth on his oath make the following Declaration in order to obtain a Benefit of the Act of Congress passed June 7th 1832.

That he enlisted in the service of the United States under the following named officers and served as herein stated. That on the first of August in the year 1778 he enrolled himself as a volunteer for the term of nine months in the militia or state troops of North Carolina to serve as a private therein the Company of Captain David Cowan . . . and he was enrolled for the term aforesaid under an offer from the Congress of the United States or the State of North Carolina of a Bounty of one hundred Dollars. [After duty guarding Guilford Court House, the Dan River, a brief furlough, and marching to Briar Creek] The deponent was in the Battle fought There where Gen[eral] Ash was defeated. . . . The Light Infantry and all that Escaped with us swam the River and joined General Rutherford's Army on the Carolina side. Col. Lytle Lost Many of his Men. Some were killed and others were drowned in attempting to swim the River. And after our defeat at Briar's Creek we were marched to and engaged in the assault on Fort Stono in the summer following Gen. Ash's defeat.

. . . I was born in Frederick Town in the State of Maryland and in the year 1763 from the best of my information. I have no record of my age. My Father Died when I was about thirteen years old. I went to Salisbury, North Carolina where some of my relatives lived and I resided there when I first entered the service.

Perhaps it was like this:

George Hofstalar fell to the ground exhausted. The order to rest had finally been given. It was the evening of March 3, 1779, and darkness had long since fallen. It was a cold, damp night, and his clothes were still wet from his swim across Briar Creek and his struggle through the swampy ground where the creek flowed into the Savannah River. His company and other North Carolina and Continental troops were in full flight from British and loyalist soldiers. Before he gave himself up to sleep, he looked around and noticed how few of his friends were with him. Some, he was sure, would catch up with them during the night. But the afternoon had been confusing. He had no idea how many of his company had been killed or wounded in the short battle, but he knew that some had drowned crossing the creek. Despite its name, Briar Creek was really a river, more than sixty feet wide with deep, fast-moving water. Once they had made it to the other side, they marched away as quickly as they could and later heard British soldiers calling to each other as they searched the swamp for patriot stragglers. At one point, he thought he smelled smoke, and his sergeant told him that the British had probably lit the brush in the swamp to light their way and flush out anyone hiding. But now all was quiet. The British had given up their search for the night, and they were temporarily safe. He knew he should sleep, but he strained to identify the strange sounds he heard in the darkness. His old home in Maryland seemed a long way away.

His father's death two years earlier had led to a lot of changes in his life. He had been born and raised in Frederick Town, Maryland, a small but bustling county town founded in 1745 by German immigrants. When his father died, Hofstalar was sent to live with an aunt and uncle on their farm in Salisbury, in Rowan County, North Carolina. It was awkward being in a new family, but he was familiar with farm labor, and he pulled his weight when he worked alongside his cousins. Like his hometown, Salisbury was small but lively. It was only recently settled, but it was the county seat and had a small courthouse, public buildings, and farmers and traders passing through. But he had to adjust to his new community. His relatives were closely tied to other German families in the area, and they argued all the time over minor differences in Lutheran Church doctrine. Hofstalar listened carefully, kept quiet, and learned which families shared his relatives' opinions, who he could speak to and who not, and tried to fit in. In the summer of 1778, when he heard that there was a bounty of one hundred dollars to anyone enlisting, he was eager to go. He was not sure if his uncle would consent, as Hofstalar was only fifteen, but he did. His uncle went with him to the recruitment post at the tavern in Salisbury to sign his enlistment paper to serve for nine months. They said their farewells, and the boy went to stand with the other recruits.

The soldiers set off in high spirits, but their first few weeks of service were challenging. They marched in the summer heat more than sixty miles to Guilford Court House and from there to the Dan River (another sixty miles), carrying heavy packs and muskets. But the next weeks were better. Hofstalar made friends among his fellow soldiers and enjoyed their company. And they stopped marching great distances. Instead, they stayed around the Dan, standing guard and scouting until his unit made its way home on furlough for a few weeks.

When his company was called out again early in 1779 to keep a close eye on British movements south of Augusta, Georgia, their hard marching took him to the limits of his endurance. They tramped for miles day after day and food ran short. Hofstalar's pack seemed to get heavier and heavier. His shoulders ached, and after one particularly rainy and miserable day, his skin was raw where the straps rubbed his shoulders. This was his condition before the British attacked at Briar Creek and the company had to flee.

Now he laid in darkness, his body aching, listening for sounds of the enemy until finally he fell asleep. The next morning, he woke slowly and heard the order to march. He staggered to his feet; an older soldier showed him how to make his pack more comfortable on his painful shoulders, and the company walked on at an easier pace now that their lives were not in danger. Soon they met a wagon carrying food supplies, and that lifted everyone's spirits. Hofstalar dragged himself along; after a few days, he felt he had almost recovered from his ordeal. Over the remaining months of his enlistment, his company continued to wear out a lot of shoe leather. They tracked the movement of British troops and engaged in a few small skirmishes. Hofstalar returned home in September 1779. Overall, his months in the army had been tiring but satisfying, and the following year, a mature seventeen-year-old, he enlisted again, only this time in a mounted unit. He never wanted to march again.[1]

DETAILS DRAWN FROM HOFSTALAR'S pension application, from community records, as well as from facts surrounding the battle at Briar Creek allow us to imagine Hofstalar's experience during his first year of service and to consider the ways in which young soldiers were both useful and encumbering to an eighteenth-century army. Hofstalar was eager and resilient. Like many boys his age, he had worked before joining the army. But he had neither the knowledge nor the stamina of an older youth or man. He was probably unaware that his presence had worried his officers and some of the older soldiers, all of whom kept a special eye on him. He was strong enough to use a musket in combat but struggled to carry it long distances. After only a mile or two, he began to slow down, altering the pace of the entire company.

Having the stamina for a march was important. In the eighteenth century, and for many centuries beforehand, armies often did little fighting. They engaged an enemy when they had to, or when it was to their obvious advantage, but commanders usually avoided clashing with one another, because that could be expensive in manpower and matériel. During the American Revolutionary War, in particular, where both sides needed to mobilize political and logistical resources in creative ways, the opposing generals preferred to target each other's strategic posts, supply lines, or foraging parties, and otherwise wear each other down.

These generals led armies in states that were able to purchase and deliver supplies in the field. But even experienced quartermasters, the officers in charge of these well-developed administrative systems, often found this difficult to accomplish. It took a combination of political will, money, manufacturing ability, and transportation networks to keep an army equipped and fed on a campaign. Yet even when these elements were in place, the rebellious colonies and then the new United States were often short of horses and wagons. In November 1776, when thirteen-year-old slave Peter Brooks Nelson—enlisting for three months in Massachusetts with his master's permission rather than at his request—set off to join Washington's forces in New York, the troops had virtually no equipment. A few weeks earlier, Washington had written to Congress to report that the soldiers coming to join him were without "a Single Tent or a necessary of any kind . . . not a pan or kettle." Fifteen-year-old soldier Joseph Plumb Martin of Connecticut confirmed these hardships. His company joined Washington's forces at the same time, and he was sure he got sick after sweating from exertion during the day and then lying on wet, cold ground at night. It was a happy moment when he found some dry leaves and "made up a bed of these and nestled in it." A friend foraged some food for him and found turnips and "some boiled hog's flesh." Intermittent shortages of basic necessities made life grueling.[2]

It was these tasks of survival that occupied soldiers through much of history. They had to be able to repair their equipment (or even make it), to endure the inefficient supply lines that delivered food of uncertain quality, to forage for food when none arrived, and finally to cook whatever they had been able to garner. When not doing these tasks, soldiers had to march great distances, carrying all the tools of their trade and their own few possessions, turn their hand to building the structures in which they might live and the defensive works they might guard. They would cut trees, build roads, and haul themselves and the army's war matériel across great swaths of territory, and feel, alternately, content, miserable, bored, exhausted, and frightened.

If this were not difficult enough, tired and poorly fed soldiers, often living closely together in camp, were vulnerable to disease. There was no clear knowledge yet of the direct connection between poor hygiene and illness, although experience indicated there was one. Poor sanitation led to a variety of illnesses such as dysentery, bloody diarrhea, typhus, a flea- or tick-borne fever, and typhoid, contracted from drinking contaminated water. Any respiratory infection spread quickly among them. Soldiers' lives were at much greater risk from disease in the army than in civilian life. For example, during the Seven Years' War (1756–63), the last major war before the Revolution, Massachusetts provincial troops, in a few short months of service, were four times more likely to die from disease than they were in a whole year spent at home. European armies routinely lost three times more men to illness than battle, and these statistics became much worse if the army was operating in an unfamiliar climate, exposing the troops to new pathogens. Soldiering was a hard life, and that meant the preferred recruit for any army was a man who could withstand its rigors.[3]

Could boys under sixteen be good and useful soldiers? They certainly could not carry loads as heavy or march as far as some of their older comrades, but they were hardy and could recover quickly from the demands placed on them. Mostly coming from the countryside with little exposure to the pathogens of the larger world, boys were vulnerable to the diseases of camp life, but probably no more so than older soldiers if they also had previously little contact with crowds. But boys' health and long-term stamina was not on recruiting officers' minds. They focused instead on boys' lack of physical strength. For example, in 1779, fourteen-year-old Simeon Hewitt stood before Connecticut militia officers hoping to be taken as a substitute for his father for two months of service. The militia was a force drawn from the community to deal with local emergencies for brief periods. But even for this short period of time, the officers wondered whether he was strong enough to do the job. His father had come to see the officers the day before to suggest the substitution. The officers consented to it provided, Hewitt later recalled, his father agreed "to return if I did not answer the purpose." The boy duly presented himself, and the officers looked him over. They concluded that he would indeed "answer the purpose," and the boy served.[4]

But senior officers were always annoyed to see boys in the lines. They simply did not think they were useful. Lord Barrington, the British secretary of war at the beginning of the American Revolution, thought "young boys" were so useless that recruiting them was an "abuse" that amounted to a "fraud on the public." George Washington felt the same way. In 1776, he ordered that when "any boys or decripid [sic] persons are brought into the Service," they would be discharged. The officer who enlisted them would, he threatened, "be chargeable with the Expence they may be to the publick." This threat was not carried out, but other senior officers shared his sentiments. Barrington and Washington probably had no particular minimum age in mind or much information about the troops recruited for the service when they complained of boys in the line. They were simply looking at troops and noting that among them were those who looked too small and young to be useful. American General Arthur St. Clair was probably equally ignorant of the exact age of his soldiers when he lamented that many of them were "mere boys, altogether incapable of sustaining the fatigues of a soldier." St. Clair, writing to Governor James Bowdoin of Massachusetts, explained why he had ordered his forces to abandon Fort Ticonderoga in the summer of 1777. Surveying his troops, he had noted their youthfulness, assessed what they might be capable of, and acted accordingly.[5]

Not surprisingly, the boy soldiers themselves had a higher opinion of their abilities. When they were old men applying for pensions, they and their witnesses emphasized their physical strength. Samuel Branch, who enlisted at age fourteen, insisted that even though he had been "very young for a soldier," he was a "pretty good size for my age." Thirteen-year-old Bishop Tyler "was a great boy and stout & strong." Virginian Robert Gale, in the militia at age twelve, "was very young but was able to bear arms." Thirteen-year-old Nathaniel Warner of Connecticut was "a stout rugged boy of sufficient age and capacity to bear arms as much as any man." Of course, these veterans wanted pensions and had to convince the pension commissioner—just as years earlier they had to convince recruiting officers—that they could do a soldier's work. Thus, they emphasized their physical maturity and usefulness.[6]

When Washington and Barrington railed against boys' presence in the line, it was because they knew a soldier's life was hard. Yet recruiting officers enlisted them. They did so not just because they had different opinions about work and war, about who was a useful soldier, or because they were under pressure to fill the ranks. Military leaders and junior recruiting officers had differences of opinion because they stood at an unusual juncture in history. In previous centuries, boys would have been as worthless as Barrington and Washington believed. However, since the seventeenth century, there had been changes in weaponry, communications, and military life that made service by boys possible and, to a degree, brought boys into the military community.

IN THE CENTURIES before the American Revolution, there is little data available on the ages of soldiers. Kings and their nobles raised armies, but they and their chroniclers thought there was little worth noting about the soldiers who fought—not their names, their places of origin, or their ages. William Shakespeare, in his play *Henry V*, written around 1599, demonstrated this state of affairs: after the battle of Agincourt, King Henry asks the number of the English dead. Handed the information on a piece of paper, he reads aloud: "Edward the Duke of York, the Earl of Suffolk, / Sir Richard Ketly, Davy Gam, esquire: / None else of name; and of all other men / But five-and-twenty." The men named in this speech were ordered by social rank from nobleman to gentleman. Those beneath that rank were nameless.[7]

While Shakespeare was not a good historian, he was in this instance quite accurate. After the battle of Agincourt in 1415, in which the French and English clashed in northern France, chroniclers of the event named only the most illustrious figures and the age of no one. One Englishman recorded the French dead as two named noblemen, three dukes, seven counts, "100 barons, 1,500 knights, 7,000 men of gentle birth," and listed the English dead the same way—the Duke of York, the Earl of Suffolk, and "more than 30 common people." French chroniclers offered no more, naming a few men of high birth, then noting a number of "knights and esquires" or "men entitled to banners." This social convention is played out in military records throughout the medieval and early modern period and indeed through much of the eighteenth century.[8]

Since information about soldiers is missing from most muster rolls, which indicated only (often inexactly) the number of men enlisted and present, enterprising historians have tried to glean the identities of soldiers from other sources. Medieval records are complicated by the fact that many people in European feudal societies owed their lords *service*, yet the records are vague about what exactly that service was. The word had a wide range of meanings; for males it might include farming, paying taxes, administering the lord's estate, and traveling and fighting on the lord's behalf, but it is not clear who was doing what, when, and at what age. Documents such as receipts for lords' payments to garrison commanders have revealed a few names, but even these have been difficult to cross-reference with other kinds of information such as tax or baptismal records. Petitions for assistance and court documents on a variety of matters such as property disputes have revealed fragments of information about soldiers, but little to indicate the age at which they first served.[9]

The weapons and the nature of warfare itself present the best evidence for the lack of boys in battle. The weapons of war, whether broad swords, axes, pikes, spears, bows and arrows, or armor were simply too heavy for them to wield or to wear. Thomas Despenser, the future earl of Gloucester, was twelve when he served England's King Richard II in his campaigns against Scotland in the fourteenth century. However, Despenser was a nobleman leading his troops, not marching with them. Most soldiers were men serving for a season or a campaign and returning to their homes and farms at the first opportunity to serve their lords in another capacity. But some of them liked the life or needed the money and served year after year against a range of enemies. Boys may have occasionally been present with their fathers, working as servants, running errands, or taking care of horses, but the medieval chroniclers say little of them. There is little evidence they fought until they were old enough and strong enough to be effective.[10]

In the meantime, boys needed to train so they could fight when they were grown. Legislation in England encouraged young boys and youths to develop military skills. A law passed in 1388 ordered "servants" to give up their "useless and dishonest games," such as dice and cock fighting, and instead practice archery in their spare time. In the sixteenth century during the reign of Henry VIII, legislation required fathers with boys between seven and seventeen to train them in archery—using child-sized bows, however. The adult archer's longbow stood between five and six feet high. It had a draw—the pressure needed to pull the bow back—of between seventy to one hundred pounds. It required immense physical strength to use. While boys were obliged to train to be warriors, they were not expected to fight.[11]

In northeastern North America, Native boys, like their European counterparts, trained for war but did not participate in battle. Again, the physical demands of carrying and using weapons restricted their participation but, more importantly, for warrior societies such as the Iroquois, becoming a soldier was a part of other rites of passage that took a boy from childhood to youth and adulthood. At about age fifteen, a boy would go on a "vision quest" that involved physical endurance as well as spiritual revelation. Only after this was he ready for war.[12]

The introduction of gunpowder weapons in the late fifteenth century did not immediately bring boys into military service. The weight alone of the new musket, about fifteen pounds, was beyond a child's capacity. Because loading and firing the musket with a matchlock firing mechanism was a slow business, musketeers needed protection from enemy cavalry while they were doing it. This was provided by soldiers carrying pikes, long wooden poles with spears at the end. While a pike only weighed three to five pounds, it was between thirteen to eighteen feet long, awkward and unwieldy, and needed two hands. No slight youths or boys could use either of these weapons.

There continued to be scant information about soldiers' ages, or indeed anything else about them in the first centuries of the gunpowder era. In England, militia legislation required only men over sixteen to serve. And military handbooks confirmed the military preference for mature men. Gervase Markham, in his circa 1630 pamphlet, "The Muster Master," said that while soldiers should have the "strength and vigor of youth," those under sixteen were simply "too young" to be useful.

But perhaps this reminder indicates that a few boys were slipping into the ranks.[13]

However, one source—the Port of London registers of 1634 and 1635—confirms it was still rare for boys to be in the service in any capacity. Fearing that skilled craftsmen were leaving the country, the English Commission for Foreign Plantations ordered the agents at the port to record the names, ages, and professions or trade of everyone boarding ships for either Europe or the colonies. Among the travelers were soldiers who had been recruited for military service in the Low Countries as part of what would become known as the Thirty Years' War. About fifteen hundred soldiers embarked over several months. The harried clerk wrote down the soldiers' names and ages as they filed past him. While more than half the soldiers were under twenty-four, very few of them were under nineteen. The rest were twenty-five or older, with a few well above fifty. As the men filed past him, one caught the clerk's attention. When Robert Sanders stood before him and gave his age as fourteen, the clerk paused and questioned him. Beside Sanders's name is the additional information, "Capt[ain's] Page." No other soldier that young had passed before the clerk or aroused his curiosity enough for him to record this kind of information.[14]

In the crisis of the English Civil War in the 1640s both royalists and parliamentary forces needed all the men they could find. There are records for how communities raised their forces, but little is known of individual soldiers. Soldiers' names appear occasionally on officers' lists of deserters, or on their lists of those who were sick or taken prisoner, but no ages were given. Garrison records also reveal little. In 1645, in the parliamentary garrison at the town of Malmesbury, the officers and local tradespeople were named in the account books—for example, "Mr. Washington for 2 locks," "Parker for a load of straw"—but soldiers were not. The garrison record simply notes that "Major Fawkenor" received 120 pounds "towards the payment of the soldiers 3 weeks pay."[15]

It is impossible to give the age range of the armies in the English Civil War. The first commander of the parliamentary forces, the Earl of Essex, complained that in one county, the royalist recruiters had already taken every man "from 16–60" (the age range for militia service) leaving no one for his own side. This indicates the preferred age range for service, but a few boys almost certainly went with their fathers or other male relatives. And parliamentary and court records indicate that some "Silly younguelings," as one member of Parliament called them, were caught up in the excitement, particularly servants and apprentices, but their exact ages remain elusive. One parliamentary committee heard how a schoolboy, sixteen-year-old John Cundy, "was induced" to leave his studies and "join the King's party" but then moved over to fight with the parliamentary forces. Cundy was fined for his initial royal sympathies. Few other boys appear.[16]

Youths were active on the political side of the struggle. London apprentices, mostly in their early teens to twenties, were involved in the rioting that accelerated the political crisis and turned out regularly to practice drilling. But there is no evidence they played an active military role. The physical stamina required to carry a pike or musket meant that commanders needed men.[17]

BY THE TIME George Hofstalar was born in America in 1763, the military world had changed. Military arrangements, technology, and communication had all been transformed over the previous century. The sizable permanent armies of the Revolutionary era brought boys into the military in large numbers, while innovations in the musket and the introduction of new musical instruments to military life made boys useful.

European armies of the eighteenth century expanded as states consolidated power, developed distant trading interests, and engaged in wars. Armies had previously existed for a season or a campaign. Now Britain and its European rivals and allies of this period created standing armies that existed year-round, winter and summer, in peace and war. This meant that soldiers now served long terms. This could be for a period of a few years or the duration of a war or for life—or at least until they were too old or frail to be useful. Because there was often no mechanism to send pay home to their dependents, married soldiers and those who married while serving, often brought their families with them into camp and on campaigns.

Armies became large communities of enlisted men and their families. There are no good data for most places, times, or armies. However, there was one census done for part of the Prussian army in 1776 when it was billeted in Berlin. Accompanying the approximately seventeen thousand soldiers and noncommissioned officers were about fifty-five hundred women and sixty-six hundred children.[18]

The Continental army, the main patriot army during the American Revolution, had fewer women and children with it than European armies. This is partly because when Congress initially created an army in June 1775, it was ambivalent about having a standing army at all. Many American patriots, drawing on political ideas going back to the English Civil War in the seventeenth century, feared that a standing army, used by an ambitious general or tyrannical leader against citizens, might be a threat to liberty. Consequently, soldiers were initially limited to three-, six-, nine-, or, at most, twelve-month enlistments, and many married soldiers left their wives and children at home. Even after the fall of 1776 when Congress permitted soldiers to enlist for three years at a time, there were still a variety of short-term options available.[19]

Short enlistment periods gave families options. If a man served for a few months and had financial resources or relatives who did, he might serve and leave his wife and children at home knowing there was money available for their support until he could return with his pay. Families without such resources traveled with the army. For example, when Patrick Cronkhite enlisted for three years in January 1777, his wife, eleven-year-old son, and baby came into camp with him. And these children were not alone. As the war progressed, camp commanders tried regularly and usually fruitlessly to get an accurate count of "all the Women and Children in Camp" so they could calculate the necessary rations. While there are no exact numbers available, children became a noticeable part of the patriot military community as the Continental army became a seasoned, longer-serving force.[20]

At first, George Washington felt that women had no place in an army camp. He had observed the roles that women and children played in the military when he served alongside the British as a young man in the Seven Years' War. He saw they provided necessary services for soldiers, earning money doing laundry, sewing, or taking care of the sick, and they did so with their children playing around them or doing small tasks. He had also noted that they could be disorderly, create tension, and use up valuable rations. He felt these disadvantages outweighed the advantages, and, at the beginning of the Revolutionary War, he tried to restrict the presence of women. However, he soon realized that some men would not join unless they could bring their families, and that, in fact, while some women were disorderly, the tasks they performed were critical. Girls in camp could work alongside their mothers. But what about the boys?[21]

For decades, senior commanders and policy makers in European armies had come to see boys as future recruits. For example, in 1758 in Prussia, there were two thousand soldiers' children in the Potsdam Military Orphanage. The boys, presumably 50 percent of those who lived there, were destined for military service. This might not be a bad prospect for boys who had spent much of their childhood around soldiers. For them, the army was likely a familiar and comforting place. British army captain, Bennett Cuthbertson, observed that such boys, "being bred in the Regiment from their infancy, have a natural affection and attachment to it, and are seldom induced to desert, having no other place to take shelter at."[22]

However, two important changes were under way that made some recruiting officers decide not to wait for the boys to turn sixteen. The first was a change in military technology. By the end of the seventeenth century, the introduction of prepared cartridges that wrapped gunpowder and a musket ball in a paper package and the development of the flintlock firing mechanism made the musket simpler and safer to use. That, together with the invention of the socket bayonet that could be easily fitted to the musket barrel, dispensed with the need for a soldier carrying the unwieldy pike. The new musket, ten pounds in weight and about five feet in length even before the bayonet was attached, was not easy to manipulate, but a boy could, if necessary, carry and use it.[23]

There was another change taking place that opened a plausible role for a boy in the ranks. It was a seemingly innocuous development in music that transformed military communication and became an iconic symbol of boys and war—the widespread introduction of the snare drum.

IN MARCH 1776, when fourteen-year-old Reuben Woodworth of Saratoga County enlisted in the New York Continentals as a drummer, he had no idea he was part of a dramatic transformation in military communication. In his young lifetime, martial music was ubiquitous. Before he enlisted he had probably seen soldiers arriving in Albany, marching in step to rousing music, with a drummer, on an officer's command, setting the pace, signaling the arrangement of the line and the halt. However, the sight of troops marching in step to the command of a musical instrument was a relatively new phenomenon.[24]

In previous centuries, music had been only a small, formal part of military life. A collection of horns or wind instruments, often oboes, entertained officers or were used on ceremonial occasions. Soldiers in camp provided their own musical entertainment with songs perhaps accompanied by a whistle. On the battlefield or on the move, the trumpet or drum sounded the calls to action. The trumpet had come to be closely associated with the royal court, knights, and chivalry, and by the eighteenth century only cavalry moved to its command, certainly not the lowly infantry. Soldiers moved to a drumbeat in the field or on the road. For much of western history, the beat was pounded on a large drum carried by a strap at shoulder height to support its weight and size and was struck by hand or by a drumstick. Though it was physically possible for boys to carry it short distances, youths or men more commonly did so.[25]

But drum use became more important with the introduction of gunpowder weapons as officers needed to give soldiers more complex instructions. In the early seventeenth century, some commanders such as Gustavus Adolphus of Sweden had their musketeers and pike men execute complex maneuvers on the battlefield, each stage signaled by a drummer. The men could execute maneuvers more perfectly if they marched in step, but this took a while to catch on. Even by the end of the seventeenth century most soldiers would never have seen this kind of marching or done it themselves.

This changed in the eighteenth century after the snare drum appeared on the scene. Since the fifteenth century, a whole range of new percussion instruments, such as the snare drum, cymbals, and triangle, had slowly been introduced to western armies by observers of Ottoman Empire martial practice. In contrast to earlier percussion instruments, the snare drum, with a body made of ash and with calfskin drumheads, had gut snares across the bottom and could produce a sharp sound. The snare drum's technology improved in the seventeenth century. By adding cord or rope lacing around the ash casing and wooden hoops with tension screws around the drumhead, drummers could easily change the drum's tautness. This meant that a single drummer, armed with a couple of wooden drumsticks, could produce not only a snappy sound, he could also split the beat into multiple small units. This allowed him to play a range of easily distinguished patterns, using faster, more complex rhythms.

The snare drum became the means by which a whole range of signals were conveyed to soldiers. In camp, this included the morning reveille, assembly, and changing of the guard. On the march, the drum set the pace and instructed soldiers how to arrange themselves in a column. In the field, the drum covered every order from advance to retreat and all maneuvers in between. As the English writer Francis Markham,

Gervase Markham's brother, observed in his 1622 *Five Decades of Epistles of Warre*, the drum had become "the very tongue and voyce of the Commander" to which every "Souldier should wholly attend."

Musical accompaniment was added to the drumming, especially at the beginning of marches. At first this was provided by the oboe and the newly invented clarinet. But these instruments were difficult to learn and the reed mouthpieces did not hold up well in bad weather. They soon gave way to the simpler fife, a cylindrical, transverse, side-blown instrument with six holes. Its limitations (it could only play tunes in three keys—A, D, and G) were outweighed by its advantages: it was easy to learn to play; it could be simply and cheaply made from hardwood; it was almost indestructible; and its sound carried. By the eighteenth century, most infantry companies had at least one drummer and fifer and a complex system of signals around which life was organized. Providing music for the army was an important task that boys could do.

But new muskets and musical instruments did not mean that European regular armies suddenly recruited thousands of boys. There was a limit to the amount of signaling an army needed, and the difficulties and fatigues of military service were unchanged. Gervase Markham's earlier opinion that boys were not useful was still widely held by a variety of advice-book writers, officers, and policy makers. In 1756, an anonymous pamphlet sent to Lord Barrington proposing conscription rather than voluntary enlistment for the British army emphasized the importance of size and strength. Soldiers should be in their twenties and at least five feet six inches tall. To prove their strength, they must be able to "carry thirty pounds weight in each hand for thirty yards." But recruiting officers should be given a little leeway. At their option, the writer proposed, they could enlist "a stripling under the age of 20 likely to grow." The British never turned to a draft in the eighteenth century, although Parliament did pass emergency wartime Press Acts that impressed men without gainful employment into the army. However these acts did not target boys.[26]

Some officers and policy makers even had mixed feelings about formally recruiting boys as army musicians. One advantage of doing so was that, as they grew up, they could be put to the real business of soldiering. Not only did Captain Bennett Cuthbertson think that "Soldier's [*sic*] children in most regiments can afford a sufficient supply" of musicians. He also believed it important for all these young musicians to be formally enlisted "on first entering the regiment." That, he noted, would "obviate their refusal, to serve in whatever capacity the commanding officer may think proper" as they got older. Musicians, he wrote in his military instruction manual, should be a "little nursery" for future soldiers.[27]

But not every European army followed this advice. Neither the French nor Austrian armies enlisted their young musicians until they were sixteen. Without them, there were virtually no boys in the ranks. One census of almost sixteen hundred French soldiers from 1716 shows that only two (0.1 percent) were under sixteen and only twenty-five (1.5 percent) were under eighteen. In the Prussian army, about 1 percent of those enlisted were under sixteen. Even in the British army, despite the presence of boy musicians, regimental reports of soldiers serving in the Seven Years' War show an average age of just over thirty with an average enlistment age of early twenties. Ten percent of the soldiers were under twenty, but the exact number of boys is unknown. Unfortunately the British only collected data on their soldiers irregularly, and then usually reported it only in the aggregate. However, Cuthbertson's and others' frequent advice about how to use them (or avoid using them) indicate boys were present.[28]

In the colonial armies of British North America, neither officers nor policy makers thought boys made useful soldiers. In the Seven Years' War, boys serving were exceedingly rare. Legislation and recruiting orders stipulated a minimum age of sixteen, and muster rolls that include ages indicate that very few boys under that age were accepted into the provincial services. Colonists would have noticed a few boys present in the ranks of soldiers of both the British regulars they fought with and the French army they fought against. Yet they did not copy them. Even though colonial soldiers could be young (for example, the median age of recruits from New London County, Connecticut, was only twenty-one,) boys made little appearance among them, either in Connecticut or elsewhere. While the extant Virginia records for two years of the war show that about 10 percent of the soldiers were under twenty, few were under eighteen. And only one thirteen-year-old and two fifteen-year-old boys appear on the rolls at all among hundreds listed. The New York provincials were similarly mature. They recruited no boys in their early teens at all. One sixteen-year-old, Nathaniel Cook, might possibly have been younger. He is explicitly labeled a "boy" and stood only four feet nine inches. Another is humorously noted as aged "16 3/8," perhaps to indicate his being the baby of the company. The surviving rosters of

Pennsylvania provincials tell the same story. Of the hundreds of soldiers listed in the surviving muster rolls, only three were aged fifteen (there were none younger), and even the sixteen-year-olds can be counted on the fingers of one hand.[29]

As the British North American colonies raised troops over the course of the war, recruiting officers rarely thought boys answered the purpose in any capacity. Perhaps as they recruited in the coastal towns and villages, they realized service would begin with a march of hundreds of miles to fight in distant places. Service was going to be physically demanding even before the enemy was engaged. Additionally, there was no incentive to enlist boys in the hope of retaining their labor as they grew up. With soldiers serving only for short terms of a year, and even that, in practice, meaning usually only for the fair-weather campaign season, most soldiers' wives and children stayed home so there were few boys under foot to be put to work. Not even critical manpower shortages drove legislatures to eliminate age minimums or caused desperate or enterprising recruiting officers to fill the ranks with boys.

The armies that enlisted a few boys as musicians found that there were still drawbacks. Even drummer boys needed stamina. The new snare drum was light, only weighing about eight pounds, but it was awkward to carry. It was sixteen inches in diameter and eighteen inches deep, much deeper than those of today. The carrying sling was over the shoulders, and the drum rested against the thigh. This meant that walking and playing at the same time was a balancing act. Some boys could do it, but Cuthbertson admitted that those "much under fourteen, unless they are remarkably stout, are rather an incumbrance to a regiment (especially on service) as they are in general unable to bear fatigue, or even carry their drums on a march."[30]

Indeed, some boys in the Continental army were daunted when they saw the snare drum at close quarters. In the mid-nineteenth century, Augustus Meyers, who enlisted as a musician when he was twelve years old, was given a choice between becoming a drummer or a fifer. He chose the former. But his sergeant, looking at his "slim and youthful appearance," told the lad to think over his decision. The next day, the young Meyers watched closely while the drummers practiced and took a good look at the weight and size of the snare drums. He quickly "resolved to become a fifer" instead.[31]

In fact, the extant muster rolls show that while many boys in the Continental army were musicians, most musicians were not boys.

The majority of musicians were often significantly older. The drummers in an available small sample from New Jersey troops in the Continental army had an average age at enlistment of nineteen. In the British army, the usual complement for a company was two drummers, and if a boy was one of them, he was paired with someone much older. For example, the British Thirty-First Regiment of Foot had a thirteen-year-old drummer, Alexander Hogg, serving in the same company as his father, a sergeant. But the second drummer was forty-three and a veteran of almost twenty-five years' service. In one Prussian army regiment, the average age of all the musicians was about twenty-nine, and one fifer was sixty-four years old. Drummer boys attracted the attention of artists, such as the French painter Nonce who included one in his imaginative representation of the American victory at Saratoga in 1777. This created a romantic scene but was not very realistic. The drummer in any regiment was much more likely to be significantly older.[32]

Whatever the age of musicians, boys and their older fellow drummers and fifers needed to learn and practice their musical skills. This quickly became apparent to General Andrew Lewis, who commanded a regiment sitting outside of Williamsburg, Virginia, in March 1776. He appointed regimental fife and drum majors to teach their charges how to play. The majors had to gather the musicians from the various companies into a band, a word applied to military musicians in the eighteenth century for the first time, and "practice the young Fifers & Drummers" for two hours every day from eleven in the morning until one o'clock. A month later, Lewis complained they had to be more diligent about practicing, although the practicing was probably not always easy to listen to. The young nineteenth-century fifer Meyers, mentioned above, thought the sound of fifers practicing was a "shrill din." Lewis also found that his fifers were careless with their instruments and threatened that a fifer had to pay if he should "render his fife unfit for service." Lewis's musicians, young and old, were a great source of aggravation to him.[33]

Even when the musicians acquired musical skill, it did not necessarily lead to harmony. At Valley Forge in the spring of 1778, General George Weedon could not tolerate the chaotic sound of signals beating at variable times and locations across the camp. He detailed in the orders of the day exactly which signals had to be given at different times, the order in which the regimental drummers should beat, and where they needed to be in relation to each other so that chaos did not result if soldiers responded to a drum beat near them but not directed at them. In 1780,

Major Moses Ashley, with his Massachusetts regiment camped near West Point, told all drum and fife majors to meet and bring with them "all their old fifes for the purpose of having them properly sorted to the same Keys." One can imagine what these mismatched fifes sounded like to Ashley and the soldiers.[34]

But in deciding whether to recruit boys as musicians, some officers may not have had their musical talent or strength in mind at all. They may have been concerned with the beauty of a military line. Efficient commanders in the eighteenth century struggled to make uniforms practical but recognized the importance (to officers particularly but also to soldiers) of looking stylish according to the fashions of the day. Monarchs, generals, and many officers admired what historian John Lynn has called "the elegance of war," the beauty of the line, the neat formations of troops, and even the graceful lines of a well-built fortress. When they were reviewing troops, senior officers often commented favorably on a "tall, well made, strong Body of Men," and were sure to note in their reports if they saw several of them "rather low." Captain Cuthbertson had exactly this in mind when he advised recruiting only boy musicians who "promise a genteel figure." But it was important they not be too small in order not to be a "disadvantage to its [the regiment's] appearance." Sometimes, perceptions of beauty mattered as much as utility.[35]

There was another factor recruiters needed to consider: traditionally, drummers were tasked with inflicting the lash punishments handed out by courts-martial. The lash was the foundation of military justice in all European armies, and the American Continental army followed suit, although limited its use. In the British army there was no legal limit to the number of lashes inflicted, and, during the Seven Years' War, court martial sentences averaged above 720 stripes, with about 40 percent of sentences involving a thousand lashes or more. Awful as this was for the recipient, it was hard work for the drummer. These high-lash sentences might be carried out over several days or weeks so the soldiers could survive them. Still, it was demanding work.[36]

Drummers needed to be sturdy for another reason. The recipients of lash punishments might later seek revenge. Thus, a drummer might need to defend himself. In the American Revolution, where for most of the war the standard punishment was a hundred lashes, one Delaware soldier, Abram Meers, was court-martialed for assaulting a drummer who had done his whipping too enthusiastically. Before striking the drummer, Meers warned him he should be more moderate so as not to "get the ill will of the whole comp[an]y." Older drummers could defend themselves better from aggrieved soldiers.[37]

Most patriot boy musicians did not serve long enough to grow into other work or even to become older musicians. Fisk Durand of Connecticut enlisted at age ten as a drummer in 1776 along with his brother William, who was sixteen. Both boys enlisted for two eight-month terms. However, at the end of their second term in 1777, William was ill and had to be helped home. Neither served again for the duration of the war. Aaron Day of New York also did not mature in his role. The fourteen-year-old drummer served one nine-month term in the Continentals, had a few months at home, then served another nine months in a different regiment, and after that, once he turned sixteen, only served periodically in the militia. A few musicians, such as John Vaughan, who enlisted as a drummer at about age thirteen in the Connecticut Continentals, served for years in that capacity. However, the majority of young musicians were like Reuben Woodworth, brief sojourners in military service. Without giving the army a long-term commitment, they were not especially desirable recruits.[38]

WITH THESE MIXED opinions about the usefulness of boys, it is not surprising that in European armies and colonial armies before independence, boys only slowly entered the lines as musicians and occasionally soldiers. Hessian, French, and British armies continued to have only a few boys present, whether formally enlisted or not. The data available for one company of Hessians showed an average age of twenty-four and included only one sixteen-year-old. In other companies, soldiers were much older, on average over thirty, and already with years of service behind them. The French army was younger. Data from 1789, just before the French Revolution, show about half its soldiers as under twenty-five. Only 1 percent was under fifteen, and they were almost all sons of soldiers, serving as musicians. Boys are concealed in the British army's aggregated data, but on average its soldiers continued to be mature. Their average age was about twenty-eight with only 4 percent even under twenty. During the Revolutionary War, not surprisingly, serving British soldiers aged, and new recruits were hard to come by. A few officers complained about the quality of the new arrivals, but they were reluctant to discharge "any Man that could be made of the smallest use." Few boys appeared, however. By 1782, data for four regiments indicate soldiers now averaged over thirty years old, and only 3.5 percent were under twenty. There are a few companies in one of these regiments for which there are detailed records, and these show that about 1 percent of those serving were under sixteen. Boys in other forces were only present in small numbers.[39]

When it came to recruiting boys from outside the military community, much depended on the attitudes of individual recruiting officers as to whether they accepted any boys who came before them. Recruiting officers in the eighteenth century went where they believed recruits would be. This might be a neighborhood where officers were known and had influence. Over the course of a war, they had to cast their nets wider. British recruiting records from the Seven Years' and Revolutionary wars indicate that, in their homeland, officers searched for recruits where they might find craftsmen buffeted by a downturn of the economy, or others, such as shoemakers, suffering from the dislocations of early industrialization. Large numbers of such men in surviving muster rolls indicate both the men's need for work and resourceful recruiters.

The data that exist for the patriot forces indicate that boys made up a larger percentage than in the armies of their European counterparts. However, the scant information available limits the focus to a few particular moments in place and time. One Massachusetts descriptive roll for 1777, augmented by other local sources, indicates that out of 576 soldiers whose ages are known, fourteen of them (2.4 percent) were fifteen and younger. In a study of all men from Morris County, New Jersey, who served at any time during the war and whose ages are known with certainty, 1.6 percent were under sixteen when they enlisted. Adding the few servicemen born in 1765 or later (likely candidates for boyhood enlistment), but whose enlistment date is not known, brings the percentage to 2.4 percent here also. Genealogist Bobby Gilmer Moss has determined the dates of birth of 634 of the patriot soldiers who fought at the October 7, 1780, Battle of King's Mountain in North Carolina, on the South Carolina border: 2.2 percent of them were under sixteen as they fought that patriot victory. Even more striking, of this group, seventy (11 percent) had first enlisted in military service when they were boys. While the percentages of boys present indicate that they remained only a small portion of the patriot forces, these were significantly higher percentages than in the European armies they fought with and against.[40]

WHEREVER AND WHENEVER boys enlisted in the patriot forces, they were promptly put to work. But, apart from being musicians, what could they do that might answer the purpose? There was no single role they played, and there were almost as many different tasks as there were boys. One position often assigned to boys was that of waiter to an officer. Joseph Rundel was given that job even though he was about sixteen because he was small for his age. Rundel had intended to be a soldier when he enlisted in 1778 in the Connecticut Continentals, but the next day General Israel Putnam saw him and, Rundel remembered, "told me I looked too young (I was then in my sixteenth year) to go into the line and said he would take me as his waiter." That duty did not just mean laying out an officer's clothes. A waiter also performed military tasks such as standing guard and a range of other duties. Israel Trask, who was ten when he waited on his father, brought him cooked food, took care of his baggage whenever the army moved, and managed his mess (living space) when it was stationary. When Cordilla Fitch was a waiter to his father, Lieutenant Jabez Fitch, encamped outside Boston in 1775, he visited a sick sergeant in the hospital on his father's behalf. This was not a quick task. The hospital was about four miles away, probably the reason his father did not want to trek there. When Cordilla went, he stayed overnight and came back the next day.[41]

Despite the opinion of many policy makers and officers that boys were a waste of taxpayers' money, many of the boys, especially the older ones, performed a range of essential noncombat jobs. Many, such as Timothy Blackmore and Jacob Diefendorff, fourteen and thirteen respectively, stood guard at camp. This involved not only keeping an eye out for enemy activities but also monitoring soldiers and officers who were coming and going from camp. Even slightly older youths occasionally found it tricky to assert their authority in this capacity. When seventeen-year-old John Adlum of Pennsylvania was standing guard one night he challenged some junior officers heading out for "a frolick" against orders. Adlum's attempt to arrest them led to a scuffle. Fortunately, a brigadier turned up at that moment and backed up the youthful guard. Adlum, enjoying the moment, even went so far as to demand an apology from one of the officers who had cursed him. Under the senior officer's eye, the apology was duly given. It was not only the enemy who could present a young guard with tense moments.[42]

Other boys kept watch over anything that needed protecting. Fourteen-year-old Reuben Blankenship guarded Tory prisoners in

Western Virginia; Stephen Hammond, in 1777 at age thirteen, served as a guard in Providence, Rhode Island. In Massachusetts, Eli Jacobs kept watch over the coast, Chester Morris guarded military stores, while William Guest in North Carolina guarded the frontier. Young as they were, they may not have been much of a deterrent to a potential military threat. However, like Connecticut fifteen-year-old Samuel Aspenwall who looked out for "cowboys"—British or loyalists raiding cattle or other supplies around New York—they could raise the alarm when necessary.[43]

Boys performed a host of other tasks. Ebenezer Atwood built barracks for the Connecticut troops as they went into winter quarters. Jacob Gundy, at age thirteen serving in the Pennsylvania Continentals, was "hawling provisions from Morristown New Jersey to the troops at New Windsor & other places in New York." Gaines Hitchcock never went far from his home in Springfield, Massachusetts, when he served, but he stayed busy preparing cartridges—wrapping powder and musket balls in paper. Nathaniel Warner, a fourteen-year-old in Connecticut, chopped wood. John Collins, about thirteen and living on the North Carolina frontier, was useful even "before it was thought I was able to carry arms." He carried news and messages around the backcountry for patriot leaders. "Confidence was placed in me," he remembered, because "I was a good rider and knew the byways through the woods." Finally, his soldier-father decided the boy needed to enlist for his own protection in case he should be captured. The boy then did the same work but as a private. In Virginia, fourteen-year-old William Coff, a free African American boy, on one occasion helped to bury a French colonel killed in a duel with an American officer. But his usual task was as the assistant to a camp butcher employed in "slaughtering beef for the army." Isaac Bedell of New Jersey, also fourteen, brought meat from the slaughterhouse to camp. In short, boys did many of the jobs that older soldiers did.[44]

Boys were also assigned to care for the wounded. Fourteen-year-old Samuel Younglove fought in the Battle of Bennington in August 1777, and afterwards helped "moving our arms, ammunition and taking care of the wounded." In September 1781, thirteen-year-old William Addison of South Carolina was in the Battle of Eutaw Springs. Addison was "within a few paces of" General Andrew Pickens when the general was shot. The boy carried him "about fourteen miles from the battle ground." A few weeks later, George Paul, a fifteen-year-old Virginian, was sent to Yorktown right after the battle there to attend to the sick and wounded, one of whom was his father.[45]

Not every boy always acted in accordance with military law. Some solved the problems of hunger and hardship on a march by acting as soldiers had for generations before them, by taking what they needed from hapless civilians. That is what fifteen-year-old Ebenezer Fox did. Fox, an apprentice, was serving as a substitute for his master in the militia for three months. Any man drafted for the militia or other military service could send a substitute. One might hire someone from the neighborhood, send a son whose labor was not needed at home, or, as Fox's master did, send his apprentice because business was slow and he did not need him in the workshop. As Fox's company marched from its mustering place on Boston Common to Peekskill, New York, neither he nor anyone else in his company had any qualms about stealing geese from a local farmer when they came across them "enjoying themselves in a pond near the road." One was quickly killed and concealed in a snare drum. This hiding place was so effective that when the owner came to complain of the theft, not a feather of the goose was found when the company was searched. The soldiers also stole chickens from a farmer who had refused them food when they had asked. Fox, as an old man remembering these petty thefts, did not comment on the humor of himself, a fox, getting into the henhouse. Rather, he felt some remorse and offered these incidents as examples of the "losses and vexations" people are prey to from soldiers passing through. But at the time he did not care, and, while the chicken soup they made was not a grand feast, "it was not to be despised by a company of hungry soldiers." Fox was prepared to do what he needed to do to get food just like any other soldier.[46]

Some boys paid a high price for their service and suffered from illness and injury. From his fourteenth birthday onwards, Elijah Lacy had served for multiple short terms in the Virginia militia, first under his older brother Matthew, an officer ten years his senior, and then under his cousin, Elliott. Even though his relatives were there to help him, and his tasks, guarding prisoners and horses, were not too arduous, the campaigns were hard. Exhausted, he was finally "[so] afflicted with the Rheumatism, that he was compelled to accept a discharge, and by slow and painful travelling [sic] to return home." He never fully recovered. In western New York, fourteen-year-old Adam Gerlock's horse fell with him on it, and the boy broke his leg between the knee and ankle. "I have been lame from this injury my whole life," he reported. David McCance of South Carolina got so sick he had to be "hauled home in a waggon." Samuel Hancock was so ill from dysentery that his comrades "lost all hope of his recovery." News of his death had even reached his family. Sadness pervaded the Hancock home. Three Hancock sons, Simon, Samuel, and Edward, had enlisted together in 1776. Simon had died in camp within a few months. Edward had returned home, too ill to continue in the service, and now it seemed Samuel had been taken from them as well. But fortunately the boy did not die. After languishing for several months in the hospital, Samuel was taken to an uncle's where he stayed a few more months. Finally his father came to carry the boy home, but even then he was still too weak "to rise from his bed" for some time. Richard Frost, who had enlisted in the Massachusetts Continentals in 1780 at age eleven as a drummer, was at the Battle of Yorktown the following year when a musket ball passed through his arm, an injury that left him "lame," without the full use of his arm for the rest of his life.[47]

Some boys paid the ultimate price, dying in service, although usually only particularly moving or shocking circumstances made others think it noteworthy. For example, outraged witnesses recorded the death of fourteen-year-old Joseph Williams. In November 1781, the South Carolina militia was defending Hayes Station from a loyalist attack. Realizing they could not hold out, they surrendered. But the loyalist leader, William "Bloody Bill" Cunningham, did not respect their surrender. Instead, confirming the reason for his nickname, he attempted to hang the two patriot officers, Colonel Joseph Hayes and eighteen-year-old Captain Daniel Williams, from a pole. But the pole broke, and in his frustration, Cunningham took his sword to the two officers and others within reach. One of those was Daniel's younger brother and fellow militiaman, fourteen-year-old Joseph Williams. Fortunately, most boys avoided that kind of fate.[48]

But like Joseph Williams, boys occasionally found themselves in the thick of action. Samuel Aspenwall of Connecticut was fired on when he was with a party out foraging for food. Fifteen-year-old Doctor Bostwick (he was not a doctor, just a boy with an unusual first name) was assigned to "protect the inhabitants from the depredations of the British Cow Boys," trying to raid supplies. Virginians Thomas Groves and John Meany enlisted at age fourteen "in the musketry," in Thomas's words. John fought at Guilford Court House and in battles at Ninety Six and Eutaw Springs, and Thomas saw action at Gibbons Lane near Savannah and watched the British evacuate Charleston.[49]

A few boys did what the British Captain Cuthbertson hoped they might do—they began their military careers as young musicians and ended them as soldiers. Moses King of Massachusetts was a thirteen-year-old fifer when he enlisted but when he turned fifteen, he became a private in the ranks. He was wounded in action and lost his right arm. Christopher Loring enlisted as a thirteen-year-old drummer in the South Carolina Continentals. By 1781, he was a sixteen-year-old private at the Battle of Eutaw Springs where his hand was almost severed by a sword. These boys, and many others, answered the purpose.[50]

But despite these many contributions, boys' lack of physical strength limited their capacity. And even their employment as musicians and waiters did not occupy them all day long. Senior officers sometimes struggled to find tasks for them. In 1781, Brigadier General Edward Hand, the adjutant general, complained about the soldiers he saw who were too small and young to be put to work. But as the useful administrator he was, he did more than complain. He acted. The following year, working with Baron Von Steuben, the army's drill instructor, he formed some boys in camp into a company and found a noncommissioned officer to keep them in line and be a schoolmaster to them so they were not getting up to mischief. For these boys, service may have meant months of schoolwork that left them longing for adventure.[51]

A few boys had more excitement than they wanted. One of these was John Piatt, the young fifer we met in the introduction. His first year of service was grueling as he traveled hundreds of miles on foot and by bateaux from his native New Jersey to Canada and back again, returning home injured after being kicked by a horse. But that just marked a pause in his military career. Four years later, still only thirteen or fourteen, he was again with his officer father and took part in the Battle of Springfield, New Jersey. This was triggered when the British and Hessians moved to attack Washington's army still encamped at Morristown, where it had been for the winter. Piatt fought in the battle, and although it was a patriot victory, he and some others were taken prisoner. Fortunately for the boy, he was released shortly afterwards, "being a youth," and he made his way home for good.[52]

In North Carolina, fourteen-year-old John Burchfield also found life adventurous. He was living on the frontier at the Catawba River when he enlisted; his company marched to South Carolina and after some time joined General Daniel Morgan's troops. In January 1781, now fifteen, the boy fought at the Battle of Cowpens where he received a bad cut on his forehead from an enemy sword. Afterwards, he remembered Colonel William Washington (a distant cousin of the commander in chief) coming to "view the wounded," presumably to lift morale. Burchfield was able to rejoin his company and to march home a few weeks later. When he recovered, he enlisted again and was assigned to the "spy service," observing the Cherokee Indians.[53]

When they were not drumming and fifing, boys guarded coast-lines and prisoners, waited on officers, dug latrines, chopped firewood, slaughtered livestock, hauled wagons, built defensive works, spied on enemies, carried messages, tended to the wounded, marched for miles, foraged for food, and fought. Indeed, they did everything older soldiers did. Despite the fears of Washington and others, boys performed work that advanced the army's success.

CHAPTER TWO

A Strong Desire to Enlist

State of Vermont
Probate District of Bradford
in the County of Orange

At a court of Probate held in Bradford in and for the District
of Bradford before the Hon. William Spenser Judge of said
court—on this 7th day of August 1832 personally appeared in
open court before the judge of said court now sitting Samuel
Aspenwall a resident of Bradford in the County of Orange
and State of Vermont aged sixty six years who first being duly
sworn according to law doth on his oath make the following
declaration in order to obtain the benefit of the act of Congress
passed June 7th 1832.

... That in the month of March 1782 he joined the company
of Captain Allen and a regiment of the Connecticut Militia.
[He lists several officers.] That he joined this company as a
substitute for one Daniel Hibbard of Windham in the county
of Windham and State of Connecticut who was drafted for one
year's service. That he immediately marched to Horse Neck—
near the southwest (CHK) corner of Connecticut—to guard
the lines from the depredations of the Cowboys—Refugees and
Skinners—[loyalists or British troops and thieves foraging from
Long Island].[1]

This was all Aspenwall had to say about his enlistment. However,
his sister Mary Truman, giving a deposition in support of his claim,
remembered the events of that spring vividly. She recalled her brother
had "a strong desire to enlist" before he was sixteen (he celebrated that
birthday six months after he joined). She listened to family conversations,
knew that her father was worried about Samuel catching smallpox or
finding his fellow soldiers too rough for a young boy to associate with.
She could also remember his return a year later because he came back
just as the family welcomed a new baby sister.[2]

Perhaps it was like this:

In 1782, Samuel Aspenwall was fifteen years old. He could barely remember a time when his country had not been at war. He had lived all his life in Stonington, Connecticut, and even though it was not the site of any major battles, he had regularly watched the men in his community march off to serve in the Continentals, the state troops, and the militia. They had been fighting since the earliest days of the war. Stonington was only a hundred miles from Boston—close enough to help the Massachusetts militia and other troops respond to the British army's attacks at Lexington and Concord.

That fateful spring, Aspenwall had only been nine years old, and much of what he knew about the war he learned from stories repeated around the fire at home in the evening. In the intervening years, news of the great events of the day—the defeat of patriot forces in New York and New Jersey in the following two years, the victory of General Horatio Gates at Saratoga, New York, in 1777, and the triumph of General Washington and French General Rochambeau at Yorktown in Virginia in 1781—came to Stonington from a variety of sources. Local men serving in the armed forces wrote letters home, and their families shared the news. The soldiers themselves added details when they returned. And thirdhand reports appeared in the weekly newspaper, which his father or a neighbor occasionally bought in the port town of New London, about fifteen miles away, when they went there on business. Samuel took all this in, sometimes reading the newspaper himself, listening to his parents' conversations, or being with his father when he met relatives, friends, and neighbors to talk about politics and the war.

Some of the events of the war happened close to home. Since 1776, the British had occupied New York. New London and the neighboring fort at Groton Heights overlooked the mouth of the Connecticut River and Long Island Sound, just a few miles away by water from British forces. There were regular alarms along the coast that required the militia to turn out when enemy ships appeared on the horizon or raiding parties landed hoping to forage supplies. In 1781, the British, led by the traitor Benedict Arnold, had attacked Groton Heights and overwhelmed its outnumbered defenders, killing dozens of men and taking the wounded prisoner. Some of those defenders were from Stonington and neighboring towns, and a few had been boys around Aspenwall's age.

The following year, he felt he had been on the sidelines long enough. He now had a "Strong desire to enlist" for a year's term in the Connecticut state troops. He thought his father, a man sympathetic to the patriot cause, would fully support him. But he was wrong. His father vehemently objected; he thought Samuel was too young for the military. He was worried about the boy going far away from home, living a hard soldiers' life, and keeping rough company. He also knew that many soldiers had contracted smallpox and died in army camps in the early years of the war.

But Samuel was so eager to go that he regarded his father's disapproval as a temporary stumbling block. A determined fifteen-year-old can be a force to be reckoned with, and Samuel launched a campaign to change his father's mind. It took so much effort that, decades later, his sister Mary could still remember the regular family discussions about whether her brother could go or not. Finally, their father relented and seized what control he could of the situation. Mary remembered that a couple of weeks before her brother left home, their father arranged for him to be inoculated against smallpox "for the purpose of joining the army with more safety." Their father was also determined the boy should serve with men who would not corrupt him. Mary recalled her father traveling to the recruiting post with Samuel to make sure he enlisted "in a company agreeable to my father's mind." However, no matter what his father's efforts were on his behalf, the boy was just glad finally to be a soldier.[3]

IN HIS PENSION APPLICATION, Samuel Aspenwall did not say anything about his early boyhood. He began his account of his service, as did his sister Mary in her supporting deposition, with recollections of the family arguments about the lad enlisting. He said nothing about why he wanted to serve. We can imagine war news swirling around him, his family, and his town during his boyhood by reading other historical sources: local newspapers, local muster rolls that indicate that veterans were coming and going, and understanding the interactions of town life. What veterans' anecdotes or ministers' sermons he heard, what games played, songs sung, or books read that caused this "Strong desire," is something difficult even to guess. We know that Aspenwall was not the only boy excited about going off to war. Orphaned Thomas Painter, who enlisted at sixteen in the summer of 1776, had, he remembered, "(as is common for Boys) an inclination for a Soldier's life." The same year, fifteen-year-old Joseph Plumb Martin was eager to enlist and "be called a defender of my country." In 1780, twelve-year-old Bishop Tyler was also "anxious to go." Like Aspenwall, he had first to get around his reluctant father. For a year, Bishop "continually importuned" his father, apparently a man with strong powers of resistance. Mr. Tyler finally relented only after arranging for his son to serve one Captain Miles as his waiter. Miles was a neighbor and friend of the family and might be able to offer the boy some protection against the dangers of war or the corrupting influence of his fellow soldiers. Bishop Tyler was thrilled.[4]

But where did this enthusiasm for service come from for boys in the American Revolution? The distant excitement of war and the stories told by returning soldiers, relatives, neighbors, or friends are the most obvious sources of this enthusiasm, but boys had also surely heard of the illness, death, and hardship that accompanied military life. Military service provided order and daily discipline yet also permission to do things often not otherwise permitted, such as destroying property, and even killing. It could be tedious and tiring. Yet, at the very least, to a boy otherwise doing chores and going to school, it offered excitement, contact with the larger world, and the opportunity to experience intense emotions. Even though in the army he might be doing work similar to what he did at home on the farm or in the workshop, he would be laboring in different locations and with new friends.[5]

Given the scarcity of sources for this period, it is impossible to delve into the psyches of boy soldiers of the Revolution as much we would like, but the culture that surrounded them gives us clues about the forces that gave them the inclination to enlist. The exact connection between culture and individual actions is unclear even today and of course is hard to reconstruct for the distant past. But by examining the ideals of manhood boys wished to emulate, the toys they played with, the adventure stories they read, the songs they sang, and the sermons they heard, we can see the forces that combined with the news of the day and veterans' anecdotes to encourage them to see war as a great adventure.

MANY BOYS GROW UP wanting to emulate their fathers or other men in their families or communities, and boys in British North America were no exception. While there was no single ideal of manhood in colonial

America—for example, in New England, Christian piety played a more important role than in other regions—there were widely shared sentiments regarding what a man should be. Families everywhere valued self-control, economic independence, and, finally, becoming the head of a household. In aspiring to these attributes, white boys saw themselves as fundamentally different from white girls, slaves, and Native Americans, who were seen as permanently dependent. While gender and race shaped this perception, girls' and slaves' dependence was a legal fact sufficient to make white males see them as inferior. Native American youths were seen as more savage and uncontrolled. Of course, that was not how any of these groups saw themselves.[6]

For white boys, it was especially important to have self-control. It was believed to lead to diligence and economic independence, ideally by following a vocation of boys' parents' choosing. Later, as heads of households, husbands, fathers, and managers of labor—slave, bound, or free—men should be able to control their emotions and gain the respect of those around them, perhaps taking on civic responsibilities. Legal authority rested with men in family and public matters. Even though in practice men may not have always exercised the authority the law gave them, not all men married, and some marriages may have been more companionate, the community ideal and the law were clear that men were in charge.[7]

Despite the importance of self-control in colonial culture, there were times when violent outbursts were considered acceptable for boys and men. Violence was allowed in disciplining children, servants, slaves, and other dependents. It was also permitted in defense of property. When, in Malden Massachusetts, Thomas Shepherd's pigs somehow got past a fence to feed on the corn in his neighbor Samuel Blanchard's field, the two men had a heated exchange that quickly escalated to blows. When the matter came to court, the court recognized that each man had a right to defend his property with force, and the magistrates mediated the dispute rather than punishing the violence. Servants, sons, or other family members who came to the defense of property or a property owner were often gently treated too. But if they had no such good reason for fighting, the courts punished them.[8]

A more socially acceptable way to channel restless, violent impulses was wrestling. On the New York frontier, just after the Revolutionary War, Levi Beardsley learned to wrestle, and on picnic days, men gathered to watch and cheer the boys on. Beardsley was good at it, and "in a rough and tumble scuffle . . . there were but few of my age I could not throw." Native boys were also encouraged to play this way. Jesuit priest Pierre de Charlevoix observed when he lived among the Miami and Potawatomi peoples that boys "learned to wrestle together." Slave boys wrestled for fun too, but not necessarily with their parents' approval. One slave, remembering his early-nineteenth-century childhood, recalled that his parents had forbidden play wrestling in slave quarters because wrestling between slaves was at times staged for white entertainment.[9]

There was another outlet. Organized violence—war—was central to life in colonial North America, and enlisting as a soldier and displaying military valor were important components of manhood. Warfare had been a regular feature of colonial life, but it escalated in the eighteenth century as regional wars between European settlers and Native peoples became enmeshed in European imperial struggles. Particularly from the 1740s onward, tens of thousands of men in the colonies fought in a range of forces—militia, rangers, and provincial—and more than a few had joined the British army in wars against Native and imperial enemies.

One result of this warfare was that military skill and the willingness to serve became celebrated alongside other manly virtues. Service had long been part of Christian manhood. In the late seventeenth century, the Reverend Samuel Nowell reminded New England artillerymen that not only was it lawful, in the eyes of God, to "take up arms for the defence of friends and allies," it was also "in no way unbecoming a Christian to learn to be a Souldier."[10]

The regular mustering of troops over the decades provided plenty of opportunities for ministers to develop this message. Ministers emphasized the justness of war and reminded men that their service was the epitome of manly virtue. As the Massachusetts minister Thomas Ruggles observed in a 1737 sermon, it was "a Duty for men to become Expert and Valient Souldiers." That way, they could "fight the Lord's battles, and be Courageous for themselves, for their Land, and for their Families." There was, he noted, "true Manliness and grandure in military exercises," and men should make themselves "Masters of the Art of War." During the Seven Years' War, John Lidenius noted that it was a man's duty "to revenge God, reason, and Christianity," and he reassured his listeners that an offensive war was just when all other means of establishing safety and security had failed.[11]

Failure to serve could even jeopardize men's standing as good Christians. When the Reverend Samuel Davies preached to the Virginia militia during the Seven Years' War, he asked them to consider whether a failure to enlist was not "an enormous *Wickedness* in the Sight of God, and worthy of his Curse, as well as a scandalous, dastardly Meanness in the Sight of Men, and worthy of public Shame and Indignation?" If any disagreed, they did not speak up.[12]

Military service could cement a man's reputation. Warriors on all sides celebrated their own manhood and derided their opponents by comparing them to women, children, or animals. For example, during the Cherokee war of 1759–61, Cherokee leader Attakullakulla mocked the British Colonel James Grant as a "corn puller," someone who performs a traditionally female task. The Creeks, making fun of a British defeat at the hands of the Cherokee, claimed that the British had not been beaten by real warriors but by Cherokee "Boys and old Women," and chided the British for being "Dunghill Fowls." And a British cartoon mocked the French after they were defeated at Louisbourg by British and colonial forces in 1755. In it, the French were depicted as chickens, cooped up in a cage.[13]

All this had shaped grandfathers and fathers and had been passed on to boys in the Revolutionary era. But these boys were also directly exposed to this rhetoric. Ministers of patriot sympathies addressed everyone within hearing when they exhorted and blessed troops as they assembled at taverns, churches, and town squares. Reverend John Hurt addressed Virginia troops as they served in New Jersey, telling them their service would "not only meet with the applause of men, but also the approbation of God." And in 1781, Reverend Joseph Willard in Massachusetts reminded the soldiers and others he addressed of the duties of the "good and faithful Soldier" with his text for the sermon from 2 Samuel, "play the men for our people and for the cities of our God." Just as for boys of earlier generations, military service was an obvious way to claim the status of a man.[14]

Boys would also have heard soldiering and military life celebrated in song. Songs were central to life in early America and could be heard everywhere, in town and countryside, tavern and home, in church, in the fields, and on ships. Indeed they were sung anywhere where there was repetitive labor to be done, entertainment needed, or time to be whiled away. The ability to sing well was greatly valued in many communities. That skill had not always mattered. But in New England at the end of the seventeenth century, some ministers began lamenting the poor quality of singing at services. A few encouraged their congregants to take lessons, and books such as Thomas Walter's *Grounds and Rules of Music Explained* became popular. These books taught singers how to read music and encouraged people to take pride in their abilities. Men and women attended new singing schools and formed singing societies. In 1721, Massachusetts judge Samuel Sewall went to hear such a group sing at the schoolhouse one night where Reverend Cotton Mather was preaching. Mather noted in his diary that the singing was done by "a Society of persons learning to sing" and that there had been a large crowd present. Sewall thought the singing "extraordinarily Excellent, such as has hardly been heard before in Boston." Most people, either adults or children, would not have sung in such a formal setting, although choirs proliferated in towns in the eighteenth century. More commonly, songs were sung around the fireside, in the tavern, or at any public occasion.[15]

Songs that celebrated military glory and honor and reminded singers and listeners of soldiers' hard lives and made fun of their reputation for bad behavior were common at military musters. The mustering of British and Provincial troops during the Seven Years' War and the subsequent British military presence made soldiers' songs a part of daily life long before the Revolution. In Boston in the early 1770s, the band of the British Sixty-Fourth Regiment performed by itself and alongside local performers. One popular song was the aria known by its first line, "The soldier tir'd of war's alarms," from British composer Thomas Arne's opera, *Artaxerxes*, which had been performed in New York and Boston in the 1760s. The song celebrated the soldier who, weary of war, still responds to the trumpet's call when he is needed.[16]

Most boys, though, would be more familiar with songs of an older vintage that celebrated the soldiers' life. One popular song recounted how hard it was for soldiers to leave the comforts of home and part from their sweethearts. The song's hero goes to the aid of his "Country Bleeding" but has to leave behind his "Weeping maid." He tells his love: "I go where glory calls me & danger points the Way / Tho coward Love upbraids me, yet honour bids Obey." A humorous song made fun of soldiers' shady reputations. In "Soldier, Soldier, won't you marry me?" a soldier pretends to woo a young maid. He extorts valuable clothing, a shirt, new pants, a coat, and boots from her, all of which she has found in her grandfather's old chest. But she discovers in the final line of the song that the soldier is already married and she has been duped.[17]

All these songs, old and new, were part of the entertainment wherever soldiers gathered, and they transmitted the values and traditions of military life in accessible and sometimes humorous ways. Young Bishop Tyler loved hearing these tunes when he saw soldiers mustering. He improvised his own instrument, a fife made out of straw, so he could pretend to accompany the singing. Surrounded by mustering soldiers, singing along with their songs, hearing the exhortations of ministers, and living in a world that celebrated the military life, boys learned about the soldiers' world.[18]

DURING THE EIGHTEENTH CENTURY, this ideal of a militarized man meshed with play, particularly war games. Some of these were played on military training days. On those occasions, boys turned out with fathers, neighbors, and other male relatives. When they were very young, they would have played around the mustering militiamen. As they got older, they may have joined the exercises. All this encouraged war games. The colonial records are scanty, but in England in an earlier period, account books show purchases of child-sized bows and crossbows, and court records note accidents in which young children were injured by errant arrows from games. A year after Wyatt's Rebellion in 1554, in which Protestant rebels challenged the Catholic Queen Mary, a crowd of boys in Finsbury, then outside of London, replayed the battle. They "made a combat in the field," dividing themselves into either the forces of Wyatt or the Queen. It is hard to imagine that such war games did not cross the Atlantic with English families.[19]

Two centuries later, toys, if they were involved at all, were still most likely improvised rather than manufactured. Toy soldiers were not yet common although there were a few expensive military toys available. The son of the French king, Louis XIV, had a complete set of soldiers made of silver. George Washington imported a single "Prussian Dragoon" from a London toymaker that cost more than a shilling as a gift for his young stepson. But most toy soldiers in this era, and probably even the one Washington purchased, were flimsy, two-dimensional figures, crudely made of tin. In the 1770s, a German tinsmith called Johann Hilbert developed a new manufacturing technique that allowed toy soldiers to be more robust and detailed. Before that, generations of boys more commonly played with tin or wooden figures and wooden or child-sized weapons, if they had playthings at all.[20]

In every society, children are encouraged to play as a means of developing skills and traits that the community values. If military skill were valued, it would make sense that such play would be encouraged. But not every community valued imaginative play. In Puritan New England, adults were cautious about play and playthings. There, people valued self-discipline, work, and religious reflection. Purposeful play was acceptable. After all, children will play with any household object and mimic its adult use. But the business of life was serious. A vivid imagination and fantasy life, today considered important ingredients in children's unstructured play, was frowned on by many who saw it as not only a waste of time but also potentially devilish. South of New England, attitudes toward play were more relaxed. It was valued for the self-discipline, cooperation, and leadership that it taught. The toys that Washington's stepchildren played with, the toy soldier, a stable, a coach pulled by six horses, and a "tea sett," reflect this mix of imaginative and purposeful activities.[21]

But by the eighteenth century, even Puritan New Englanders were beginning to recognize the educational value of play. John Locke, in his 1698 work, *Some Thoughts concerning Education*, thought that "Gamesome humour," that is play, could help children develop "their spirits and improve their strength and health." That was, of course, always provided that such play showed adults due "[r]espect to those that were present." It was not unstructured play that Locke thought important. Rather, it was play that might help inculcate important values such as obedience and cooperation. Slowly, Puritan attitudes grew more accepting.[22]

In other cultures, play had long been used to develop traits the society valued. Indian children were encouraged to play so they would develop toughness and independence. The priest, Charlevoix, noted that Miami and Potawatomi parents trained boys through play and "put the bow and arrow into their hands" when they were very young. These, of course, were hunting skills as well as skills for war. White boys in less constrained places than urban New England were also encouraged to hunt. Southern boys practiced hunting with bows and arrows. And children everywhere played tag and a variety of other games that could be played with toys easily whittled from pieces of wood, such as tip-cat (played with a small bat and stick), a spinning top, or skittles. One boy, Levi Beardsley, when he was about six or seven, went out with his uncle, himself a boy about fourteen, to kill snipe, a waterfowl, using sticks and stones.[23]

And children of all communities, slave and free, found ways to add play to their day even when otherwise hard at work. Many tasks, such as collecting kindling from the woods or gathering fruit from trees, especially if done out of sight of adults, could be interspersed with hide-and-seek or tag. Play would have been enjoyed for its own sake, yet toys, games, and roughhousing all shaped boys' attitudes toward leadership, cooperation, and discipline. These were useful qualities for many fields of adult endeavor but they were especially useful for military life.[24]

CHILDREN ALL OVER the colonies overheard adults talking about the great political ideas behind the war, and, in as much as they could understand them, these too helped boys become excited about serving. Boys would not have been immersed in the arguments of the great pamphleteers in the years of the crises surrounding the Stamp Act and Townshend duties in the 1760s. After all, those who were boys when they joined the military struggle were born after 1760. Most were born after 1764 with the youngest about 1770. Still, the ideas of the age circulated and continued to be the talk of the dinner table and public gatherings as the political crisis deepened. Ebenezer Fox, who was born in 1763 and ran away to sea in 1775, was barely a toddler when these crises erupted. However, he was later sure that he and boys like him were inspired by the political ideas they heard. He recalled that it was "perfectly natural for the spirit of insubordination that prevailed should spread among the younger members of the community." While children like him would not have had a complex understanding of the issues of the day, they could absorb them when they were presented in easily understood ways.[25]

Again, songs were an important medium. Simple and engaging lyrics were quickly written to familiar tunes to celebrate the patriot cause and call men to action. They became a ubiquitous and vibrant part of Revolutionary political culture. John Adams noted in his diary in 1769 that song was a wonderful part of a large gathering of the Sons of Liberty, a loose political group of colonists opposed to British parliamentary policies. The meeting, and others like it, served to "impregnate them [the people] with the sentiments of Liberty." On this occasion, the festive spirit was dampened only by the rain. But as they ate and drank toasts in honor of various people, the "Liberty song was sung— that by the Farmer . . . and the whole company joined in the Chorus. This," Adams observed, "is cultivating the Sensations of Freedom." The farmer he referred to was John Dickinson, whose anonymously published political work against actions by the British parliament, *Letters from a Farmer in Pennsylvania*, had been widely published and distributed in the colonies at the end of 1767. His "Liberty Song," written the following year and first published in the *Boston Gazette*, was one of many new songs that appeared in the prewar and war years. Written to familiar folk tunes, these songs had new lyrics that celebrated political actions by colonial groups and demonized parliament, its representatives, and British soldiers. Former slave Jehu Grant of Rhode Island remembered that one of his inspirations to run away from his loyalist master to join the army was exactly the "songs of liberty that saluted my ear." Such songs were sung at political gatherings, taverns, and military camps, and distributed as broadsides throughout British North America.[26]

These songs (loyalists had their own versions) were quickly transmitted because the lyrics were written in a simple ballad meter and could easily be sung to familiar tunes. One song, celebrating "Godlike WASHINGTON," was sung to the tune of a well-known British army marching song "The British Grenadiers." John Dickinson's "Liberty Song" was, with deliberate irony, set to the tune of the patriotic British song "Hearts of Oak." That was part of a recently written opera that celebrated British victories in the Seven Years' War. "Hearts of Oak" fêted the traditional liberties of Britons as "freemen not slaves." Approximately three hundred songs (Dickinson's included) composed in the years leading up to the Revolution indicated the tune to be used either at the top of the published broadsheet or in the song's first line that mimicked the original melody.[27]

One popular wartime patriotic song that was set to original music was "Chester," written by William Billings, an impoverished Boston tanner, composer, music teacher, and choirmaster. Billings never prospered from his musical activities, but his zesty, tuneful music, printed in his 1770 book, the *New-England Psalm-Singer*, sold well. "Chester" was part of that collection, but it was the 1778 version, written with new wartime lyrics, that became popular. It honored the political cause, military valor, and, in a line guaranteed to appeal to the young, honored the "beardless Boys" of the American troops. Whether patriotic songwriters composed their own music or used familiar tunes, the songs were enjoyed by old and young alike. Patriot boys up and down British North America sang along.[28]

BOOKS, BOTH ADVENTURE stories and political works, were another source of boys' enthusiasm for military service. Children of all backgrounds heard the glorious tales of ages past around the fire. Charlevoix observed that Indian families told boys of the "exploits of their ancestors

or countrymen." Other boys on colonial farms and in towns were beginning to learn these stories more from reading than listening, but it was
a transition that had only recently begun.[29]

In the years before the Revolutionary War, the number of printers
and the number of books they printed and imported increased dramatically, and the titles available now included a new genre: children's
books. However, no young child recorded what he or she was reading,
and not many children's books and special "small books" or chapbooks,
as they later came to be known (usually about twenty or so pages with
stories, poems, or riddles), have survived. It is only printers' records,
newspaper advertisements, the account books of some wealthy men
who noted what they bought for their children, and a few memoirs that
provide evidence of the existence of children's books at all. These last
two sources are frustratingly vague. For example, Washington bought
books for his stepchildren through his London agent just as he did for
himself. When his stepson, John Parke Custis, was about five, he bought
"6 little books for Childn. Begg [beginning] to Read," and when John
was about ten, he purchased "Children's Books" for five shillings. Silas
Felton, recalling his Revolutionary War childhood, noted that he loved
"boy books" and read them voraciously in the "evenings and Stormy
Days" when he did not need to go to school or work on the farm. But
neither said what the books were.[30]

Such "boy books" were a new phenomenon. For most of the eighteenth century, if a household owned books at all, these were usually the
King James Bible and the *Bay Psalm Book*. Other popular titles, widely
available and shared by children and adults alike, were allegories like
John Bunyan's *Pilgrim's Progress*, *Aesop's Fables*, and novels such as
Gulliver's Travels by Jonathan Swift. But, slowly, these household staples
were joined by a trickle, then a flood of books written especially for
children, offering everything from religious passion to silly entertainment, folk tales, and adventure. These joined spelling and instruction
books, such as the best-selling *New England Primer*, aimed specifically
at children.[31]

By the second half of the century, the number of children's books
increased exponentially. Enterprising printers geared their bookbinding
techniques to customers with a range of disposable incomes. Wealthier
buyers probably preferred leather-bound copies of the children's books
they purchased. But most were sold with so-called "trade bindings," with
pages simply saddle-stitched rather than leather-bound. This made them

cheaper. Occasionally, and even more cheaply, single sheets could be purchased for home assembly. By these various means of production, books entered a range of households, and children were introduced to characters such as Dick Whittington and his cat, Robin Hood, Leo the Lion, and the good giant Benefico. These heroes were virtuous, brave, honorable, but violent when necessary. Robin Hood was brutal and destructive to the greedy but generous to those "that toil at cart and plow" and to "the widow and the fatherless." These stories did not always have a happy ending. Robin Hood was killed by his enemies who had to resort to treachery to catch him. But readers knew whom to hate.[32]

Children and adults also shared a delight in reading about the adventures and escapades of pirates and highwaymen. Even though accounts of their lives came in the form of cautionary tales, the appeal was as much in the recalling of their evil deeds as the certainty of pending divine punishment. The last words of pirate Joseph Andrews provided lessons about the evils of drunkenness, greed, and violence, but also included the sordid details of his "Sundry excesses and depredations upon innocent people." Accounts of Captain Edward Teach, alias Blackbeard, entertained readers and listeners by the "pitch of wickedness [to which] human Nature may arrive." Poems about the 1701 execution of the "noted pirate" William Kidd still delighted readers decades later. And despite the details of evildoing, the stories often conceded that the villains, such as the pirate Sir Henry Morgan, had a "large share of personal courage and Bravery."[33]

In addition to these works that celebrated derring-do, escapades with the law, and occasionally violence, there were also books, enjoyed by children and adults, with heroes who defied strict fathers or anyone else who opposed them. As the colonists were resisting parliamentary levies, flexing their economic muscle in boycotts and nonimportation agreements, novels appeared that celebrated the independent action of individuals. For example, in Daniel Defoe's *Robinson Crusoe*, the fictional hero, shipwrecked on an island, became the epitome of the independent man. Crusoe, having foolishly rejected the guidance of his wise parents, had gone off to sea. He was alone (at first) to organize his society as he wished, with only God to guide him. Although Defoe wrote the book in 1719, the New York printer Hugh Gaines brought out an abridged North American edition in 1774 (about half the size of the original and aimed at younger readers) that was immediately successful. During the war, in 1779, an enterprising Boston printer brought out an even shorter chapbook version for still younger children. All these versions celebrated a child growing up to be able to think rationally and independently.[34]

Boys also had access to the same political works their parents did, and some of these, such as the best-selling *Common Sense* by Thomas Paine, were deliberately written in simple language to appeal to the largest possible audience. Older children could easily grasp the concepts. Some of these political works presented the colonial political struggle using the imagery of a family quarrel with the colonists as children who had outgrown their dependence on their father, an argument that may have had a special resonance for the young. One of these was Francis Hopkinson's humorous allegory, *A Pretty Story Written in the Year of Our Lord 2774 by Peter Grievous, Esq.*, written in 1774. Hopkinson presented British intransigence and the colonists' struggles for their rights as a drama between an aging farmer on an old farm and his youthful children on a new farm. One of the problems the "children" suffered was a tax on their favorite drink, "water gruel."[35]

Children's books and those on political matters were readily available at bookstores and circulating libraries. In 1768, John Mein's bookstore in Boston offered for sale Dickinson's *Letters from a Farmer in Pennsylvania* and David Dulaney's *Considerations in the Propriety of Imposing Taxes in the British Colonies*, two great expositions of colonial grievances against Britain, at the same time as *Giles Gingerbread* and *The Story of the Cruel Giant Barbarico* were available. A parent with some disposable income could have bought both.[36]

Some children had limited access to this material. This might be due to poverty or their distance from booksellers. Sometimes even bookish households did not have children's books. One boy, Samuel Goodrich, born just after the Revolution, lived in Ridgefield, Connecticut, and although there were many books in his minister father's library, they were all either on theology or in Latin. Samuel's parents were raising a large family on a small income, so there was no money for extras. The boy read his primer, some religious texts, and other books for school. But, as he noted in his memoir, he "had made little acquaintance with literature." He was about age ten or so when his father brought home some children's chapbooks and adventure stories for him. Samuel was stunned by the morally compromised heroes he was supposed to admire, such as Jack the Giant Killer, who accomplished good things but only through trickery and deception. This boy was probably unusual, but he reminds us how hard it is to be certain about what any boy might have got out of reading.[37]

In the backcountry, access to books and newspapers was more limited. Even the printers of the most successful newspapers only printed at most a few thousand copies. Most printed significantly fewer, and their distribution was usually local, with delivery boys taking copies to regular customers. The very act of buying books was complicated. It required a trip to town or having an intermediary, friend or agent, make the purchase. Missionary societies, such as the Anglican Society for the Propagation of the Gospel, were one source of books and pamphlets in less settled areas, but they were more likely to distribute sermons and other religious texts than tales of piracy or adventure, no matter how morally virtuous their heroes.[38]

But would boys such as Bishop Tyler and Samuel Aspenwall have been able to read these political or adventure books? The answer is most likely yes. Literacy rates were surprisingly high in the colonial period. But first we should break down what we mean by literacy. In this era, reading was taught separately from writing. Reading was taught at a very young age, often well before age six. Writing and arithmetic came years later, if at all. Reading was considered a simple but essential skill, greatly valued in New England for spiritual reasons. There, Puritans believed a personal understanding of the Bible was critical to their faith. Children were expected quickly to learn to read it and other religious texts. Reading was also the gateway to finding information on other subjects, and lastly, and least importantly, it was a source of entertainment. In contrast, writing and arithmetic were primarily needed for commercial activities and managing large households and were acquired as needed by older children or adults. So many people could read without knowing how to write. While being able to sign their names to documents (veterans' pension applications, for example) meant people could read, not being able to write their names (signing with a mark instead) did not mean they could not.[39]

Of those children who learned to read, they commonly did so in their own homes, taught by their mothers. Or they might go to a dame school, run by a widow teaching small children in her own home. For example, in 1691, when Joseph Sewall was three, his father, Samuel Sewall, sent him off to be taught to read by the mother of his neighbor, Captain Townsend. Joseph's older cousin, Jane, walked him there, carrying his spelling book. John Barnard attended what he called a "reading school" or dame school until he was six years old, and he proudly recalled that before he was seven, he had already "read my Bible through thrice."

Many schools expected children to have some elementary skills when they arrived. At James Twifoot's school in Philadelphia, his most elementary class was for those children who "have been but imperfectly taught to read." But he did not expect to have to start from scratch. This class aimed only to "correct all bad habits in reading" and improve "pronunciation."[40]

Sewall and Barnard were children at the end of the seventeenth century and were from prosperous New England families. But over the next hundred years, even humble families came to see the ability to read as an essential skill. This skill was more widespread in northern colonies due to the religious imperative to gain a personal understanding of the Bible, the prevalence of towns that offered more schools, and the existence of several colleges that produced more educated young men prepared to teach. There was also an increased interest in the ability to read all over British North America. Apart from the opportunities reading offered for entertainment and information, it freed people from dependence on others to read and relay information to them. Being able to read a document with confidence might improve one's social standing, indicating to those around that he or she was literate and informed. In towns, the literate had an advantage in dealing with new retail businesses or tradesmen. And in rural areas, farmers found the ability to read useful when negotiating leases, arranging credit, or selling crops.[41]

Not only ambitious or prosperous families saw the advantages of literacy. Courts handling the cases of the community's neediest children came to feel the same way. In the 1670s in Talbot County, Maryland, no contract in which the courts bound out a boy or a girl (when the children were orphaned or otherwise impoverished) required the master to teach reading or writing. By the 1740s, all orphaned boys bound out by the court were required to be taught to read, and almost all had to be taught to write, too. This did not mean that all boys could read. There was no enforcement of this requirement, and delinquent masters, further instability, and poor instruction or ability might all delay or prevent a boy from learning, but the court expected him to learn. It had similar ambitions for orphaned girls. By the middle of the century, of the girls the court bound out, 94 percent of them were required to be taught to read. However, no contracts required them to be taught to write. Reflecting the prejudice of the community, only a small minority of the contracts for "bastards" required them to be taught to read, and almost none added writing, condemning those children to a future in the lowest-level jobs.[42]

For black Americans, there were limited opportunities to learn. In New England households, servants and slave children were often taught reading alongside the children of the house. In Lincoln, Massachusetts, enslaved Peter Brooks Nelson was sent to school about age five along with the niece and nephew of his owners. In Philadelphia, African American James Forten, born free, learned to read at an early age, probably taught by his mother, Margaret, who was celebrated as having a "fine mind." In the South, a few slave owners taught slaves to read. That became illegal in South Carolina after the bloody slave uprising there in Stono County in 1739. Despite this prohibition, in 1741 young Eliza Pinckney, living on a plantation in that colony, happily taught "a parcel of little Negroes" to read. Schools for enslaved children were established by Quakers in Philadelphia, and in New York, the Anglican Church opened a free school for "30 Negro children" five years and older in "reading, and in the principles of Christianity, and likewise knitting and sewing." The organizers encouraged masters to send their young slaves, "especially those born in their House," in the interests of the children's souls and future "usefulness."[43]

A few Native children living in or close to white society also became literate. Samson Occom, a Mohegan Indian, always remembered fondly the man who taught him to read when he was ten years old. Missionaries had built a succession of schools for Native children whose families had converted to Christianity. These were founded by white missionaries such as James Fitch among the Mohegan, Eleazar Wheelock with the Narragansett, and David Zeisberger in Delaware and Cherokee country, and by Mohegan teachers Occom himself and Ben Uncas. But all these endeavors to teach slaves and Native children were small-scale and reached only a handful of individuals.[44]

High sales for spelling books, such as the *New England Primer* and imports such as Thomas Dyche's *A Guide to the English Tongue*, indicate that many people wanted their children to learn to read. We do not know if children did so willingly or reluctantly, easily or haltingly, but in New England, reading literacy may well have been near universal for white boys and surprisingly high for white girls, with significantly lower rates elsewhere. Among slave and Native American children reading ability was certainly much lower but is impossible to estimate. Despite this widespread ability, we cannot say with any certainty what children read. But there were many books around to inspire them to see action and adventure as noble and virtuous.[45]

One boy, Stephen Burroughs, was explicit about the role reading played in his dreams of military service. His "romantic ideas of military prowess" and desire for "an opportunity of signalizing myself in that department," he claimed, came directly from novels. He found the adventures of Guy, Earl of Warwick, particularly inspiring. The hero of this legendary tale needed to prove himself against dragons, giants, and ordinary mortals in order to become a knight and win the hand of his beloved. Guy's military exploits had "a direct tendency to blow the fire of my temper into a tenfold rage," and Burroughs felt "an enthusiastic ardor" to copy the legendary Earl. The boy imagined himself "at the head of armies, rushing with impetuosity into the thickest of embattled foes, bearing down on all who dared to oppose me." Dreaming of glory, many boys were probably similarly inspired.[46]

BOOKS, READING, SONGS, and stories all played their role in drawing boys into the service. These voices went alongside those of parents with patriot sympathies. Bishop Tyler was particularly influenced by hearing his father's outspoken political convictions. Benjamin Peck's mother was politically committed to the cause too. Peck remembered that she had "induced" her husband and three sons to serve, including Benjamin who was then ten years old. John Romer's mother was also a "warm whig" who had encouraged male relatives to enlist. And, at age fourteen, Gaius Stebbins was encouraged to serve by his father, a man "uncommonly zealous in the American cause."[47]

Other adults in their communities, such as schoolmasters and ministers, also led boys to think about military life. John Tileston, the teacher at the Boston North Writing School, did his part to encourage patriot fervor among his students. Tileston was exactly the same age as patriot leader John Adams, whom he knew slightly from childhood. Every year since the Boston Massacre in March 1770 there had been solemn anniversary speeches to mark the event. On the anniversary in 1775, Tileston let his students out at ten o'clock in the morning and cancelled class for the rest of the day so they could all go and listen to what he noted in his diary was an "elegant and spirited oration" by Joseph Warren, another leading patriot figure of the city.[48]

Aspenwall and other boys from New London County, Connecticut, may not only have been encouraged in the political struggle by their own schoolmasters, they may also have been inspired by the stories they heard about the local schoolteacher-turned-officer, Nathan Hale. Hale, a passionate patriot, graduated from Yale at age eighteen in 1773 and became a teacher at the Union Grammar School in New London, where he taught both Latin and writing. He may well have directly influenced some of his students although no evidence exists of it. He was young, just twenty, when war broke out, and he became an officer, first in the militia and then the Continental army. Boys such as Aspenwall were too young to have been in Hale's class. It was Hale's execution by the British for spying a year later in September 1776, rather than his teaching, that may well have shaped the hearts and minds of boys in and around New London.[49]

Ministers too played a role in encouraging males in a community to go off and serve, not only by connecting service to manhood but also by regularly expounding on the virtues of the cause in church and at troop musters when soldiers marched off to war. Bishop Tyler particularly remembered regular sermons at which his clergyman had encouraged the congregation to pray "for the success of the righteous cause." Tyler was also moved by the congregation's fundraising efforts to support the troops. Most ministers conceded, as Nathan Perkins in Connecticut did in the early days of the conflict, that politics was not the true purpose of the pulpit. "But when necessity calls," he argued, "it may with propriety address us on civil liberty." And so he encouraged those ready to "hazard their lives in the defense of their country" to go and do it.[50]

Boys in the backcountry from New York to the Carolinas may not have heard many such sermons. Few clergy worked in those areas at all and church institutions were weak even if religious passion was not. Formal sermons were few and far between, and when ministers were present, they usually did not write down their sermons but spoke extemporaneously. However, people later remembered ministers cajoling the faithful to continue with their efforts in the cause. The parishioners of Presbyterian minister James Hall on the North Carolina frontier remembered that he regularly spoke to them "and inflamed their love of liberty." Hall, who had responsibility for several congregations in a swath of territory between the Yadkin and the Catawba Rivers, was a staunch patriot. After the British entered South Carolina in 1780, his parishioners remembered him addressing them "in the most thrilling manner [about] the wrongs of his country, and the sufferings of their friends and countrymen." Hall regularly served with the local militia as its chaplain; such a man would certainly have inspired boys in his community to action.[51]

BOYS MAY ALSO have been encouraged by the stories they heard of the political involvement of other youths in the years before the war. In some communities, boys had long been part of local festivals that had a political edge, such as Pope's Night on November 5, marking the anniversary of Guy Fawkes's attempt to blow up the British Houses of Parliament. To mark the occasion, boys made effigies of Fawkes or the Pope or any other locally unpopular figure, and carried them around town and finally burned them. These parades sometimes ended in brawls as rival groups of older boys, most famously those from the North End and South End neighborhoods of Boston, tried to outdo each other.[52]

From 1768 onward, when colonial committees encouraged merchants not to import and sell British goods, boys became an important part of the groups of youths harassing traders who did not join the boycott. How much of their activity was set in motion by the adults around them is not clear. Certainly some people suspected that was what was happening. William Gordon, a minister of the Third Congregational Church in Roxbury, Massachusetts, was sure that boys "small and great, and undoubtedly men, have been and were encouraged, and well paid by certain leaders, to insult and intimidate" those who imported British goods.[53]

Whether paid or not, their participation became apparent when events spiraled out of control, as they did on February 22, 1770. According to an edition of the *Boston Evening Post* printed a few days later, a group of "Boys and Children" (meaning older youths and younger boys) set up a "large wooden Head, with a Board faced with paper, on which was painted the figures of four of the Importers who had entered into, and violated the Merchants' agreement" not to import goods. However, the boys were soon sidetracked. A local man, Ebenezer Richardson, an "infamous Informer" to the customs' office, came upon them. Perhaps he tried to dismantle their construction, but he certainly chided them. They reciprocated. The group followed him home, taunting him, and at some point were joined by eleven-year-old Christopher Sneider, the son of German immigrants, who was on his way home from school. Once Richardson was inside his house, the children pelted it with what the sympathetic newspaper described as "light rubbish." It was not as light as the newspaper claimed, as the boys "broke some windows." Richardson, more "provoked than endangered," as the Reverend Gordon later remarked, reached for his gun and fired out the window, wounding a nineteen-year-old, Samuel Gore, and killing Sneider. It was not clear whether Sneider was drawn in by the politics, by friends, or just by the crowd. But he was the first political fatality in the city as the crisis escalated.[54]

Christopher Sneider's death and the killing of five men in Boston two weeks later, immortalized by sympathetic writers as the Boston Massacre, were felt deeply by the community in general and boys in particular. Thomas Perkins, aged about six at the time, remembered a family servant taking him to the site of the massacre to see the dead. Joseph May, in 1770 a ten-year-old "scholar at the public Latin school," remembered seeing the victims being buried and was so deeply moved that, as an old man, he could still walk to the exact spot.[55]

Some boys living on the frontier were also no strangers to political violence. Those who served in the Revolution from the western Carolinas were born too late to have witnessed the war against the Cherokee over land and trade, but a few may have recalled the Regulator crisis. That struggle pitched some western farmers against the governor and colonial militia, in other words citizens against citizens. The Regulators wanted to "regulate" the area, remove some corrupt officials, bring routine administration of justice to the region, and receive better representation in the colonial assembly. When petitioning and rioting had not brought change, they resorted to open conflict. Violence escalated after 1768, and in 1771 culminated in a pitched battle in which the governor and militia suppressed the rebellion. Regulators had destroyed property, acted as vigilantes, and humiliated their opponents. The governor in turn had executed the movement's leaders. Historians debate whether its causes were religious, ideological, regional, or class-based, but there is no disagreement that the movement left old scores to be settled when local residents chose sides in the Revolutionary War.[56]

The positions people in the area chose regarding independence did not clearly follow the divisions of the Regulator movement. The former Regulators had no love for British authority. But they hated equally the colonial political leaders who had suppressed them, and it was these same men who led the patriot cause in the region. On whatever side they fell, some families, to paraphrase the Scottish poet Robert Burns, had nursed their wrath to keep it warm. Boys would have heard stories about these old grievances around the fireside that would have helped shape their understanding of what side to take and what military conflict looked like.[57]

And when war came, many young boys had a chance to watch the activities of soldiers for years before they enlisted themselves. However, where they lived dictated the kind of war they would have seen. In the backcountry, especially in New York and the Carolinas, boys would have witnessed irregular warfare as bands of loyalist and patriot militias and their respective Indian allies fought each other and destroyed settler and Native villages. Civilian men and boys could especially find themselves the targets of this violence, and they and their families fled to hastily constructed forts for safety when the enemy attacked.

Boys in the East, in contrast, may have observed soldiers muster and march but were unlikely to have seen any fighting or felt at risk, even when military operations were being carried out near them. In that region, American and British military commanders fought a more conventional war. With a few exceptions, their forces were generally kept under tight control, respected civilians, and tried to minimize property damage. Each side had reason to nurture civilian support and present itself as an upholder of law and order. Both sides also avoided fighting wherever possible. They preferred to conserve their resources and target small strategic locations or interfere with the enemy's supply lines in limited engagements. However, boys could still feel bitter about property damage and the resulting dislocation. Samuel Boyd of South Carolina was eager to serve because of "the abuse I and my family had Received from [the British.] I was resolved, never to submit to them." He enlisted as soon as he turned sixteen in 1780.[58]

But even boys living some distance away from the thunder of muskets and artillery were no strangers to the sights and sounds of military life. Before the war, John Greenwood in Massachusetts earned a little pocket money playing his fife for the local militia when they trained, as the political crisis escalated. On those occasions, he "imbibed the ardor of a military spirit." During the war, Bishop Tyler saw soldiers regularly when army recruits and the local militia assembled at his father's tavern. Fourteen-year-old Jonathan Keeler of Ridgefield, Connecticut, watched British regular and loyalist forces march to transport ships waiting for them on Long Island Sound. Keeler especially remembered the occasion because the "soldiers were so exhausted." Abraham Weeks was impressed by the civility of French officers and soldiers and their "[s]trict discipline" when they were in his neighborhood in Westchester County, New York, and especially because they paid hard money for everything. And Josiah Quimby remembered a party of loyalist troops passing through and staying nearby "where they fed their horses with the meadow grass and went on next morning." And so boys learned about the military world even when war itself was distant.[59]

By these many means—singing songs and listening to sermons, reading adventure stories and political tracts, playing games and rough and tumble sports, absorbing community ideals of military manhood, and watching or experiencing the tumults of war itself—boys were drawn to a soldier's life. For some, any one of these would have been enough to encourage enlistment. But for other boys, there were also factors at home that made the army seem appealing. For them, the complications of family life and the exigencies of war added to the lure of the military and made service an appealing escape from difficult circumstances.

CHAPTER THREE

My Father Caused Me to Enlist

State of New York
County of Orange

On this twenty fifth day of May in the year one thousand
eight hundred and eighteen before me the subscriber [the
undersigned] one of the judges of the Court of Common Pleas
in and for the County aforesaid, personally appeared John Jenks
aged forty nine resident in the county aforesaid who being by
me first duly sworn according to law doth on his oath make the
following declaration in order to obtain the provision made by
the late act of Congress entitled an act to provide for certain
persons engaged in the Land and Naval service of the United
States in the Revolutionary War.

That the said John Jenks enlisted in the spring of the year
one thousand seven hundred and eighty as a drummer into a
company commanded by Captain Poertree [?] being the seventh
company in the fifth Regiment in the Connecticut Line [of
the Continental army] commanded by Colonel Sherman . . .
[He served three years] after which time he was honorably
discharged by General Huntington at West Point in the State of
New York. That he is in reduced circumstances and stands in
need of the assistance of his country for support and that he has
no other evidence in his power of his said services.[1]

John Jenks was among the most effusive of the former boy soldiers who
applied for pensions. With a sarcastic tone, an energetic style, and a bliz-
zard of exclamation points, he remembered some of the circumstances
of his enlistment and his years in the army. Even though he, like many
other veterans, could produce no evidence, such as a discharge certificate, his name appeared in the available Connecticut records, and his
pension was quickly approved. However, Jenks had to repeat the process
several times. After an early corruption scandal in the pension office,
all applicants of 1818 had to reapply, and a veteran also had to reapply whenever he moved to a new state, which Jenks did, moving in the

mid-1820s from New York to Pennsylvania. Over the years, he filled out the account of the circumstances of his enlistment and his service, duly noting every officer who ever gave him an order, the drummers and fifers he messed with, and where they all stood on parade in relation to one another.

Given his age when he gave the deposition above and his age on his next petition to the courts two years later when he was fifty-one, he would have been born in 1770 and age ten when he enlisted in 1780, and indeed he offers that as his birth year. A few years later, some of Jenks's neighbors suspected him of being a fraud as he was so young. The first age he gave, ten, was probably the correct one, but we will never know with certainty. Concerns over fraud led to his pension being rescinded, but it was reinstated in the early 1830s.[2]

In his defense, he repeatedly explained how he came to enter the army at such a young age, and he offered sections of that story over several years. Drawing on his own extensive correspondence, what we know about the army, and the options for impoverished children in this era, we can imagine Jenks's journey into military service.

Perhaps it was like this:

John Jenks was restless. He was bound to a master who expected him to earn his keep and who did not spare the rod in instilling household discipline. Jenks was ready to get away. And so, in 1780, when he heard that a recruiting party for the Continental army had arrived in the nearby town of Lebanon, Connecticut, he wanted to run off and enlist. But he was not sure if the army would take him. After all, he was not even close to five feet tall, and he was only ten years old. His grand plan might not work.

Life had not always been filled with such uncertainty. John's early childhood with his parents and two siblings had been carefree. As far as he was aware, they had not been poor. But in the early months of the war, when he was about five years old, John's father was killed in battle, and the Jenks family was "reduced to a state of penury." Impoverished, his mother bound out John, his older sister Sabrina, and younger brother Obadiah to various relatives in Windham County, Connecticut, to work in exchange for their support. John landed with one Samuel Whipple, who seemed to feel burdened by the obligation, even though he was a distant relative by marriage. The boy knew how to read, but it is unlikely he had access to many books or the time to enjoy the comfort and escape of reading amidst the work that was expected of him. The next years were lonely, and John probably missed his siblings. When he discovered the recruiting party was within walking distance of Mr. Whipple's, he realized this might be an opportunity to escape.

Jenks slipped away without anyone noticing. When he arrived at the recruiting post, he hoped he would be accepted. There was no point trying to lie about his age. That would be clear to everyone given his "infancy & size, [and] being very short of Stature." John was delighted when, at first, a sergeant agreed to enlist him. But then an officer decided he really was too small to be useful and promptly returned him to Mr. Whipple, who gave him a beating for his trouble.

But shortly after, there was a lucky turn of events: Mr. Whipple was drafted. Whipple was loath to enlist but needed to serve or provide a substitute. He immediately saw the solution: Jenks could go in his place. Whipple took the boy back to the recruiting officer, and, Jenks recalled, his master somehow "managed the affair so as to get me enlisted and mustered" in his place. The boy found himself standing again "among some recruits from whom but a short time before I had been mustered out!!!"

And so Jenks became a drummer in the Continental army, even though when he was first given a drum, it seemed to be almost as big as he was. A special small blue drum was quickly found for him, and he enjoyed becoming a favorite of the older soldiers. He loved everything about his military service. He was fed, clothed, and paid; he made friends; he played music. And he stayed for just over three years in his new army home.[3]

JENKS OFFERED NOTHING in his correspondence about his life in the years before his service with Samuel Whipple or the texture of his relationship with him. Jenks did not say if Whipple was a laborer, farmer, or craftsman, if he was married, if there were other children, servants, or apprentices in the household, if Whipple was a hard man or a caring one. The only hints that Jenks provided were that he ran away to enlist; that he was whipped on his return; and that he was shortly thereafter delivered as a substitute when Whipple himself was drafted. Draftees could provide a substitute to serve in their stead, and there was no shame in hiring one or being one. Some draftees hired substitutes from the community. Others preferred to draw on labor they did not need to pay, such as their dependents, nephews, or other male relatives; for Whipple, that was Jenks. While his guardian's actions seem harsh to a twenty-first-century sensibility, Whipple may just have been a pragmatic man or a man with a short fuse who felt the child in his care did not appreciate the home he was offered. The nuances of Jenks's experience are lost to us, and we can only imagine the way his daily life with Whipple might have been. In his adult recollection, he framed it as an interlude between his happy early childhood and later military service. His story, and those of boy soldiers like him, offer us a window into the lives of the period's most unfortunate children.[4]

THE INSTABILITY IN JENKS'S young life did not make him unusual in the Revolutionary era or for many years before and after. Death, poverty, or illness often led to the breakup of families as surviving parents, extended family, friends, or the courts found homes for children buffeted by the vicissitudes of fortune. And among boy soldiers, there were a number who enlisted to get away from difficulties and instability at home. A few, like Jenks, seem to have been motivated by unhappiness and a desire to escape servitude. Others were simply rebellious, enlisting to get away from strict fathers. Some wanted to avoid conflict with a new stepparent. A few were enlisted by their fathers, sometimes against their will or without their consent. Others enlisted voluntarily to find stability and safety amid the chaos of war; some were forced into the service by officers responding to wartime events.

When these boys were old men, they were frank about the forces that pushed them into the service. After all, they were telling their stories in order to receive a pension or, if writing a memoir, to have the recognition of their families and friends. It would have been natural for them to couch their enlistment in patriotic terms. Also, in the period in which they were writing, from 1818 onward, they had become the nation's greatest generation. They were generally admired, sometimes revered, and their sacrifices appreciated.[5]

It had not always been that way. In the years following the war, public festivals to mark great events such as Independence Day, the defeats of the British at Saratoga and Yorktown, or other patriot victories, celebrated only the great men of the era, such as George Washington and General Richard Montgomery who was killed in action early in the conflict. If soldiers were honored at all, it was men of the militia, those valiant men of property who had stood up for their rights. The other branches of the service were largely ignored. All patriots had struggled and occasionally suffered during the war years. Soldiers had been paid for their trouble. What other acknowledgement was required?[6]

But as the revolutionary generation aged, these political celebrations, like the society at large, became more democratic. The veterans, ordinary men, sometimes very poor men, began to be recognized for their service. At first, they—and later their sons— began to be recognized at the ballot box. Many of the veterans, at the time of the war, had been unable to vote. The boys, of course, had been too young, well under the legal voting age of twenty-one. Others had been too poor to vote, most states having requirements to own property, to be a taxpayer, or to pay a poll tax in order to do so. The expansion of the franchise was uneven over time and place, but in the decades following the first broad pension legislation in 1818, voting rights steadily broadened. Aging Revolutionary War soldiers and victorious veterans from the War of 1812 joined together in arguing for political inclusion. By 1840, only three states in the union—Virginia, Rhode Island, and Louisiana—still had property requirements and poll taxes, and other tax requirements were quickly disappearing from the political landscape. White male suffrage was almost universal, and four northern states—Massachusetts, Vermont, Maine, and New Hampshire—extended voting rights to free black men.[7]

Grand public occasions, such as Independence Day parades and the anniversaries of important patriot victories, began to reflect this more democratic impulse. Initially, after the war, only surviving high-ranking officers led parades. But with national confidence soaring after the War of 1812 and the aging Revolutionary generation attracting sympathetic attention, elderly veterans (whatever their lowly social origins) were now sometimes invited to take center stage. They were toasted at public gatherings, commemorative events, and indeed sometimes when they went to apply for pensions. New school textbooks celebrated the role of many Americans in the Revolutionary struggle, not just Washington and a handful of other patriot leaders.[8]

Given this shift in public perception, former boy soldiers might be expected to celebrate their heroism in memoirs and pension applications. Surely they would highlight their political reasons for fighting in what one orator in 1838 called "the most august event . . . in the political annals of mankind."[9]

But they did not. Despite their newfound glory, or perhaps because of it, many veterans gave pragmatic rather than fervid ideological reasons for enlistment. They used the pension process as an opportunity to step off the pedestal onto which the public now placed them. Perhaps in doing so veterans were quietly protesting years of public neglect. They wanted to let the world know what the reality of their lives had been. Reflecting on the hardships of war after a lifetime, these former boy soldiers may have felt more aggrieved in retrospect than they did during their military tenure. And it may have been therapeutic to tell their stories at all.

Finding a home and stability in the army perhaps had its own kind of glory. Jenks's experiences illustrate the ways in which instability could rock young lives in the Revolutionary era. But they also show the possibilities and limitations for children to shape their own destinies. Prior to his military service, Jenks had experienced a perfect storm of death and grief, and probably loneliness. Not every child was so unfortunate, of course, but elements of his life experience were common to many children. Death was a regular companion, and instability and insecurity were frequent sequels. Some felt driven from home and sought the army as a safe haven from a tumultuous home life. Others were pressed into service by fathers or by the chaotic military situation that swirled around them. But whatever pushed boys into the service, some of them found the army an oasis of support and friendship in difficult times.

EVEN THOUGH JENKS lost his father in battle rather than to disease, he was not unusual in losing a parent at a young age or in having his home and family broken up as a result. Children in the happiest, most loved, and most seemingly secure circumstances could find themselves similarly tossed. There are no good mortality statistics for British North America in the eighteenth century, but in the United States in the early nineteenth century, average life expectancy for white men and women at birth was about age forty, meaning that many adults died when their children were still young.[10]

Among children too, early death was common, adding to the difficulties and insecurities that surviving siblings and friends faced. Data for the early nineteenth century show that children under ten years of age accounted for fully 40 percent of all deaths. Indeed, for Jenks, the loss of his father may not have been the first family death he had encountered. For many children, few years passed without experiencing the loss of a sibling, parent, or other near relatives. Death could strike at any time, and parents and ministers encouraged children from a young age to prepare for their own deaths and that of those around them. Some of the earliest children's books published, such as James Janeway's, *A Token for Children, Being An Exact Account of the Conversion, Holy and Exemplary Lives and Joyful Deaths of Several Young Children*, encouraged children to reflect urgently on the state of their souls. The subject was a regular part of sermons, and even contemporary guides to good manners such as *The Friendly Instructor* offered information to children on how to prepare spiritually to "submit with Cheerfulness to the Will of God whatever it shall be." Funeral rites and services helped survivors cope with the death of a loved one, and family, kin, or the larger community offered the needed comfort or support, whether out of love, friendship, or at the direction of the courts.[11]

Jenks certainly would have known children who had died. Colonial mortality rates varied over time and place, and exact data for children are hard to calculate as the deaths of newborn infants were not always noted in diaries, family Bibles, or church records. However, in New England between 1640 and 1759, probably about 25 percent of all children did not live to see their tenth birthdays. At the beginning of the eighteenth century in Charles Parish, Virginia, 18 percent of children died before they reached age four. Epidemic years took a particularly heavy toll when diseases such as smallpox, influenza, or diphtheria (called throat distemper at the time) swept through communities. Native towns and villages were particularly hard hit by these Old World diseases. Not only did the indigenous population have little resistance to these contagions, their impact was compounded by the dislocations of conquest. Slave children too experienced higher mortality rates than free children probably due to poorer early childhood nutrition. But all over the colonies, ministers' diaries logged a steady stream of deaths. For Lutheran minister Henry Muhlenberg in the village of Trappe, Pennsylvania, about thirty miles west of Philadelphia, it was a rare week when he did not officiate at the funeral of at least one child. There were many weeks when he buried several, and at some services he buried two children at a time.[12]

Children died from accidents as well as diseases. The hazards of home and hearth, such as open fires, boiling water, and uncovered wells, all took a sad toll. As an infant, John Tileston's hand was badly burned when he crawled into a hearth where a fire was burning. When Samuel

Dewees was a young soldier he witnessed the death of a girl aged about six whose apron caught fire in her family's kitchen. The flames quickly spread to the rest of her clothing, as the child, in her panic, ran outside where the flames were whipped by the wind. People rushed to help but could not prevent the fire from engulfing her. It was, Dewees recalled, "a distressing sight."[13]

The deaths of siblings or parents from disease and accidents were some of the upheavals that regularly swept through children's lives, but other forces also undermined family stability. For slave children, their parents might be sold. To cope with this crisis, children were encouraged to address older slaves as aunt or uncle and to take a broad, inclusive view of family. But sometimes the bonds of family were severed before any such lesson could be taught, as it was for boy soldier Peter Brooks Nelson. Nelson was a slave in Massachusetts; he was born a twin in the summer of 1763. The owners of his mother, Peggy, thought that twins presented too great a demand on her time and decided that one of them should be taken from her. Nelson was sold to a childless white couple for four pounds when he was nineteen months old, presumably as soon as he was weaned.[14]

Death of a master could be equally disruptive to slave children. Distribution of a slave owner's estate to his heirs might result in families being broken up. In South Carolina, where some planters enjoyed immense wealth and could own hundreds of slaves, families had a greater chance of staying together or at least in the same neighborhood upon a master's death. But if an owner's estate was burdened by debt or if a master owned only a few slaves, bondsmen and women and their children who may have lived as a family for years could be scattered to heirs or sold to meet the demands of creditors.[15]

For free children too, parental death could quickly lead to the breakup of the family, as Jenks knew all too well. Another young soldier, Thomas Painter, lost his father when he was six, and that plunged the family into poverty. For a few years his mother had to "work hard and fare hard" to keep her three children with her, but finally she succumbed to a fever and died. Thomas was then dispatched to his grandmother for several years, and at age eleven, he apprenticed to an uncle who was a shoemaker. William Conner, who was born in Isle of Wight County in the Tidewater area of Virginia in 1763, faced similar instability in his young life. His father died when he was about seven, and he could "remember seeing his father's coffin." After his father died, William and his mother moved north to be near his aunt in Fauquier County, and four years later his mother died. A much older brother came and took him to his house out in the frontier settlement of Surry County, North Carolina, about three hundred miles to the south. It was a world away from his early childhood home.[16]

Samuel Smith of Rhode Island also faced an early childhood surrounded by death and instability, though he conceded that some of the latter came from his own poor judgment. His father had died when he was very young, but the family stayed intact. Then a terrible illness at age eight resulted in Samuel never again having full use of his right arm. His mother died when he was thirteen, and he was sent to the home of a neighbor for one year and then to another for three. From this last, Smith ran away—not because his master was unkind, but because the boy thought he could get better terms elsewhere, an unsuccessful gamble he deeply regretted. Smith later found himself "destitute of home . . . [and] in a lonely condition." An opportunity to enlist solved his problems of where and with whom to live.[17]

Being from a rich family and having loving relations nearby did not protect children from such buffeting, as Martha Laurens, the daughter of the wealthy South Carolina planter and merchant, Henry Laurens, discovered. She was five when she lost her sister Eleanor, four years her senior, eight when her infant brother Samuel died, and eleven when her mother died in childbirth, an event that she later described as "an immense loss." Her mother's death prompted her father to scatter his flock. Martha and her new baby sister went to live with their aunt and uncle, and her three surviving brothers were dispatched across the Atlantic for their education. Martha joined her brothers in London when she was sixteen, arriving in time to visit her youngest brother, ten-year-old James, a few weeks before he died after falling from a balcony.[18]

Perhaps high mortality rates worked against the development of strong connections between siblings, and, of course, not all surviving siblings got along. However, bonds could remain strong. For all colonial children, siblings and other close kin were the primary companions of daily life, whether working, playing, or learning. This was especially true for children raised in rural areas, where about 95 percent of the colonial population lived. Household duties and the tremendous physical isolation of rural places forced siblings of this era into each other's company a great deal.[19]

In her memoir, years later, Martha Laurens recalled that her surviving siblings and her faith were a comfort to her during periods of loss and dislocation. Her brother, John, five years her senior, had been her constant solace. He was interested in her well-being and education, and became a "dearly beloved brother." However, that consolation did not last long. John was killed in action during the Revolutionary War when Martha was twenty-three. Following the death of her mother, Martha had become deeply religious. After John died, she sought relief again in her faith, and "found the comfort of having secured a friend in her maker."[20]

As a child, Samuel Younglove had formed a strong bond with his beloved sister. After the war, when he was about nineteen, his mother died, an event that he "lamented much." He was also deeply pained by his father's subsequent remarriage, something that he later recalled "drove me almost to distraction." In his sadness, he fell into a "great vortex" of despair and dissipation, and even the love and assistance of his closest and "favorite sister" could not help him. Years later, when he had regained his usual high spirits, the memory of the grief he had caused her gave him great pain.[21]

Few people left such explicit records of their feelings for their siblings, but their actions spoke for them. Jonathan Burrows and his brother, David, had enlisted in the army together but, during their service, David died of smallpox. Jonathan was burdened with grief, but it was some months before he was free to head home. While he had been away, his wife had given birth to a son whom she had named, Jonathan, after her husband. But when Jonathan Burrows finally returned, he renamed the seven-month-old boy, David, in his brother's memory. Perhaps inspired by the friends, David and Jonathan, in the biblical story from the book of Samuel for whom they were named, Jonathan "was knit to the soul of David." Thomas Painter similarly grieved for his brother, Shubel. Both boys went to sea in their late teens, working together, trying their luck on a privateer. When Shubel became ill and died on board the vessel, Painter was bereft. In his memoir, decades later, he remembered with great emotion the ceremony committing his brother's "mortal remains to a Watery Grave, never more to be seen until the Sound of the Arch Angel's Trump, shall cause the sea to give up her dead."[22]

Siblings were separated by circumstances other than death but found the parting equally difficult. Samuel Dewees noted that it was a "painful trial" when he was separated from his family at age five when his impoverished father bound him out. And John Jenks, who may not have seen his siblings for many years, if ever, after they were separated in 1775, did not forget them. Forty years later, he made a point of mentioning them by name in his pension application, even though they were irrelevant to his claim. In such recollections and actions, we can hear the whisper of sibling bonds.[23]

Many children, then, were buffeted by instability. The most important, formal way the community coped with this was the system of binding out children to others. Long before their enlistments, young soldiers such as Jenks, Fox, Dewees, and others had been sent to live and work in the homes of relatives or neighbors when their parents were either dead or unable to care for them. Sometimes this was an informal arrangement, such as when William Conner went to live with his brother or Martha Laurens with her uncle. But it was also common for a child to be bound by a contract even if a relative was involved, such as with Jenks and his distant uncle, or a member of the community, such as Fox. If parents or surviving family could not make the necessary arrangements themselves, the courts stepped in to do so.

The practice of binding out existed in all the colonies. Sometimes the process was initiated by courts, concerned about the welfare of a child, and, in others, it was begun by a parent or relative in need of assistance. After being bound, children began a period of servitude, owing masters their labor until they were twenty-one, although the age limit for girls was sometimes a little lower, often their late teen years. Like contracts for other indentured servants, those for impoverished children also spelled out the details of what was required of them, namely work and obedience, and what was required of the masters. This was a longer list and included that masters support, educate to some degree, perhaps teach a skill, and provide some parting gift of money or clothing when they sent the adult children on their way. These were the local systems in place to protect and provide for poor or orphaned children.[24]

Binding out was not the only way poor families could cope with providing for their children. By the middle of the eighteenth century, families living in and around the few colonial cities had another option: the charitable school. Among the earliest and most rural of these was founded by George Whitefield, the Anglican evangelist, who raised money on his speaking tour of colonial North America in the 1740s for the Bethesda Orphan House and Charity School that he was building just south of Savannah, Georgia. In his 1740 pamphlet, Whitefield stated that his school was a place where poor children spent the same number of hours at schoolwork as they did at "labor in their respective stations," and he proudly noted the amount of cotton the children had picked. Some charitable schools, such as the Friends Schools in Philadelphia, found it costly to sustain a broad mandate to educate the truly poor. Families who could afford to pay or make a contribution to their children's education did not want their children mixing with the poorest in the community. Consequently, the Friends and schools like them offered the poorest children only the most rudimentary education, kept them in separate classrooms, and focused on training that would ready them for domestic service and other labor. Charity schools of the period did not offer opportunities for class mobility; rather they, like the binding-out system, reflected and perpetuated existing social arrangements. In the twenty-five years before the Revolution, hundreds of children passed through the doors of such charity schools and most probably fared no worse than poor children bound to labor.[25]

Being bound out was not necessarily a bad experience. When seven-year-old David Perry's mother died, his father "broke up housekeeping" and sent the boy to live with an uncle who treated him "very kindly." And, according to the evidence left by Elizabeth Drinker, her charge, young Sally Dawson was not unhappy about her situation. Three weeks after Dawson's mother died, her father bound her to Drinker for eight years. Drinker noted in her diary at the time that the girl was "9years [sic] and ½ old—a pritty looking Child." Two years later, Drinker and Dawson were still mistress and servant, but Drinker's note in her diary that she was sitting up late reading with the girl "sleeping in a chair by me" hinted at a more companionable relationship. Of course, Dawson may have been quietly miserable, without the means or opportunity to express it. Still, even though tales of disaster litter the court records, probably the most common relationship between master or mistress and bound child was reluctant cooperation in the hope that a skill could be learned that would allow for later independence.[26]

In remembering their time as bound children, some veterans recalled their unhappiness. Some also acknowledged that those rough times had served them in good stead. Thomas Painter thought his life was "a hard lot" when, as noted earlier, he was apprenticed at eleven as a shoemaker after both his parents died. However, before he was twenty-one, he accepted that this might have actually been to his advantage as he was not spoiled and had been "oblig'd to shirk [*sic*] for myself." Ebenezer Fox, bound to a neighboring farmer by his impoverished father at age seven, realized years later that this fate had not been so terrible. However, his account of this period began bitterly with a barb directed at his father, sarcastically chiding him for thinking "that my physical powers were adequate, at this time of life, to my own maintenance." Fox also noted that, while bound, he experienced "many privations." However, as an old man of seventy-five, he was philosophical about these hardships and thought that "boys are apt to complain of their lot, especially when deprived of the indulgences of home. They do not estimate their advantages or disadvantages by comparison; but view them in the abstract." Fox felt he should have appreciated his "comparative blessings." But he remembered the sadness he felt at the time very clearly.[27]

Jenks may have entered Mr. Whipple's household philosophical about his circumstances, and he may not have seen his uncle's use of the whip as unusual or excessive. Being whipped for disobedience—and many lesser infractions—was par for the course for many children in colonial America. In the eighteenth century, public whipping was still the most common punishment courts handed down for offenders of all ages. Few colonial children, no matter how prosperous, beloved, or privileged, were spared the correction of at least a sharp smack, often by a birch branch or hickory stick, and occasionally a horsewhip.

Jenks probably did not know that children in some communities were never beaten at all. Observers from all walks of life encountering eastern Native peoples noted the gentleness with which parents treated their offspring. As one Jesuit priest observed of the Huron, they "know not what it is to punish them." But Indian children did not go unpunished. Father Jean de Lamberville simply did not see the punishments that were taking place because they were not corporal. Indian parents instead used ridicule, making fun of disobedient children, or threatened them with evil spirits. Some sprinkled water on children's faces. A very young child might be denied the comfort of the cradleboard where he or she usually slept. But in no community did parents beat children in a way de Lamberville would have found familiar. David Zeisberger, a Moravian missionary among the Delaware and Cherokee, observed that parents felt corporal punishment produced "bitterness, hatred and contempt." They feared that children so embittered would revenge themselves when grown-up. Whatever the reason for eschewing the whip,

Zeisberger noted that children responded to this "mild treatment" and were "wellbred" and showed "great attention and respect to parents."[28]

Quaker parents, members of the Society of Friends, also rejected corporal punishment for their children. They believed that a child's salvation and natural obedience would come about from loving "holy conversation," not coercion. They wrestled over whether this principle should extend to servants and slaves. One master, John Warrell, was chastised by his Pennsylvania church, the Chester Meeting, for whipping his servant. He knew the meeting was justified in its actions but felt the servant deserved it as he was a "worthless" fellow. Gentler means of encouraging obedience needed to be found. The meeting developed a system whereby masters gave servants certificates when their bound time was over that served as a job and credit reference. Servants who wanted a certificate needed to be dutiful. It worked. Of course, slaves could be offered no such inducement for good behavior, but Friends exhorted each other to withhold the lash and spoke out against the institution of slavery generally.[29]

Most other children in colonial America were familiar with corporal punishment, having either received it or having observed it used on others. Many parents found it a necessary tool for disciplining children. As historian Karin Calvert noted, this did not mean these parents loved their children less. Rather, they loved them in different ways, believing that punishment at best trained children to be obedient and dutiful and at worst did no harm.[30]

Of course, children's experiences varied considerably, not only among different families, but also within them. This was especially true given that parents did not cluster their childbearing into a few years as is usual today. In this era before reliable and easy birth control, couples had children throughout a woman's childbearing years, and the surviving oldest and youngest children could have radically different experiences in punishment and many other aspects of life. In blended families, the differences could be even greater. Paul Revere, the famed Boston silversmith of the Revolutionary era, had sixteen children—eight with his first wife and another eight with his second (eleven of whom lived beyond early childhood). Deborah, his first child, was born almost thirty years before her last half sibling. In the years before her own marriage, she helped her mother and stepmother and would have been disciplined and been a disciplinarian in turn.[31]

In Puritan New England, families saw children and servants, slave and free, as willful beings who needed to be coerced into becoming obedient and malleable. Ideally this was done by example and explanation, but the next reprimand was physical. In the late seventeenth century, Joseph Sewall knew this from an early age. One day, when he was four, his father, Samuel Sewall, was particularly displeased with him. The boy had played at prayer time, started eating dinner before grace was finished, and hit his older sister, Betsy, on the head. For these infractions, Mr. Sewall "whipd him pretty smartly." Fifty years later, the infant Sally Burr received an equally sharp lesson, though perhaps with less awareness of her wrongdoing. Sally was the daughter of Esther Burr, who was herself the daughter of Sarah and Jonathan Edwards, the great New England preacher and theologian of the eighteenth century. Even though Sally was not yet quite ten months old, Esther thought that the baby knew "the difference between a smile and a frown as well as I do." Thus, Esther told an old friend that she had "begun to govourn Sally" and had already "Whip'd" her for disobedience. Her friend's letter in response has not survived.[32]

Slave children, of course, were also familiar with corporal punishment, which could be inflicted by their parents as well as their masters. It was imperative that slave parents quickly taught their children the self-control necessary to survive the complex interactions with white masters and their families. When masters and overseers punished slave children, their parents were helpless to protect them.[33]

If Jenks thought the army was a refuge from corporal punishment, he was mistaken. Soldiers of any age were whipped for crimes such as theft or drunkenness and for breaches of military regulations such as being disrespectful to officers. Not all soldiers were punished this way. Militiamen, who were usually property owners or the sons of property owners, were required to pay a fine for any infraction. But soldiers in the Continental or state troops were often poorer men who were paid little and who were usually short of funds. Consequently, the courts most commonly sentenced them to be whipped by a lash with knots in it, the cat o'nine tails. One hundred lashes was both the maximum punishment allowed and the sentence most commonly handed down by military courts.[34]

Children, servants, and slaves knew that corporal punishment needed no magistrate, judge, or jury to be handed out. Any adult, master, parent, or teacher, had the right, and indeed responsibility, to give them appropriate "correction." But the courts did reprimand people whose actions seemed too harsh. In 1682, Philip Fowler faced a court in Ipswich, Massachusetts, for punishing his servant by "hanging him up by his heels as butchers do beasts." The judge cautioned Fowler about using this kind of punishment in the future and required him to pay the court's costs. In New York in 1726, a court sided with an aggrieved apprentice who had been "Immoderately corrected." The apprentice was released from his contract, and the inconvenience that this gave the master was considered reprimand enough. Of course, punishment of slaves brought no judicial review, and the slave's only protection was his or her labor value.[35]

Soldiers could also be disciplined without the courts being involved. Most officers had no objection to fellow officers or noncommissioned officers, sergeants, and corporals casually smacking young troops in the course of training them. When thirteen-year-old David Granger became a soldier in the New Hampshire Continentals, he lived in fear of the sergeant major who rousted the soldiers out of bed in the morning. When it was the boy's turn to do early morning guard duty, he made sure all his things were ready the night before so he could leap out of bed and be ready quickly so as to "not get a caneing from him as some others did." And Samuel Dewees, a fifer, and three other musicians each received a punishment of "12 lashes each upon our bared buttocks" after a brawl in which they gave a soldier they knew some "rough treatment." The next day the fife major cornered the boys and gave out the punishment—or rather had the musicians lash each other so he did not have to exert himself.[36]

By the middle of the eighteenth century, some parents and officers were becoming sensitive to the emotional impact of corporal punishment and were using it less. One Connecticut court-martial panel was sensitive "to the Wound the Whip inflicts on the character of a young soldier," and gave the youth on trial simply a warning. In South Carolina too, officers worried about the effect of the lash on the young. When seventeen-year-old Oliver Mahaffey was found guilty of being absent without leave, the court sentenced him to sixty lashes but recommended "him to Mercy being a young Soldier." The commander agreed, and Mahaffey received twenty lashes instead. But no boy soldier could count on such leniency.[37]

In civilian life, enlightened parents (who may yet have used corporal punishment on their servants and slaves) increasingly tried guiding their children using reason and love. While these parents preferred not to discipline their children harshly, they were not above having servants or teachers do it. In the late seventeenth century in Boston, Massachusetts, John Barnard's parents and later his stepmother guided him gently though life. It was his schoolteacher who wielded the whip. Barnard recalled that at school he was "often beaten for my play, and my little roguish tricks." But he was a good student, and he was pleased that he was not "beaten for my book more than once or twice." In particular, Barnard recalled the time his schoolmaster asked him to translate some of *Aesop's Fables* into Latin—a task he found difficult despite his proficiency. Mistaking Barnard's lack of "poetical fancy" for a lack of effort, Barnard's teacher whipped him for his poor translation. His parents, however, refrained from physically punishing their son.[38]

Unlike Barnard, many children found that beatings, floggings, and whippings were tasks in which their parents were happy to share. Bob Carter, the second surviving son of wealthy Virginia planter Robert Carter, was whipped by both his father and his tutor. The boy, according to the tutor, Philip Fithian, was "extremely volatile and uncertain in his temper" and "often flog'd by . . . [his] Pappa." But Fithian did his part and regularly gave his charge a "smart correction," usually for impertinence, fighting, or other infractions.[39]

Most of these reprimands were probably quickly forgotten. But Hiram Hill, growing up shortly after the Revolution, remembered "receiving three severe floggings" from his father and, more than thirty years later, could recall the circumstances in great detail. The first flogging, at age eight, he accepted, as he had deliberately not responded to a straightforward question. But this punishment was delivered with such passion that the boy's mother and sisters left the room until it was over. The second thrashing he thought was unjust. Late one evening, his father had required silence from him and another boy, Robert, a visiting relative, with whom he was sharing a bed. Hiram knew to be still right away, but Robert tickled him and told him a funny story that made Hiram laugh. His father gave him a beating with "a good size stick." The third time, Hiram again accepted the punishment as deserved; he had absentmindedly left an axe out in the rain overnight after being told especially not to. That beating left "marks on my back for a good while." As a middle-aged man looking back, Hill advocated restraint. He "would not advise parents to flogg their children except in such cases as may seem absolutely necessary." The adult Hill did not think any of his floggings had qualified.[40]

Not only parents, masters, governesses, tutors, and teachers could punish children. Sometimes entire communities made sure a wayward child was punished. Before he went off to the army, young Stephen Burroughs was a trickster who, for his own amusement, delighted in "pestering others," especially adults. He remembered he became "a terror of the people" and certainly "the worst boy in town." It became a badge of honor for others in the community to get him whipped. But, he recalled, "repeated application of this birchen medicine [a switch made of birch wood] never cured my pursuit of fun."[41]

No boy, not Jenks, Hill, or Burroughs, would have expected any different treatment for such conduct. Indeed, *The New England Primer*, the most popular spelling book used by schools, tutors, and parents all over British North America, reminded children of the connection between learning and punishment. Brought to them by the letters *F* and *J*, the alphabet rhyme reminded them that "the Idle *Fool* is whipt at school" and that "*Job* feels the Rod yet blesses GOD." John Jenks could not have imagined there was any home without corporal punishment and certainly not the army. But perhaps he hoped to find some friendship to make it bearable.[42]

NOT EVERY BOY driven to enlist by unhappiness at home was fleeing instability or a difficult master. Having both parents still alive or living with a parent and stepparent was not a guarantee of happiness. Eli Jacobs ran away from home to join the army after an argument with his stepmother. But his father made no attempt to retrieve him. Mr. Jacobs perhaps preferred the new domestic tranquility of his home and told a neighbor that he hoped the army "would make a Steady man" of young Eli. George Blackmore, living in Maryland with his mother and stepfather, also found his new stepparent a trial and ran away to join the military when he was seventeen. Stephen Burroughs, being regularly whipped at home for being naughty, "eloped" from his minister-father to enlist at age fourteen. However, in Burroughs's case, his father quickly came to retrieve him.[43]

While these boys had taken the initiative to flee to the army, others found themselves enlisted against their will. Fourteen-year-old William Deane of New Jersey was an "unruly child." His parents were presumably dead or unable to care for him. Family friends decided that Deane must enlist so that the army might "break his unruly spirit and prevent his ever acting so again." It apparently did the trick. Before Deane turned sixteen, his guardians felt that the desired change "is effected" and tried to arrange a discharge so the boy could return home. In 1780, in Surry County in the North Carolina backcountry, Obadiah Benge, fifteen or sixteen at the time, found himself enlisted for a nine-month term. He was, he remembered, "forced" into the service "by his step-father, John Fielder, as a substitute for one James Green, [and] his said step-father received from said James Green a horse, bridle and saddle for the same." His stepfather had bartered him away. Fourteen-year-old James Ayres also found himself in the army in 1775, having been enlisted by his father. That led to a difficult day in the bitterly divided Ayres household. James's father was a "good whig," serving in the military himself, and he was eager for young James to go out with him. Mrs. Ayres, however, was "in great distress." She was angry and distraught over the enlistment as James was still "quite small[,] about a good size to send to mole." Since a mole catcher had to be able to collect traps from this small insectivore's network of tunnels, young James Ayres was slight indeed. Mrs. Ayres's tears were in vain, and the boy left with his father.[44]

A few boys who went to the battlefield as waiters to their officer-fathers may have had some choice about enlisting. In 1782, before twelve-year-old Cyrus Allen left with his father, Captain Daniel Allen, his service had been the subject of regular conversations in the household. A neighbor, Daniel Carpenter, an old veteran of twenty-one who had enlisted for his first term at age seventeen, "talked to him about his going into the service so young." Unfortunately Carpenter did not say how he advised him, but young Cyrus enlisted.[45]

Most who served under their officer-fathers probably had little say in the decision. John Piatt, who entered the New Jersey Continentals, remembered that at the time "he was quite a youth, under the guardianship of his father," implying that matters were out of his control. Cordilla ("Dilla") Fitch was taken into the Connecticut Continentals to be his father's waiter probably when he was about twelve, but he was sent home a few months later after a long bout with fever. Ten-year-old Asahel Durkee also seemed to have had little choice, but he enjoyed his first six months of service and signed up for another year. Shortly after Asahel began his second term, he was sent home (perhaps because the boy was ill or there was some need at home). His family hired a substitute for him, and he did not serve again until he was fifteen.[46]

Would the enslaved Peter Brooks Nelson have had a say in his enlistment at age twelve? His owners were Josiah and Elizabeth Nelson of Lincoln, Massachusetts, a childless couple who bought him when he was a toddler. In some ways, Nelson was treated as their child. He attended the local school and played with the Nelsons' nephew and niece and other children in the neighborhood. But he grew up knowing the true place of slaves, however affectionate the treatment he received at home. There were more than twenty-five slaves in Lincoln, a village with fewer than seven hundred inhabitants. In church on Sundays, Nelson would meet his mother from whom he had been sold and who still lived with her owners in nearby Lexington. They, with other black worshipers, had to sit in the gallery of the church. The social and legal strictures of the period were stark. But these stark routines were dramatically interrupted on April 19, 1775. British soldiers marched through Lincoln as they headed to nearby Lexington on that fateful day. The men of the village were actively involved in the battle in which the first shots of the war were fired. The community was in an uproar. Within days, Josiah Nelson and other men in his community rushed to join the troops gathering to trap the British in Boston. Peter Nelson, along with another slave, Cato, who was owned by the local militia captain, were also going. Given the excitement of those days, it is possible that Peter was eager to be in the thick of things with his master, his neighbors, and his fellow slave, whom he certainly knew. No enlistment papers have survived, and Nelson did not live long enough to apply for a pension, when he might have documented his account of those earliest moments of the Revolution. As a young boy and a slave, Peter Nelson's papers would have been signed by his owner, Josiah Nelson. And we will never know whether Peter hurried to battle of his own will or that of his master.[47]

However, four years later, in 1779, when he turned sixteen, it was certainly Peter Nelson himself who was eager to go to war. The year before, the state of Massachusetts had authorized the enlistment of blacks and had offered freedom to slaves who enlisted in the Continental army. It is doubtful that his master wanted him to leave. Peter Nelson's labor was needed at home on the farm, but the community, as well as his master, was under pressure to supply men for the army. Nelson became free at his enlistment, but it was his master who received the bounty, and it was probably his master who signed the enlistment paper, though it has not survived.[48]

For some free boys, the situation is clearer. Samuel Dewees "was enlisted" into the Pennsylvania Continentals at about age fifteen by his recruiting sergeant-father. John Cronkhite enlisted in the New York Continentals as a fifer when he was eleven as part of his whole family's involvement in the army. His father joined as a sergeant, his mother was in camp as a paid laundress for the officers, and at least one sibling, a baby still in his mother's arms, also came along. John's service was part of the package.[49]

Some boys found themselves enlisted by their fathers with safety in mind. Gaines Hitchcock of western Massachusetts recalled that his father "caused me to enlist" as soon as he turned fourteen; Mr. Hitchcock was concerned that his son might soon be drafted and subject to a harsh soldier's life. So when a local captain was looking for a waiter, Mr. Hitchcock thought this would be easier service and the boy, "under my father's direction," duly enlisted—although as an old man he could not recall whether he or his father had actually put his name on the enlistment paper. On the Carolina frontier, ten-year-old Thomas Price served with his officer-father (Captain Thomas Price) as a fifer, and Captain Price strongly preferred that the boy be with him. Young Thomas was tall for his age, and his father thought "there was great danger in leaving a boy of his size at home," as Tories (loyalists) were intimidating patriot families. Thomas's older brother William, age fourteen, was also joining the service leaving Thomas without his nearest companion. It was a better and safer solution for the younger boy to enlist.[50]

A few other boys also joined for safety, but they were refugees from the shifting tide of war. A number of these were French Canadian. After the patriot invasion of Canada in December 1775 and spring 1776, some French Canadians and a few English colonists who had married local women joined the patriot forces. When these troops were driven south back into New York, the Canadians rightly feared reprisals from the British and gathered up their families to join the patriot army on its retreat. In these circumstances, boys enlisted with their fathers, joining whole companies of soldiers and officers made up of refugees from Quebec. Eleven-year-old Alexander Ferriol was one of them. He became a fifer in the same company as his officer-father and served in one of two Canadian regiments of the Continental army. And, of course, there was a host of other refugee children in camp. Ferriol was friendly with many of them. One of these was Theotist Paulin, about age five when her family joined the army. Another was Sally Robenet, who was eight when her American father and French Canadian mother fled to the patriots. For these children, this was no short-term participation in the military community. They had no home to which to return.[51]

For one teenager, the war raging outside his home mirrored the one within it. He lived in the North Carolina backcountry, and, in that region, communities split sharply during the war over patriot or loyalist allegiance. Families did too. Josiah Brandon was fifteen when independence was declared, and, at that age, he might be expected to have held the same political opinions as his father. But he did not. The boy was a patriot; his father was loyal to the British crown. In 1776, they may have served together in the militia in an expedition against the Cherokee Indians. But, in 1777, the militia split into patriot and loyalist groups with each side targeting the other and its supporters. His father now served as an officer with the loyalists. Brandon, who had turned sixteen, went out with the patriots. His actions were, he later remembered, "contrary to the will of his father." This was probably an understatement. Over the next few years, they both were frequently out with their opposing units, and one can only imagine the grief this caused the family. When Brandon came home, he probably stayed with friends rather than in his father's house.[52]

Their family conflict came to a head in 1780. In late spring that year, a large British force landed in Charleston, South Carolina, defeating patriot troops in the area. With that British success and the army's continued presence, the loyalist militia turned out with greater confidence, and the guerrilla war in the backcountry escalated. Josiah's father felt more confident too and reasserted his authority over his son's life. His father now compelled the youth, who turned nineteen that summer, to join the loyalists. Father and son served side by side, and, in October, found themselves together in the heat of the Battle of King's Mountain. Josiah was unscathed, healthy apart from a foot problem, and was taken prisoner. His father was killed. Fortunately, a few days after his capture, Josiah was recognized by a patriot officer who arranged his release. Word was sent to his mother who came and took him home. Brandon was not sentimental about the cause in which his father had given his life. Freed from his father's authority, he rejoined the patriot militia for the remainder of the war.[53]

In his pension application, Brandon made no attempt to conceal this brief change of sides. He had served in the patriot militia for many years and hoped to be rewarded for it. But his letters to the pension office, and those of his supporters, reflected the varieties of opportunities and obstacles he had faced. One advocate stated that the young Brandon, in 1780, was "then a minor and under his [father's] absolute control." Yet, in another letter, Brandon referred to the switch to the loyalist side as "an indiscreet act of my youth," implying that he had had some choice in the matter.[54]

Not many boys faced decisions such as Brandon's that would tear their families apart. However, some boys were reluctant to fight despite the pressing exigencies of war, William Walton of Virginia among them. Walton served alongside his father, and both were "drafted or impressed" by a Continental officer, something William deeply resented. The boy worked with his father hauling grain to the troops in the Virginia backcountry, and in "this most disagreeable service I was compelled to continue twelve months, finding my own horse & fixtures, thinly clad in homespun furnished by my Mother, in one of the coldest Winters almost ever known." He was still angry testifying about it fifty years later, while applying for a pension for this same labor.[55]

Two boys from the New York frontier remembered their service with equal bitterness. Fourteen-year-old Henry Eckler and his father sought refuge at Fort Plank after their family was captured by Indians in the Mohawk Valley and Henry's sister was killed. At Fort Plank, officers of the New York militia were urgently having men repair and reinforce the fort. Eckler recalled that he was "compelled to do duty" even though he was only fourteen. Perhaps he made a point of mentioning it because his thirteen-year-old friend, Jacob Knouls, who was also in the fort, did not have to work. Similarly Adam Gerlock, also in the Mohawk Valley around the same time, was clear that he was "ordered into the service" and had not volunteered. He "was regularly armed" doing a soldier's work, going on scouting parties looking for Indians, British, or Tories, and standing guard at the fort.[56]

Some boys were pressed into service even when the community was not in the midst of a military crisis. In 1780, Benoni Baker had traveled from his home on Cape Cod to Boston to enlist in the army, and despite being old enough (age seventeen), he was rejected for being too small. Wandering around Boston and not sure what to do next, fate decided for him. Baker "was seized by the press gang and carried on board" a Continental navy frigate. He was on-board ship for five months before he was free to leave. Back in Boston, Baker found a recruiting officer who would enlist him in the army (perhaps he had grown in the intervening period), and he now voluntarily served for six months. Andrew

Ferguson and his father, both free African Americans in Virginia, were also pressed into service. When Andrew was fourteen, he and his father had been harassed by the British. They ran away and then fell in with patriot General Nathanael Greene and his troops. Ferguson recalled that Greene told them "that if the British ever got us they would kill us and that he had better draft us." Andrew Ferguson and his father thus joined the army.[57]

As old men applying for pensions, these veterans need not have said anything about the terms under which they served. They simply had to give details of their time in the military. Yet veterans took the opportunity of their pension applications to vent long-held grievances over instances of forced military service in language that was blunt and without patriotic sentiment. While most of them volunteered for later stints in the military, pension applicants were careful to note the difference between willful and coerced enlistment—and veterans expected pension credit regardless of the terms of service. Even Ferguson saw no need to assert his political motivations in the struggle for liberty. When he applied for a pension, he was living in Indiana, a state without legal slavery, yet he was deprived of many civil liberties; for example, he could not vote or serve on a jury. Indeed, the military service of black soldiers was rarely acknowledged at public events in the decades following the war. Ferguson had every reason to feel insecure about his circumstances and the strength of his pension claim. Yet he did not exaggerate his reasons for enlisting even though he had been wounded at the battle of Guilford Court House in March 1781 and could have emphasized that hardship. Adam Gerlock had only bitter feelings about his service, but perhaps that was because, later, in 1782, when he was a seasoned soldier of about fourteen, the horse he was riding fell, and he broke his leg badly. It was an injury that plagued him all his life. Gerlock's claim was turned down for lack of proof of his service. He made repeated petitions to the courts, but he never chose to portray his service in more heroic language or claim any political motivations in order to get his pension.

EVEN THOUGH EXTERNAL factors often pushed boys into the service, some found there a sense of family and security they had not found at home. Joseph Plumb Martin, a Connecticut boy who was living with his grandfather when he first enlisted at fifteen, wrote years later that, after a long period of service together, he and his fellow soldiers had become "a family of brothers." This bond not only came from fighting the enemy. That, after all, only happened on rare occasions. But as soldiers the boys had learned to live as a community, care for each other when they were sick, bury their friends and enemies, forage for food, mend clothes, be resourceful, and otherwise cope with all the hardships of army life. Those who served for long periods grew up together. William Creamer, a New Jersey fifer who enlisted in 1777 when he was about thirteen, spent the next six years in the army, emerging a mature youth on the cusp of independent manhood. Thomas Craig of Maryland enlisted at fifteen in 1776 and was twenty-two, a legal adult, when he was discharged at the end of the war. As Samuel Morrow of South Carolina reflected, "I mite say the army was my home." It was certainly home for the refugee children, whether soldiers or not. In 1783, as the war neared its end, the children were still with the Carolina regiment. Sally Robenet, now about fifteen years old, married another refugee, soldier John Chartier. And Alexander Ferriol, a growing eighteen-year-old, attended their wedding. And even the unfortunate John Jenks, not otherwise inclined to be sentimental, felt a close bond with those with whom he served. Decades later, he could remember the names of all his fellow musicians.[58]

Instability, family tensions, and the exigencies of war all pushed boys into the service. Faced with upheaval following the death of family members, sometimes distressed by separation from siblings, living in tedious, tense, or harsh conditions, the army offered the possibility of stability and a destination to which to run. Others were coerced into service by family or the chaos of war. And in old age, none of these veterans felt the need to cast their enlistments in a more patriotic, political, or heroic light. Instead, their recollections bear witness to the tumultuous and unstable world of Revolutionary America in which many children grew up.

CHAPTER FOUR

He Took His Father's Place

State of New York
Ontario County

On this twenty eighth day of August 1832 personally appeared
in open court before the judge of the County Court now
sitting, Cyril Eaton, a resident of the town of Canandaigua,
County and State aforesaid aged sixty five years who being first
duly sworn in according to Law doth on his Oath make the
following declaration in order to obtain the benefit of the act
of Congress passed June 7, 1832. . . .

At Ashford, County in Windham, State of Connecticut
where he was born and lived at the time, He with Stephen
Eaton, went to Boston in the summer of 1781 and there
joined Captain Bird's company and marched to [illegible] and
Springfield and crossed over to Peekskill and there joined the
army under the Command of General Heath. He there done
duty until his time expired and having served three months, the
whole company was discharged and he went home to Ashford.

At Ashford as aforesaid in the fall of 1782, his father Samuel
Eaton enlisted in Captain Benjamin Durgee's company for
one year to go to New London and he, this declarent, took
his father's place . . . . [He] served as aforesaid until the time
expired for which he enlisted being one year and was then
honorably discharged and went home to Ashford.[1]

Cyril Eaton, whose pension was promptly awarded, served his first
three months in the army in 1781 when he had likely just turned fourteen.
If there was any family discussion around the boy serving at such a
young age, nothing in the file hints at it. Eaton, like many other boys
his age, had probably been working alongside his father, relatives, and
neighbors as part of a community exchange of labor for some time. It
is not clear what his exact relationship was with Stephen Eaton, but
he was probably a cousin. Stephen, who had also grown up in Ashford
and who was six years Cyril's senior, had enlisted for three years in

the Connecticut Continentals as soon as he turned sixteen in 1777 and finished up that term the year before. He was now about to sign up again for six months, and that the two could go to the recruitment post together may have made Cyril's parents more comfortable about sending their son off.

Serving as a substitute for his father for a year is the more unusual part of the story. As noted in the previous chapter, substitution allowed men drafted for Continental, state, or militia service to fulfill their civic duty through the service of another. A drafted man, or any man who had voluntarily enlisted, might not want to face the hardships of a campaign; service might be economically inconvenient; or he may have other obligations that made it difficult for him to leave home or continue serving. In those cases, he would then look around for someone to take his place. A substitute could be a local man hoping to earn some extra money. However, some draftees preferred to draw on labor they did not need to pay, such as their sons, nephews, or other male relatives.

Boys serving as substitutes for fathers were more common in the militia, where service was of short duration, usually anywhere from two weeks to two months. Longer service in the army, in this case for a year, put more at stake. Not only was the service probably physically more demanding, it also came with an enlistment bounty. The person who presented himself for service received a one-time bonus that included cash and often shoes and a coat too, both expensive items at the time. In Eaton's case, his father was not a draftee but had decided to enlist, and only immediately afterwards did Cyril present himself to do the duty. The boy would be paid the wages over the course of the year but his father received the bounty. The family economy was well served by the decision. But was it his father's decision alone? Had this been negotiated between them? Was it Cyril who wanted to serve and his father's idea to do it this way? Was it a source of bitterness between them? Cyril Eaton says nothing of it, but in detailing the sequence so clearly, he is noting, fifty years after the fact, that his father received the bounty.

Perhaps it was like this:

Cyril Eaton walked along beside Stephen perhaps trying to match his stride. The two had set off from their hometown of Ashford to join a company of Connecticut troops that, in the summer of 1781, lay near Boston. Even though he was barely fourteen years old, Eaton felt very grown up in Stephen's company. Stephen was twenty and already a sophisticated veteran of more than three years of service. Eaton hung on his every word. The two now had to cover almost ninety miles but Cyril knew he was strong. He had worked hard on his father's and a neighbor's farms during the spring and early summer, helping with planting, repairing fences, and chopping wood. Fortunately he and Stephen managed to get a ride on a neighbor's cart for the first leg of their journey, and, on the first night, they stayed with family friends at their farm along the way. After that it would be harder going, but Eaton was sure someone on the road would let them sleep in a barn, give them some cool water, and give or sell them some food.

After several days of travel, they arrived in Boston and enlisted in Captain Bird's company. Eaton proudly signed his enlistment papers. He was a bit nervous doing it. Stephen had signed first and done it with a flourish. Eaton wanted to do the same. He had practiced at home and was pleased with the sight of his bold signature. Because he was so young and had never been away from home before, he only enlisted for three months so he could try it out, but things were off to a good start.

Once that formality was out of the way, Eaton hoped he might have a chance to see something of Boston, but there was no time. Almost immediately, the company was on the move. They marched to Peekskill, New York, about two hundred miles away to join the army there under General William Heath. But after rushing there, nothing exciting happened. Eaton learned how to use a musket, stood guard duty, paraded, joined foraging parties that went out looking for food, and chopped wood to make fires for cooking and staying warm as fall set in. His three months were soon up. Stephen had enlisted for six, so Eaton said farewell and made his way home with other men from his company headed in the general direction of Ashford.

The boy had enjoyed his first taste of military life and was eager to enlist again, this time for a year. Serving for that length of time came not only with wages but also with a bounty. The boy felt giddy at the amount of money he might have in his pocket. It would not be a fortune, just what he could make in a few weeks of laboring, but that was certainly more money than he had ever had in his hands at one time. Strictly speaking, under the law, everything minor children earned when they lived at home belonged to their parents. However, many fathers, stepfathers, or guardians worked out some arrangement with their boys. Some were allowed to keep everything they earned and spend it or save it as they chose. Other boys shared their pay with their fathers, eagerly contributing to their families' welfare. A few never saw any of their pay. Their fathers collected and pocketed it. What would Eaton's father do?

The boy was not sure. He was afraid he and his father might not agree. The two had been at loggerheads recently, and it had done them both good for him to be away for a while. After the three months at Peekskill, he had not had much money left after deductions for his expenses, and, when he returned home, his father let him keep what remained. Now there would be more money at stake. Eaton was torn. The family could use some ready cash and the boy wanted to help out, but it would be nice to have some spending money.

His father devised an agreeable solution. Mr. Eaton went to the recruiting post, enlisted for a year, and collected the bounty. He then returned home, and young Cyril went in his place as a substitute to serve out the time in the army. The boy got to keep the wages for his service. Father and son were both satisfied with the arrangement.[2]

IS THIS TOO HAPPY an imagined account? Only Eaton's care in detailing the sequence of events fifty years later hints that, as an older man, he may have been a bit resentful. But there is no reason to suppose that the boy was anything other than pleased at contributing to the household economy at the time.

Cyril Eaton's story illustrates three important elements in the lives of boys and boy soldiers in particular. The first element is work, something boys did from a young age. The labor of boys was often unpaid, done around the home or in a family enterprise. Sometimes, boys exchanged their labor for support and training in the home of another. On other occasions, boys worked for neighbors as part of reciprocal arrangements or for cash. The second element is the importance of connections, as they followed a family member or a neighbor on the path, literally or figuratively, to whatever job they were going to do. When Cyril set off to war with Stephen, he was doing what he might have done to take on any work, such as haymaking or repairing a fence, learning a task beside an older relative, working alongside a familiar face. The system of substitution is the third element. Whether drawn through community networks, serving as substitutes, or of their own volition, military life provided work opportunities for boys that did not exist in peacetime. But families hesitated. They did not rush to enlist their young sons. Soldiering was a hard life, and, apart from the obvious dangers, it did not offer useful training for later independence. Of course, some boys did serve, and many of them had to work out new relationships with their fathers in order to do so. As with other kinds of labor, most boys served, as Cyril did initially, with men they knew. And while the substitution system relied on those relationships, it also tested them. As substitutes, boys were dependents acting in their families' interests. Such service also gave them a chance to leave home, be away from parental supervision, and perhaps even put money in their pockets.

The journey from being a dependent son to an independent man was a long and uneven one. As in many transitions, the devil was in the details. Cyril Eaton's story, and that of other boys, offers some examples of how that path played out in everyday life, within families, and within communities. Families and boys themselves had varying ideas about when independent decisions could be made. Cyril Eaton's and others' stories highlight the complications of personal relationships.

BY CUSTOM AND UNDER the law, most boys worked. Families and the boys themselves had differing opinions about whether their sons were mature enough to do the work of a soldier. Many parents—cautious before the physical demands of military life, observant of recruiting posters that requested "able-bodied men," and heedful of militia laws that nowhere required service from anyone under sixteen—kept their sons out of the military until they reached enlistment age. Meshack Burchfield explained that he had not gone out with the North Carolina militia at fifteen because he was "only a boy" and too young to serve. Also in the Carolinas, unhappy William Conner, living with an older brother a long way from his Virginia home, with both parents now dead, waited until his sixteenth birthday to join a regiment of mounted infantry.[3]

But some younger boys not only served, but decided for themselves about doing so. Daniel Granger was thirteen when his parents left it up to him as to whether to join the army as a substitute for his brother or not. In 1775, his brother Jacob, three years his senior, had joined the Continentals. But that December, as the army lay outside of Boston,

Jacob became sick. The family believed it was due to his "not being clad for the winter." News of his illness arrived at the family home in Andover, Massachusetts, twenty-five miles away. Daniel's parents made him an offer. They told him he must "take the horse and go down and bring" Jacob home. But if the officers would take Daniel in Jacob's place, and if Jacob were well enough to ride home alone, then Daniel might stay and serve as Jacob's substitute if he wished. When Daniel arrived, Jacob was indeed feeling well enough to ride. Daniel was entirely at liberty to do what he thought fit. He approached Jacob's commanders. "The officers examined me," Granger remembered, "& were willing to receive me in his room." Granger stayed, and Jacob rode home alone.[4]

Other boys also followed their own inclinations about service, but their parents still decided to play a protective role. That was true for fifteen-year-old John Burgess of Plymouth, Massachusetts. When he wanted to enlist, his father was willing to let him go. After all, John was enlisting with his older brother William, already a veteran, and the two would be joining a third brother, Thomas, who was serving in the fort on Gurnet Point that guarded the entrance to Plymouth Harbor. With so many of his offspring doing duty there, their father decided simply to move the rest of his family the fifteen miles from the town to the point. He found a house less than 250 yards from the fort, and, apart from one brief intermission, the family remained there until the end of the war. Burgess's parents were worried about what might befall their young sons in the army and were determined to offer parental supervision of some kind.[5]

And they were right to worry. Boys so young could be naive. Fourteen-year-old Philadelphians Henry Yeager and George Lechler certainly were. While both were out serving with the Pennsylvania militia, the British army occupied their home city. When the boys' terms were up, it did not occur to them to stay away. They returned to their parents and, not surprisingly, the British quickly arrested them. Yeager's mother tagged along to find out exactly what was happening to the boys and listened as the British charged them with spying and sentenced them to death. However, British intent was presumably to frighten them, and Yeager and Lechler were released a few weeks later. But it seems not to have occurred to them that returning to the city might be risky. It is not surprising, then, that some families felt that their sons were simply not ready to embark on that kind of work and that some boys themselves agreed.[6]

But however unworldly and young, boys like Cyril Eaton were old enough to work. Children labored in many settings, usually with adults to whom they were related or whom they knew from their communities. They were, after all, being raised to be productive, independent members of their communities and were taught skills accordingly. At an early age, children were expected to take on small domestic tasks about the home according to gender. Boys learned how to chop wood, collect food for hogs, help fathers with farm work, and perhaps hunt squirrels, birds, or raccoons. Girls baked, helped with their younger siblings, and learned to sew.[7]

That children should be trained to become independent adults had the solid backing of English and colonial law. As the eighteenth-century British jurist, Sir William Blackstone, noted in his *Commentaries on the Laws of England*, only the rich were free to "breed up their children to be ornaments or disgraces to their family" as they wished. All other parents were obliged to educate their children to prepare them for adult responsibilities.[8]

Education was one of three key parental obligations. According to Blackstone, the other two were maintenance and protection. The first was an obligation that derived from voluntarily having a child, "that the life which they have bestowed shall be supported and preserved." Protection, Blackstone observed, was simply a "natural duty" about which he did not feel the need to elaborate. It was providing an education, "suitable to their station in life," that Blackstone dwelt on at length. By education, the jurist was thinking of training and he did not think the law strong enough on this point. Families failing in this responsibility would surely simply invite "griefs and inconveniences." In Britain, Parliament passed laws that required parents to find some appropriate vocation for their sons. In the colonies, such regulations could never be universally enforced, but tradition, and occasionally the courts, tried to ensure that children worked at some endeavor that would lead them to become productive adults. In New England, some town leaders were particularly aggressive about taking children away from parents who seemed not to be up to the task and indenturing them elsewhere to learn a productive skill.[9]

But obligations did not lie with parents alone. Children also had responsibilities. In exchange for receiving maintenance, protection, and education, children owed their fathers, by tradition and by law, the fruits of their labor while they lived at home. They owed their mothers "reverence and respect." Children also owed parents or masters "subjection and obedience" while minors. To parents they also later owed care and support when they might stand "in need of assistance." The law was narrowly concerned with children's economic relationship to their families and communities. That events should unfold or decisions should be made in a child's "best interest" was still an unknown legal concept.[10]

Children's labor was an essential component of their relationship with their parents, and future independence was the ultimate goal. And, at around ages eleven to fifteen, depending on need and maturity, many children took on more structured training or work responsibilities. For wealthier boys, such as New Englander John Barnard or John Laurens of South Carolina, fourteen was often the age at which they were sent off for more rigorous schooling, overseas in John Laurens's case, college near home in John Barnard's case. Apprenticeships for training in the crafts could begin a bit earlier. Benjamin Franklin was twelve when he was formally apprenticed to his printer-brother. But Hiram Hill was apprenticed to a carpenter when he was fourteen, and David Perry was fifteen when he was bound to a tanner and shoemaker.[11]

Free boys grew up expecting and hoping to grow up to be respected men. For New Englanders especially this meant identifying one's calling—that is, the task to which God called them. Guided by prayer, family advice, the amount of money and other resources available for any training or apprenticeship, this would ideally involve them using their talents. Many boys went dutifully where their fathers directed. Benjamin Franklin famously declined to follow his father into the candle-making business and preferred to follow his bookish inclinations, and his older brother, into printing. Some boys, such as Thomas Painter, went where necessity and family connections sent them. At age eleven Painter went to live with his uncle, a shoemaker, to learn that trade but was discouraged at noticing how hard his uncle had to "work to get along and support his family."[12]

More prosperous youths, such as John Adams, wanted simply to be useful, by which they meant serving their families, communities, and God. Adams, when he was in his early twenties, reflected that a man should be judged not by how much he knows or the number of his accomplishments but by how useful he has been. The great goal, he thought, should be "to distinguish between Useful and unuseful."[13]

Being useful, of course, not only meant serving one's community or God, but also becoming economically independent. Fathers were anxious when their sons did not quickly find something that might accomplish that. At the end of the seventeenth century, Samuel Sewall was worried about his son, Sam, eighteen years old and still not settled on what he would do with his life. At ten, Mr. Sewall had sent Sam to Eleazer Moody's Boston writing school so he would have that skill. At sixteen, Sam was apprenticed to a Boston bookseller to learn that trade, but his feet became tender and swollen, Mr. Sewall thought, from his standing on the cold floor. Sam then went to work as a clerk, but that situation did not suit him. Mr. Sewall prayed for Sam to find "some Calling," then he prayed with Sam for the same thing. Mr. Sewall admitted in his diary that he was very sorrowful "by reason of the unsettledness of my Samuel." The boy, Sewall knew, needed to do something useful.[14]

Poorer boys or those living on farms did not have the opportunity to choose or to take such a leisurely path. They faced steady work from an early age. Ebenezer Fox started work at age seven when he was bound out by his poor father to a master who lived some distance away. After a few years, he ran away to sea and then finally returned home when he was about fourteen. But he was now old enough to understand how difficult it was for his father to support a large family. Fox left again, "unwilling to remain at home, a burden upon him, and desirous of supporting myself." He set off with his brother James, two years his senior. The brothers took themselves to Boston where James bound himself to a baker and Ebenezer to a barber and wigmaker. In his memoir, Fox presented himself as making an independent decision, though he and James almost certainly left with their father's consent and perhaps his encouragement.[15]

Even though more prosperous children did not work in this way, most, like the hapless Sam Sewall, were not expected to be idle. Boys helped their fathers in their businesses. Laurens, at age fourteen, copied business letters into his father's letter book when his father's clerks were sick. Young George Washington helped his older half-brother Lawrence in surveying. Many prosperous girls did not sit unoccupied either. Eleven-year-old Anna Winslow was sent by her parents in Nova Scotia to her aunt in Boston to go to school to polish her manners. She spent many pages in her letters home recounting her evenings "country dansing" and noting the local fashions in hats and cloaks. But these frivolous reports belied the steady pace of work she did. She sewed shifts for her mother and shirts for her uncle. And when she was unable to sew due to a "whitloe [painful infection around the cuticle] on my fourth finger," her aunt told her it was a great opportunity for her to learn to spin flax. If Anna was disappointed at not being able to use her new free time to go out to drink tea with her friends, she kept it to herself and declared herself to be "pleased with the proposal."[16]

Many families of moderate means expected children to work. It is hard to generalize now about how the balance between work and school played out. School or home tutoring was not organized around terms or a required number of days as it is today. Detailed records are uneven and, as historian Carole Shammas has noted, most information about young children's labor lies hidden behind the "household curtain." However, one account book kept by Quincy Thaxter of Hingham, Massachusetts, offers some insight into how this son of a prosperous farmer and civic leader spent his days. Thaxter began his book, a mixture of a journal and account book, when he was twelve years old and kept it for four years. Thaxter spent more than a third of his days in school, and not surprisingly those days were concentrated between the winter months of November and February. He spent more than 25 percent of his time engaged in farm labor, working alongside a hired boy who was four years older than Thaxter, and a hired slave or free black man of unknown age named Cato. Thaxter performed the same tasks these other laborers did: plowing, harrowing, spreading manure, clearing stones from a field, and so on. Thaxter, and boys like him, performed valuable labor on his father's farm, and his account book indicates the kinds of choices middling families had to make as they weighed the value of their boys' time spent at school against time working at home.[17]

Younger children from more modest backgrounds were assigned tasks suitable to their age and abilities. A child who could barely walk might collect eggs from the hen house. Samuel Dewees of Pennsylvania learned by age five to feed cattle, hogs, and sheep and round them up into a pen at the end of the day. He also carried wood and ran small errands. At seven a boy might cut thatch or pick apples. As he got a little older, he might drive cattle to market or help plow. Ten-year-old Benjamin Franklin helped his father make candles by cutting wicks, filling molds, and running errands.[18]

Slave children began the same kinds of work at similar ages. Venture Smith, in Narragansett, Rhode Island, at age nine, was pounding corn for chicken feed and carding wool. David George, a slave born in Essex County Virginia, began his working life "fetching water, and carding of cotton." Slave children did not generally do the more physically demanding work in the tobacco fields until they were older, and this was reflected in the price at which they were valued or sold. George Washington's plantation records indicate that children were valued as half an adult. Generally, children were those twelve and under, but a few eleven- and twelve-year-olds were on the adult list, perhaps those who were more physically mature. Washington's account books show only three of the boys working at skilled work, probably in informal apprenticeships to slave craftsmen. The other children were engaged in general farm labor. At Thomas Jefferson's home in Monticello, slave children under ten cared for younger children and the sick. From ages ten to sixteen, boys made nails and girls spun, after which children either went to work in the fields or learned a trade.[19]

Free boys were also usually in their midteens when they took on more demanding work. Apprenticeship, as noted above, was one option, but boys might also begin working for others for money—laboring for a neighbor or going to sea. Even when working at farm labor or caring for animals on the family farm, a father had to be sure that his sons were strong enough, knew enough to be useful, and would not damage his reputation before either he hired them out or his sons did so themselves.[20]

Contrary to romantic folklore, few boys went to sea at very young ages, particularly on ships that took them far from home. Records of sailors in Philadelphia and elsewhere from the late eighteenth and early nineteenth centuries and from small fishing towns in New England from before the Revolution indicate that the vast majority of men went to sea somewhere between their midteens and early twenties. There were young cabin boys, working as servants to the ship's officers, and boy apprentices, learning navigation or the business of running a ship. There were even a handful of very young seamen. Eleven-year-old Benjamin Salter, for example, worked on a fishing boat out of Marblehead, Massachusetts, in 1771. But he was rare.[21]

It is not surprising that so few boys were seamen. The work was physically demanding, and other than as cabin boys, they were of limited use. While a small boy might clamber easily up the rigging, he was unable to move the weight of wet canvas once he was up there. Even handling dry sails required great physical strength. It was also dangerous. Captains' log books and tales of life at sea recorded high mortality rates from accidents and storms, in addition to the usual death toll from illness. One young seaman, John Kilby of Maryland, remembering his

Revolutionary War labors on merchant ships, privateers, and finally the Continental navy, noted a litany of fatal accidents. A few weeks after he left his first ship, a whaling vessel that had become a privateer, it went down in a storm with "every soul lost," more than one hundred men. While Kilby was held prisoner on board a British naval vessel, a gale ripped off the ship's forward topmast and swept three men overboard. After he was free again and serving on a Continental navy frigate, a seaman was killed falling from the rigging onto the quarterdeck. It is not surprising that the number of men still at sea after their twenties dropped precipitously. Some of that decline comes from the number injured or killed on the job. As those who survived got older, some sought less strenuous work if they could find it. Others found themselves less likely to be hired by masters who viewed them as too old to withstand the rigors of the seaman's life. Very young boys, like their much older counterparts, were among the crewmen, but they were few.[22]

Among these few was a nine-year-old from Boston, John Peck, born in 1770, who served as a seaman in the Continental navy on board the frigate, *Queen of France*. The boy worked alongside his father, also a seaman, and other relatives, learning the ropes, literally and figuratively. Israel Trask also went to sea very young. He signed on to a privateer at age twelve, serving with men he knew from the fishing villages of Cape Ann, Massachusetts, where he grew up. However, these boys were probably the only very young seamen on the vessels on which they sailed.[23]

No matter the job, on land or at sea, by law, boys' earnings belonged to their parents. However, that boys' labor was not always paid in wages complicated matters. Much of boys' work, such as that done by Quincy Thaxter, involved no money changing hands. And often boys worked alongside their fathers or other male relatives as part of barter arrangements with neighbors in exchange for help on other tasks and projects. Boys might work for someone in the community for cash, always a commodity in short supply in colonial America, but unless they worked out an arrangement with their fathers, many did not keep their earnings. Those belonged to their families. After the voyage taken by young Benjamin Salter, the eleven-year-old seaman mentioned above, his share of the catch of the fishing vessel on which he sailed was credited to his widowed mother's account. And that was not just because he was so young. Merchants' account books show that the shares of minor seamen, those under twenty-one, were usually credited to their parents or guardians. War did not change that arrangement. In about

1780, when Ebenezer Fox was seventeen, he wanted to go to sea on a privateer. He was still bound to his master, a Boston barber, but business was slow, and his master agreed the lad could go on the condition that Fox would give him half his wages and half of any prize money he earned. When young John Peck sailed with his father, his share of the prize money from the crew's capture of a British vessel was simply added to his father's account. It is unlikely Israel Trask kept his prize shares even though his father was not with him. When he had earlier been in the army as a ten-year-old waiter to his officer-father, his father had "supervision of all my concerns" and received both his pay and his food rations. Later, when the boy went to sea, the family had a pressing need of his earnings. His father was very ill and was confined to his bed for more than two years. Young Trask's earnings almost certainly made a difference to the family's welfare.[24]

But however diligent and hard-working, whether on land or at sea, boys never made as much as their more senior counterparts, who were pleased to have their strength, maturity, and experience rewarded. Minor seamen on fishing vessels received a smaller share of the catch than men did. On his Continental navy vessel, the share of the prize that John Peck received was a boy's share—not a man's. Free African American fourteen-year-old James Forten of Philadelphia, on-board a privateer during the war, also received only a boy's half share of any prizes taken. Ebenezer Fox earned twenty-one shillings a month when he went to sea as a cabin boy, half what the seamen were paid. Boys laboring for cash at a variety of tasks on farms and in workshops were also paid less than men. In New England, boys doing farm labor earned about 65 percent of what a grown man might earn. But even boys' reduced wages were essential to the survival of some families.[25]

For a variety of reasons, as soldiers, boys could make a man's wage. Soldiers' wages were set first by colonial assemblies, and then, during the Revolution, by state legislatures and the Continental Congress. Since these legislatives bodies did not anticipate soldiers being young children, they did not specify a separate child's wage. Twelve-year-old Cyrus Allen was thrilled about this. He made twice as much enlisted as a waiter to his officer-father than he did working for neighbors at home. Of course, his military pay went directly to his father. Fifteen-year-old Ebenezer Atwood lived with his guardian, "both his parents being dead," and when he returned from the army with his man's pay, his "Guardian received his wages for the year's service." Even eighteen-year-old Moses

Hall, who had served six months in the Massachusetts Continentals, handed the certificate entitling him to his pay over to his father. And it was his father who went to Boston "to get his wages from the state."[26]

Other boy soldiers received their pay but handed it over when they arrived home. Fifteen-year-old Jeremiah Parrish, substituting for his twenty-one-year-old brother for a year, duly handed over all the pay he received to "the family for the use of it." And all Samuel Dewees's wages went to his recruiting sergeant-father, who had enlisted him into the Pennsylvania Continentals at age fifteen in 1777. When his father died a couple of years later, Dewees, in the army for the duration of the war, made a new arrangement. "Being a minor, he chose George Sadler of Philadelphia as his guardian." Sadler "received his pay" for the remainder of his service, and no money ever came into Dewees's hands.[27]

As old men, in their pension applications, there is a hint of bitterness about this. For example, Dewees and Israel Trask both felt that they had never been compensated for their military service, as they had not seen any of the money they earned. However, they may not have felt this way as boys. Ten-year-old Trask seemed to have enjoyed his year of military service as a waiter to his father and other officers, and years later recalled it as a great adventure. Dewees may have been more resentful. After all, his father was dead, and he appears to have had no other family. By the end of his service, he was in his late teens and, with full independence approaching, he may have hoped to use the money for his own future needs. Forty years later, he grumpily recalled that "he never received any compensation whatever himself" for his service because it had gone straight to Sadler, his new guardian.[28]

Dewees may also have felt entitled to his pay because some other young soldiers received theirs directly. Military service was a murky legal area. The army assumed that soldiers were men who could enter into a contract with the state and give their labor and obedience in exchange for pay. When soldiers under twenty-one years of age enlisted, and there were many of them, they were treated as emancipated minors who were able to act as free adults. Recruiting officers, usually glad to get any able-bodied youths, made little effort to inquire into their real status. When some boys presented themselves for service and passed muster, they signed their own contracts just as adult men did and received their own pay. However, under the law, children were incapable of giving their informed consent to a contract, and it could, theoretically, be voided. This was the reason why some parents and masters could easily reclaim their charges when they enlisted without permission. Usually any contract that governed children's labor was made by a parent. The child played no active role. Dewees would certainly have known soldiers his own age who acted as emancipated minors and collected and kept their pay. Dewees, having started his service under a contract between his father and the army, was probably obliged to find a new guardian at the direction of his commanding officer.[29]

For Trask, Dewees, Allen, and most other boys in colonial America of every social level, work was a part of their lives from an early age. For families in need of cash or the labor of others, boys' work was a critical ingredient in a family's welfare.

BUT HOWEVER VITAL boys' contributions to the colonial household economy were, families kept their sons out of military service in the imperial wars of the eighteenth century prior to the Revolutionary War. They did so because they saw soldiering as arduous, menial, and poorly paid. That it was a hard life, colonists knew from their own experience and from watching the British army. Becoming a professional soldier was not seen as a worthy career, despite the celebration of martial accomplishments in time of crisis. Soldiers were perceived as men of low status, whether they were or not. One seventeenth-century Englishman who ranked the various occupations thought that soldiers were almost the lowest members of society, with only vagrants below them. In the eighteenth century, British commander Lieutenant Colonel Campbell Dalrymple agreed. He thought that the presence of an army recruiting party simply allowed neighborhoods to get "clear of their banditti." And soldiers' pay in the British or provincial colonial armies was not more than a man might make as an unskilled day laborer.[30]

Despite their shady reputations, not all or even most soldiers were so disreputable. That the life was hard there was no doubt. While some men may have been "banditti," even Dalrymple conceded there were "good men" among them. And the pay, such as it was, drew young men trapped in seasonal labor or in a place where the craft skill they had did not offer the opportunity they hoped. One British soldier, Archibald Elliot, explained he had enlisted after his apprenticeship as an apothecary "had expired," probably when he was seventeen. "My inclination led me to the Army, (as most young Men do)," he reported, and he saw in it "a fair opportunity." Robert Kirk was a cooper, a barrel maker, who similarly saw better economic potential in the ranks than at his craft.

But with this mixture of fine men and rascals, many civilians suspected the worst and kept their distance.[31]

During the Seven Years' War, colonial armies contained an equally mixed group of men, and colonists had similarly mixed perceptions of them. Finding, just as European governments did, that promises of honor and glory were not enough to fill the ranks, colonial assemblies used steadily increasing financial incentives, both wages and bounties, to induce men to serve. For example, in Connecticut, soldiers' wages rose by over 45 percent and the bounty by almost 200 percent over the seven years of the war. In Virginia, where a draft was proving both unpopular and impractical, the legislature granted a ten-pound bounty, an amount George Washington, then colonel in the provincial forces, called "greater encouragement than hath been given before." Reverend Samuel Davies, sending off a company of provincials with prayers and hoping to get a few more men to enlist before it departed, exclaimed that "the Encouragement is so unusually great, and the Time of Service so short" that men should be glad to go. It was indeed a significant sum: more money than many poor people would otherwise make in a year, and about half as much cash as even a small planter might expect to make.[32]

The good pay made some fear that it attracted men of the lowest class. Indeed, in Virginia, Reverend Davies was sure the ranks were already filled with men of ignoble character. As he addressed the assembled troops, he asked, rhetorically, whether some of them were now "addicted to Drunkenness, Swearing, Whoredom, or any gross Vice?" If they were men of virtue, he warned, they were "entering into *the School of Vice*: for such the Army has generally been." After all, he noted, soldiers "are too commonly addicted to such Immoralities." If enlisted men were as debauched as Davies feared, however, they were unlikely to be shamed and transformed by his high-minded rebukes.[33]

Nonetheless, reputable men were enticed to the military. Short terms of service meant that enlisting did not permanently interrupt craft training or other commitments that served a family's long-term security. Military service may well have offered older teens and young men a quick source of cash. And that was the age group Davies was trying to entice into the service: "Ye young and hardy Men, whose very Faces seem to speak that God and Nature formed you for Soldiers, who are free from the Incumbrance [*sic*] of Families depending on you for Subsistence, and who are perhaps but of little Service to Society, while at Home." He thought that if they embraced religion, they could remain "uncorrupted in the midst of Vice and Debauchery." Davies too saw the potential soldiers before him as a mixed bunch.[34]

With this view of soldiering, it is not surprising that only a handful of boys answered the call during the Seven Years' War. Neither they nor their families saw it as a good work option. Perhaps families hesitated to send their sons into a world of such moral and physical risk. The significant cash inducements might have overcome that reticence, as it did for some older youths. But it did not for boys, no matter how great their financial need. The short terms of service allowing for a trial run at military life might have been tempting. But they were not. The prospect of following the guns and drums and earning honor by coming to the defense of the community could have attracted some eager boys. Families, however, did not consider military service to be a worthy interruption of schooling or an alternative to labor on the family farm or other business. It offered no career path. It developed no obvious skill that might be transferred to other crafts in civilian life. Soldiering could certainly offer excitement, laurels, and some needed cash. For some grown men and older teenagers, that was inducement enough. But boys did not go. In the Seven Years' War, apart from a handful of exceptions, boys stayed home.

THIS CHANGED DURING the American Revolution. While most boys continued to live at home, studying at school or working on farms or in workshops under their families' supervision, others entered military service. In the earliest days of the conflict, young boys such as Trask and Allen went as waiters for their officer-fathers. Fathers offered their boys adventure and probably used their sons for simple tasks, such as carrying messages and collecting firewood. But boys in the military were few, and most of them went home within a year or so, finding that the army camp was a place of great sickness and that the war was more grueling than exciting. However, as that first weary group departed, others arrived and joined the ranks in increasing numbers as the war progressed. As noted in chapter one, it is impossible to come up with accurate figures for how many boys served. The few surviving descriptive or "size" rolls that record information such as age and height can only offer snapshots of a particular location or moment in time. There was significant regional variation in recruiting campaigns, in groups targeted for recruitment, in inducements offered, and in the exigencies of war all of which affected communities in different ways at different times. But all over the new United States, boys presented themselves for service.

How can we account for this shift in attitudes? The steady rise in bounty payments over the course of the war probably enticed a few boys and their families. The inducements varied by state but included such things as clothes and shoes, cash, and, later in the war, even slaves and land bounties. While high cash bounties had not drawn boys to the service in the Seven Years' War, there was much greater economic upheaval and uncertainty during the later years of the Revolution, and that must have added to the appeal of earning both hard money and other assets.

Certainly, the passion aroused by the war must have been one element in boys' increased enlistment, although hardly any veteran mentioned politics in his application, a factor perhaps too obvious to state. In ideologically charged times, in a struggle against a great imperial power, it may have seemed a cause for which some families felt it was worth placing their sons in danger. Feelings of attachment to a new state if not yet a new nation may also have been a factor in a family's willingness to risk blood and property. However, there is no evidence for these connections. The geographic range of the conflict may have facilitated boys' participation. At different times and places, the proximity of the fighting or the possibility of attack would have drawn boys into the service, especially in the backcountry. Yet there was not a consistent correlation between the location of the fighting and boys' service. Families and boys were consistently inconsistent.

Many families still preferred to keep their sons out of the military. In 1775, Benjamin Russell's father felt so strongly about this that he arranged a discharge for his thirteen-year-old son when he found he had enlisted without consent and was with the army outside Boston. To be fair, the boy had not been disobedient. He had not gone off to war—the war had come to him. Russell, a schoolboy, had become separated from his parents when the patriot forces closed off the city in May 1775. In the chaos that followed, Russell was unable to write to his parents to tell them he was safe. At first, he survived by "partaking of public and private bounty," but then he enlisted and became a clerk. At the end of the summer, his father, fleeing Boston, found him. Mr. Russell, even though a man of patriot sympathies, was unimpressed by the army's needs. He arranged his son's discharge and took him away. Perhaps realizing the events of the day might be too exciting for the boy to return to school or recognizing that he was growing up, Mr. Russell took his son fifty miles away to Worcester and apprenticed him to the printer Isaiah Thomas. Thomas's print shop had been in Boston, but he had taken his presses to Worcester just a few days before the British attacks at Lexington and Concord in April 1775. Russell's father was opposed both to his son acting independently and his becoming a soldier. However, five years later, Russell's father was dead, and the youth, turning nineteen and nearing the end of his apprenticeship, reenlisted. However, since he was still a minor, he did so "with the consent of his friends," presumably including Isaiah Thomas.[35]

Captain Roger Welles also thought boys, and especially his younger brothers, should not be distracted by the ongoing war. While service might broaden their horizons and introduce them to a range of people and tasks, it was not useful work experience. In 1783, he wrote home to his father about the education of his two much younger brothers. The "*Golden Days*" of their youth were, he wrote, "passing swiftly." He was especially concerned about his brother Leonard, now eighteen. Leonard had not been in the army, but in the disruption of the war, he had worked at odd jobs instead of pursuing either a formal or craft education. His older brother felt these years had been wasted. "Three or four years have past [sic] by Leonard which he can never recall . . . What is the value of the small pittance he has earned these three or four years, compared with the knowledge he might have acquired by proper application." Military service could provide immediate financial gain. But it was usually not time spent learning skills that could be put to any future use.[36]

Stephen Burroughs's father, a minister, also objected to his fourteen-year-old son becoming a soldier. Burroughs, a troublesome boy, ran off several times to enlist, and each time his father reclaimed him, hoping the boy would make a career in the church. Finally, his father relented, but young Stephen, full of romantic ideas of military glory and not much given to hard work, soon found army life tedious. He now begged his doting father to arrange his discharge. Mr. Burroughs agreed and in a letter to Washington argued his case. He was, he explained, still grief-stricken by the recent deaths of four of his six children. This made Stephen all the more precious. He assured Washington that he had "the cause of America sincerely at heart," yet, as the child was "so much under the age that is commonly deemed necessary to constitute a soldier" and was always destined to be an educated man, he begged

Washington for his release. The boy was discharged and duly sent off to the recently established Dartmouth College to study.[37]

Other boys who served followed the same family and community connections they would have used to go into any other employment. These were the traditional routes by which boys achieved financial independence. This goal was never an easy thing to accomplish. As the historian Toby Ditz noted, it took years of parental planning and the use of "active kin networks and careful calibration of family obligations." But few people ever really became independent. A community, after all, was a network of mutual obligations and responsibilities that covered parents, kin near and far, and neighbors. In towns and in the country-side, families were part of complex exchanges of labor and credit that were organized through extended family, church, neighbors, and civic connections.[38]

The same networks of interconnectedness surrounded boys in the military. While boys served in a range of settings, with varying degrees of danger and performing a variety of tasks, it was rare for them to be among strangers. Most served surrounded by men and youths they knew from their communities. That would obviously be the case when they were serving as substitutes in the local militia. But it was equally true for other kinds of military service, state or Continental.

That service became so enmeshed in these connections was a result of the length of the war itself. As the long years of struggle passed, many men in the community served for a variety of long and short terms in regular forces, setting off and returning multiple times. This pattern over the years folded boys into the service just as it did into other work in civilian life. It was a rare boy soldier who did not already know a number of others with whom he was serving.

The paths that boys followed into service were usually different from that of even slightly older soldiers. Older teenagers did not necessarily enlist alongside family members, although they often served with people they knew. It was the prospect of serving with someone he knew and respected that prompted Jacob Granger of Andover, Massachusetts, to enlist in a New Hampshire regiment. The regiment's colonel was Enoch Poor who had not only been born and raised in Andover but had also been a near neighbor of the Grangers. Other men from Andover joined Poor's regiment for the same reason. So Jacob, and later his younger brother Daniel who substituted for him, was joining a familiar community.[39]

Older boys sometimes enlisted together. Joseph Plumb Martin, enlisting at sixteen, did so surrounded by his friends. He remembered that at the recruiting post, "[t]he old bantering began—come, if you will enlist I will, says one; you have long been talking about it says another—come now is the time." When seventeen-year-old Austin Wells of Connecticut enlisted in 1776, he joined with seven other young men he knew. The same summer, Joshua Davis enlisted with his friend Moses Piper. The boys were already well known to each other, "being both natives of said Boston, & brought up in the same neighborhood, & schoolmates." And once in the army, Piper recognized other youths he had "known from his infancy."[40]

But younger boys were generally not drawn into the service by their immediate contemporaries. They went with older friends and relatives. Not surprisingly, in the backcountry, where towns and schools were few, kin and neighbors played a more important role in recruitment than in more densely populated areas. In Surry County, North Carolina, fifteen-year-old Peter Fulp enlisted with his twenty-year-old brother, Michael. Michael was assigned to work as a wagoner while young Peter went ahead with the regiment. But Peter was still not alone. He was serving under his neighbor Captain Minor Smith. In the same region, William Guest spent much of his time in the service, under the command of his older brother Moses, twelve years his senior. And near Albany, New York, fifteen-year-old Stephen Freeman enlisted on the same day as his brother Elijah, age twenty-two, and the two served for nine months together.[41]

Family connections may have lessened the anxiety about being away from home and among strangers for the first time, but it did not necessarily make life easy. Not all family members got along. In Connecticut, David Lockwood served on a ship commanded by his older brother, Samuel, but it was not a happy experience. He complained bitterly to his sister on his return that "he had rather be a servant to any man than a brother" because his brother wanted too much from him.[42]

And serving with family members also made it all the more painful if they died. Obadiah Benge, forced into the service by his stepfather, had been consoled by the presence of his older brother, Michael, already in the service. When Benge first enlisted, Michael was in a different company, but the boys lobbied their respective captains and arranged for Benge to be transferred to his brother's unit. Their pleasure was short-lived. They were engaged in the Battle of King's Mountain in October

1780, where Obadiah was badly wounded, and Michael was killed. Benge never served again during the war. In the same battle, largely a contest between the loyalist and patriot militias, sixteen-year-old Enoch Berry saw his father die and his brother receive a mortal wound. Serving with family brought comfort in lonely times but brought tragedy when a unit found itself in a hot spot on the battlefield.[43]

Similarly, the presence of friends and family could be both a trial and a comfort when illness struck. Israel Trask was alarmed when his lieutenant-father was "prostrated by sickness brought on by hard-ships and privations incident to a retreating army scantily supplied." Fortunately young Trask was there to nurse him. Young Cordilla Fitch had his father's loving care when he contracted the "camp distemper" and lay desperately ill. Lieutenant Jabez Fitch noted in his diary that he did no duty for a few days to "have opportunity to attend my boy" and even ordered some men under his command to help care for the child. When Samuel Dewees's father became mortally ill, young Samuel, in the absence of any other nurses or orderlies, "was ordered to attend him." He cared for him in several different hospitals, buffeted by the tide of war around Philadelphia in 1777, until finally his father died in the hospital at Allentown. With his father gone, there was no family near to comfort Samuel in turn when he fell ill a year later. He was on the march with his company, and his comrades left him among strangers to recover. The nearness of family and friends in war was both a soldier's sustenance and his curse; a sustaining presence could become, in an instant, a terrible absence keenly felt.[44]

For boys who lived in or near towns or who attended school, the army was filled with familiar faces, family, and friends. Frederick Vaughan of Lebanon, Connecticut, was "acquainted" with all his officers when he enlisted for the first time in 1780 at age thirteen. But Vaughan had also heard about military life from his family. His father was an officer who had been away from home for some time, and his older brother John, four years his senior, had joined the Continentals when he was thirteen at the beginning of the war, serving as a drummer for three years. When Vaughan enlisted for a second time, he served under his father and alongside his brother John.[45]

For one group of boys in Preston, Connecticut, born between 1758 and 1768, their relationships in the town and schoolyard drew them into the service. Schoolchildren were not yet separated into age grades, and some of them attended their one-room school, "boys together," at the same time. But they did not enlist at the same moment. Rather, each enlisted when his family either allowed or required it. But members of the group were available to offer an opinion. The oldest of them was Jacob Meech. Born in 1758, he was about eighteen when he enlisted for a nine-month term in October 1776. The following year, despite having been wounded in the shoulder, he enlisted again late in 1777 and this time served with his friend, fifteen-year-old Simeon Jones. Jones served for nine months and then did a couple of shorter stints as a substitute. When Jones returned home, he was ready to advise his friend Elisha Prentice, two years his junior, who had enlisted that summer. Both were on hand to counsel their friend Simeon Hewitt, who, in 1780, at age fifteen, had enlisted for a year. Hewitt did that year's service with his friend, thirteen-year-old Bishop Tyler. As Hewitt and Tyler left the service, Tyler was able to advise his young friend Samuel Branch, who joined just as he turned fourteen. When Branch enlisted, he joined the same company as his friend David Avery, who had recently enlisted as an old man of eighteen.[46]

Community connections encircled these boys. David Avery came from a large extended family, deeply committed to the patriot cause, with many family members already in arms. Bishop Tyler's father was a militia captain and his brother James, four years his senior, had already served six months in the Connecticut Continentals as soon as he had turned sixteen. Simeon Hewitt had already done a short stint in the militia as a substitute for his father. Many of the boys' parents and guardians had known each other for years. The interconnectedness of these boys through school, church, and play was an important element in their willingness to serve.[47]

AS THE REVOLUTIONARY WAR dragged on, these networks of boys were heavily deployed. Military action and alarms made urgent demands on the men eligible for militia or Continental drafts. Even as the theaters of the war shifted over the years, a steady stream of emergencies on the coast, Indian and loyalist attacks in the backcountry, and British and loyalist military activities around British bases of operation, such as New York, kept the patriot militia busy in many locales. The patriot victory at Yorktown, Virginia, in October 1781 lessened the scale of the fighting but did not end it. In the face of such withering demands on time and energy in this protracted battle for independence, a number of draftees exercised their right to use substitutes. Many of the boys who served during the war did either their entire service or some part of it as substitutes for others.

The practice of substitution had a long history. In the ancient Roman Empire, when the state raised troops, a landowner was expected to provide men for the army. This was understood as a tax. A property owner had simply to provide someone at his own expense, usually any free person who was a dependent such as a tenant or son, as long as he met the age and height requirements. Observers at the time thought that this practice allowed landowners to get rid of restless or troublesome young men in their families or neighborhoods. But regardless of whom they sent, the landowner's obligations were met.[48]

By medieval times, there had been a slow shift in the meaning of military service. Whether the beneficiary was a local lord or a distant king, it had become a more profound, personal obligation associated with acting in the public interest. Fines steadily increased for failing to turn out when called. However, the idea that service was a tax lingered, and the obligation to serve could still be met by providing a replacement.[49]

This ambiguity, that service in the militia was a mix of both personal obligation and tax, continued into the eighteenth century. On the one hand, militia obligations were highly personal. Belonging to the militia was seen as a badge of full membership in the community. Serving when called out in the event of an emergency certainly served the public interest, and a fine was imposed if a man failed to respond. Yet, when those events occurred, the service obligation could be met and a fine avoided by sending anyone, because the duty functioned as a tax on the household. This might be done with no cash outlay by sending a dependent son, relative, servant, or slave, or by hiring someone to do the duty.[50]

Revolutionary War records for both militia and other troops reflected this murky history. Most states used the militia as the basis for their drafts for the Continental Army, dividing men into groups (or classes) and requiring them to furnish a soldier. How any group chose to meet this obligation was up to them. They might draw straws, discuss among themselves if any one of them wanted to go, collectively hire a substitute, or the chosen man might be responsible for providing one. There was no shame in providing a substitute or in being one. Governor George Clinton of New York reflected this dual understanding in a broadside published in 1781. In it, he laid out the troop quotas that needed to be raised from several communities. He was sure the groups of men enumerated for the draft would comply "from a Sense of the Duty they owe their Country." However, he had little expectation that the men he was addressing would do the service themselves. Rather, he reminded them to send only "able-bodied Men, fit for active Service," in order that the state could avoid the inconvenience and expense of having to deal with "improper persons." Similarly, instructions from the commissioners in Berks County, Pennsylvania, instructed a group of taxpayers that they were "being classed together, to furnish one able bodied recruit for the Pennsylvania Line [of the Continental army]." When a man was supplied, honor was satisfied. Who actually served was irrelevant.[51]

In one wartime debate over the issue that took place in Pennsylvania in early 1777, those who had hired substitutes were clear they were patriots who had "rendered their Country real and essential service." The discussion happened as the war moved into the state. In the previous months, enlistments in the Continental army had declined after a series of defeats in New York and New Jersey. Although surprise victories at Trenton, New Jersey, in late December 1776 and at Princeton in January 1777 had raised everyone's spirits, enlistments still lagged. Washington and his army were in winter quarters at Morristown, New Jersey, anxiously awaiting the next move from the British commander, General William Howe.[52]

The Continental Congress, sitting in Philadelphia, needed troops. In spring 1777, it recommended to all the states that they pass draft laws raising troops through their militias. It also suggested that states offer exemptions from militia service to any two militiamen who "furnish one able-bodied recruit, to serve in any battalion of the Continental Army" for three years. In Pennsylvania, some prosperous men, in anticipation of such legislation being passed by the assembly, went ahead and hired men to serve in the army. But when the assembly passed its militia bill, requiring militia service from all males between the ages of eighteen and fifty-three, it did not include any provision for exempting those who had already hired men for the Continental army. The men who had done so were furious.[53]

These men, their ad hoc group chaired by printer and bookseller Robert Bell, met, drafted a response, and published a pamphlet, "The Rise and Continuance of the Substitutes in the Continental Army," laying out their grievances. They had, it stated, quickly secured army recruits "from the purest motives . . . and at very great trouble and expense." Now they were being doubly punished. Not only were they themselves now eligible for militia service, but the very men they might have hired as substitutes had already been contracted to the army. These well-to-do Pennsylvanians felt they were being punished for their patriotism, for their "willingness to serve the public cause." They did not expect the assembly to rewrite its militia laws. But they did hope that it would help them get their recruits back. That, they claimed, was a matter of property rights. If the men they furnished did not exempt them from service, "they are and ought to be considered as our private property, and be immediately discharged, that we may, by those means, be enabled to employ them in such a manner as to answer the purpose for which they were originally designed." This committee did not win this struggle. Events around them moved on; the Continental Congress fled from Philadelphia; and the British occupied the city. The debate over substitutes likely paled in comparison to the more pressing concerns of living with an army of occupation.[54]

The changing circumstances of the war, however, did not change the group's central point. Hiring a substitute was an honorable thing to do in the eyes of the world and met a critical civic obligation. Most former boy soldiers and others who wrote about their military service made no distinction between having themselves served or having provided a surrogate. Whenever the militia was called out, eligible men had to join, pay a fine, or provide a substitute. Having a son or other male relative serve in one's place was a cheap solution. While the boy's labor would be lost, the father could avoid a fine, save the cost of hiring a substitute, and fulfill his legal and moral commitment to the cause.

There were almost as many reasons for this sort of family action as there were boy substitutes. Thirteen-year-old William Addison in South Carolina substituted for his twenty-year-old brother, Christopher, who was exhausted and weak from a recent campaign. Joseph Brown at sixteen went in place of his father, who "was a cripple" and who could not go when drafted. Thirteen-year-old John Suddarth of Virginia took the place of his older brother James after James fell ill and came home rather than go to a military hospital. John served for three months and went home as soon as James recovered. Fifteen-year-old Daniel Bennett in North Carolina substituted in the militia for his father, who was "little accustomed to handling a gun having been a sailor most of his life." In 1777, when he was fourteen, Isaac Bedell served in the New Jersey militia as a substitute for his father, who was otherwise busy getting in "the hay and oat harvest." In the next two years, he substituted multiple times for his Uncle Henry, Cousin Abraham, and father again.

He was not unhappy, as he served with men and boys he knew. These included his friend Daniel Doty, whose family lived close by and attended the same church, and who often substituted for his father at the same time as Bedell.[55]

Sometimes a boy was swept into the service by both the substitution system and a community network, as was the case for the DeWolf brothers in Connecticut and their neighbor Nathan Gillet. Twenty-two-year-old Peter DeWolf served a short term in the militia in 1776 but was debilitated by a "camp distemper." For that reason, when he and others in his militia class had to furnish a soldier for the Continental army to serve for three years, neither he nor the others wanted to go. They hired twenty-year-old Nathan Gillet to do it. Meanwhile, in 1776, Peter's fifteen-year-old brother Joseph had also served as a soldier for a year. When Joseph completed his year of service, he substituted for Peter for short terms in the militia but was otherwise at home. Two years later, Nathan Gillet had had enough of life in the Continental army and hired young Joseph DeWolf to finish the eight months left on his contract. Joseph now substituted for the substitute.[56]

The importance of both community networks and the family substitution system in drawing boys into the service explains the relative absence of African American boys. About 10 percent of the Continental forces were black, some of whom were free men who enlisted on their own account; others served as substitutes for drafted whites. Some were slaves, serving in place of white masters, usually in exchange for freedom. For free blacks in the North or South, not eligible for militia service and probably without an extensive network of white neighbors with whom they and their sons exchanged labor and favors on equal terms, the paths to war may have been more limited. An adult or older teenage slave might direct his own destiny by agreeing to substitute in exchange for freedom, but he would not have been able to (or perhaps want to) lobby for younger brothers.[57]

A few African American boys, slave and free, did find a path to service through family or community networks. Fourteen-year-old Andrew Ferguson was with his father, both free, when they enlisted with the Continentals in Virginia. However, they were fleeing war and had traveled many miles from home. They had each other but were among strangers. In Massachusetts, twelve-year-old slave, Peter Brooks Nelson, was taken into the service in 1775 alongside his master, Josiah Nelson. While Peter's service was under his master's control, the boy knew many of the men with whom they served from Lincoln, their hometown. In Pennsylvania, community networks directed freeborn fourteen-year-old James Forten away from military service on land or in the Continental navy, and instead led him onto a privateer. The boy lived near the Philadelphia waterfront and had worked with his father, a sailmaker, since he was small. His father's death left the family in difficult straits. Tall, strong for his age, skilled, and well known to the community, Forten was able to shop around for the best opportunity and chose his captain, Stephen Decatur, whom he knew by sight and reputation. He had to plead with his widowed mother to get permission, which she agreed to give only after his "earnest and unceasing solicitations." On his maiden voyage, he not only knew his captain but probably also many of the seamen, twenty of whom were men of color from his waterfront neighborhood.[58]

These boys were unusual. More commonly, it was older slaves and free men who served as substitutes for masters and neighbors. Thirty-year-old Virginia slave Tim Jones went in place of his owner who unintentionally enlisted one day when he was drunk. In Rhode Island, twenty-year-old London Hazard substituted in the militia for his owner and others in the owners' extended family. These black men and thousands of others served in all branches of the military, but their sons and younger brothers were usually not with them.[59]

When young boys of any race substituted for their fathers and other male relatives or friends, they gave no indication later that they felt exploited. Indeed, the vast majority of substitutes, men or boys, made no comment upon it other than that it happened. Eighteen-year-old Thomas Fox substituted for two men in his western Connecticut town with whom he was at least slightly acquainted. The men who hired him were still alive to vouch for him when he applied for a pension forty years later. It was they who went into detail about how Fox was paid thirty acres of land and some cash. If anyone sounded bitter about the transaction, it was the two men who hired him, who seemed to feel that they had overpaid. For John Collins of South Carolina, the substitution system offered him a chance to support himself when he left home against his father's wishes. His first service, a brief militia tour when he was fifteen in 1776, happened with his father's consent. But when he was eighteen, he set out "contrary to his [father's] will," and, in an enterprising spirit demonstrated many times over the next two years, he went to a neighbor who was a "drafted militiaman and hired myself to him."

When young Collins was discharged from service at a fort in Georgia, he approached an arriving militia company and immediately hired himself again as a substitute. Realizing his relationship with his father was at least temporarily severed and thus "having no home," he repeated this pattern numerous times. It was in 1782 when he turned twenty-one that he finally "returned to the neighborhood in South Carolina where I was raised" but not to his father's house. The substitution system made his path to early freedom possible without having to commit to a longer and harder life in the Continental army.[60]

However, some resented such service. Sixteen-year-old Ebenezer Fox, learning the barber and wigmaker's trade in Boston, went off to the militia in his master's place for three months in 1779. His recollections drip with sarcasm. His master, he recalled, was "a firm friend to his country, and willing to do all he could to help along her cause, as far as expressing favorable opinions," but he did not want to serve when he was drafted and sought a substitute. Since he had no spare cash to hire someone, he looked for one closer to home and settled on Fox. But Fox was not coerced. He had found that "the monotonous duties of the shop grew irksome," and he yearned for a change. Still, Fox had no fond memories of his three months of trudging about the countryside, burdened by a "heavy knapsack." He recalled that "nothing would again induce me to officiate as a substitute for him or anybody else." But it was the grind of service rather than the substitution system that bothered him.[61]

Obadiah Benge of North Carolina also sounded bitter as he remembered his experiences. He had been "forced" into the service as a substitute for a neighbor. That may not alone have shaped his memories. The death of his brother, his companion in arms, and receiving a wound in the shoulder that gave him lifelong pain, no doubt also colored his recollections of that time.[62]

But the vast majority of boys offered no such comments or criticisms. The substitution system was a key mechanism drawing them into the service, and without it only a fraction of them would probably have ended up in the military at such a young age. Boys' experiences as substitutes varied greatly, depending on family circumstances, personal temperament, and military setting. But the system, combined with their community networks, ensured their presence in the ranks.

THE DEMANDS OF WORK, the practice of substitution, and the community networks around which colonial life revolved all played a role in drawing boys into the service. Boys' contributions to the family economy were often critical, and in the army boys could make a man's wage. To earn this, however, families had to overcome their prejudices against military service by the very young. High wages and bounties had not enticed them in previous wars. But in the Revolution, pay—intermittent as it frequently was—and bounties combined with economic upheaval to add to the appeal of these financial terms.

By itself, money would probably not have sufficed to overcome historic family prejudice against youthful service. But as the war dragged on, families of the Revolutionary period needed to reconcile their political commitment to liberty with daily economic realities. Men's labor could not be spared for years at a time. While long-term service was an interruption to boys' training for adult financial independence, the occasional short term of service did no harm. The substitution system allowed families to stay politically committed to the cause.

As the long war progressed, both work and substitution were interwoven with networks that were already the economic and social lifeblood of the community. Community networks adjusted to this new version of demand and supply. Just as boys migrated through these avenues to work in peacetime, so, in wartime, boys followed them into military service. In the earliest days of the war, both men and youths followed this path to service. It took the passage of time for boys to be swept into it in a profound way.

By these means, boys went to work in military service. Whether they were encouraged along these routes by dreams of glory and heroism fed by the books they had read, songs they had sung, and by the political ideas of the cause, or whether they were pushed along these paths by instability, the upheavals of war, and dire need, they enlisted. In the service, they trudged many miles, endured hardship, and occasionally had fun; they made friends, stood guard, learned to play drums and fifes, ran errands, and fought the enemy. They suffered from illness, nursed others in turn, and took their turn to bury the dead.

As they served, of course, they could not have known what the future held. Decades later, as old men, they knew they had participated in the greatest political and military upheaval of their lives.

CHAPTER FIVE

Fellow Citizens

State of Connecticut
County of New London
City of Norwich

On this 20th day of July A.D. 1832 personally appeared in open
court before the City Court of the city of Norwich now sitting,
Bishop Tyler, resident of Griswold, formerly Preston, in the
County of New London, State of Connecticut aged sixty five
years.

Who having first duly sworn according to Law, doth on
his oath make the following declaration in order to obtain the
benefit of the act of Congress duly passed June 7th, 1832;

That on or about the first day of March 1781, he entered
Service of the United States . . . in a company commanded by
Captain Charles Miles in a corps of State troops raised by the
State of Connecticut for one year. That he continued to serve
from that time until on or about the first on March, 1782 for the
period of one year, that he served for the whole of that period,
wiz one year, and was discharged at Stamford in the State of
Connecticut with rest of said company. I [*sic*] was very young
when I enlisted and my father was unwilling that I should
enlist, but being acquainted with Captain Miles, & he agreeing
that I should serve as his waiter, & being myself very anxious
to go, he finally consented & I was accepted in the capacity of a
private soldier, served out the whole time.[1]

This was Bishop Tyler's first application to the court and, at first blush,
it is a straightforward one. He explained the reasons for his enlistment
at age fourteen and his name appears in the Connecticut muster rolls.
Yet Tyler was challenged by the pension commissioner, James Edwards,
who wanted to know why he had enlisted "at the tender age of fourteen." As noted earlier, and particularly in chapter two, Tyler explained
that his enlistment was politically motivated, that his enthusiasm for the
cause had been instilled by his family, his community, and his minister.

There were two elements that make his case and his subsequent petitions to the court unusual. Unlike some veterans who had moved to other towns or states and no longer knew anyone from their earlier lives, Tyler and most of the small group of boys with whom he had gone to school and played, and who had also enlisted, had not left the state. Some still remained in the original neighborhood. Tyler, a prominent physician and leading figure in town, gave depositions in support of many of his friends' pension applications (as did they for him), and some of what we know about his young and later life in Preston appears in those depositions.

More unusually, Tyler answered Edwards's question as an outraged citizen. When Tyler went to court more than a year after his first application, he felt no need to hide his anger and mortification at being questioned in such a public way. He felt keenly that his integrity had been challenged. As he told the court, he felt:

> ... Mortification that he has not only made solemn oath to those [military] services but proved them by most respectable witnesses. He feels however some gratification that at the time when this question comes to him from Washington to be answered, he has been & is sitting in a respectable Court of Justice as Foreman of a very respectable Jury deciding the causes of his fellow citizens; that he is a practicing Physician in his native town, which town he has represented in the Legislature of the State and was employed as a surgeon in the last war at New London.[2]

Tyler's depositions in support of his own and others' pension applications and other public records allow us to imagine how Tyler may have come to respond to the commissioner's questions so indignantly.

Perhaps it was like this:

It was December 5, 1833, and Bishop Tyler was an angry man. The federal government's pension commissioner in Washington, D.C., was questioning his integrity. The problem had begun in July 1832 when Tyler had applied for a Revolutionary War pension as soon as he was eligible. Doing so was no small matter. He had ridden from Griswold, Connecticut, to the city court in Norwich, a distance of a good twelve miles, where he had given a sworn statement about his service. That was inconvenient enough, but he had also to solicit two neighbors to give depositions on his behalf. One neighbor was an old army friend, and the other was the son of one of his former commanding officers.

Now, the testimony had to be given over again, and more old friends had to be brought in, all because of Edwards. The commissioner had challenged him to explain why at the "tender age of fourteen" he had served as a soldier. That would be an easy question to answer as he could remember being caught up in the political enthusiasm of the time, watching the militia muster at his father's tavern, singing liberty songs, and hearing the local men talking politics. At least he thought that was why he had gone. Perhaps he had also been a bit jealous of his older brother James who was already serving. And he dimly remembered that his younger siblings—especially twins Amy and John who had turned eight the year he enlisted—were always interrupting him when he was reading, and he had been looking forward to getting away. Tyler had not thought to explain any of this during his first deposition, as he believed the commissioner would only be interested in his service. If he had not, over the years, regularly seen his former comrades in arms and occasionally reminisced over coffee or something stronger, he doubted he would remember anything very much at all. Still, Tyler was determined to respond to the pension commissioner as soon as possible. He rode to Norwich to give his second deposition, eager to put this business behind him.

Tyler almost regretted applying for a pension at all. In 1818, he had been pleased to read in the newspaper that the government was giving aid to impoverished army veterans. He had been saddened to hear of the straitened circumstances of some former soldiers, and thought it was only right that the government should support them, especially after the happy conclusion in 1815 of another war against Great Britain. The years since the end of that conflict had been prosperous. Tyler thought it was fitting that those old Revolutionary soldiers who were suffering from economic hardship should receive some comfort from a grateful nation enjoying the blessings of freedom. He was delighted when his neighbor David Lawrence got one. Tyler told himself that he was pleased for Lawrence's sake, and not just because it allowed Lawrence to pay him the money he owed him.

Tyler himself was comfortably settled, and had no need of a government pension. In the decades since his service, he had stayed in his hometown of Preston and prospered with it. The town had grown large enough to be divided into two, and some of his old haunts became the town of Griswold. He had become a doctor and developed a large practice. He was on the board of the local Library Company, owned a nice house and land, made some additional money from property investments, and even served as a surgeon for a week during the last war against Great Britain. In 1817, he ran for office and was elected to the state assembly. He enjoyed his time in the legislature but probably felt he had neglected his practice while he was absorbed with public business and chose not to run again.

Not only was Tyler a prosperous citizen, he also enjoyed domestic tranquility. He had waited until he was thirty and settled in his practice before he married Alice Morgan. They had two daughters, now both married, whom he adored, but he was worried that his younger daughter and her husband were thinking about moving their young family to Illinois. He and his wife still mourned the loss of their two sons. They had buried Joseph when he was just an infant, but Samuel they had lost when he was eighteen. It was a great shock, as he had been in the bloom of youth, energetic and hardworking, when a brief but terrible fever struck. It was a blow from which neither he nor Alice had ever really recovered. But despite these great disappointments, he possibly felt content with his lot in life and wanted for nothing.

But as the years passed, Tyler began to feel that perhaps it would not be a bad thing if he were to receive a small financial acknowledgment for the sacrifices of his youth. He and his friends agreed that perhaps the time had come for the government to make some payment to all the men who had won independence. At age sixty-five, Tyler was among the youngest of the war's veterans and so was more aware than most that their generation was passing. When he read his newspaper and noted an obituary headed "Another Revolutionary Soldier Gone," Tyler felt as sentimental as the next man. He believed there was growing political support for a new broad pension bill, and he was right. It passed easily in 1832. Tyler, along with many other veterans, quickly went to court to apply. As these men made their depositions, they enjoyed the fact that their neighbors and acquaintances raised glasses to their health and slapped them on the back in thanks for their wartime service.

It is not surprising, then, that Tyler was outraged when the commissioner did not believe that he had served. Now, in a subsequent sworn testimony to the court, he bitterly noted the mortification he felt at having to defend himself; that he was well known to the members of the court added to his humiliation. Tyler and two more witnesses, both fellow soldiers and boyhood friends, offered more testimony about his service. Edwards was finally convinced that Tyler was the same Bishop Tyler whose name was listed on the muster rolls. He approved the pension, and from then on, twice a year, Tyler received the grand sum of twenty-seven dollars from the government. Justice had finally been done, but, after all this, perhaps Tyler had mixed feelings about the whole endeavor.[3]

FEW VETERANS LED lives public enough to be traced, and we can only surmise what Tyler's service meant to him. His actions and language in court indicate immense pride in his participation in his public duties, which he explicitly notes are those of a citizen. Whether his youthful military service meant more to him in shaping those feelings than the many other accomplishments of his life, we can never know.

Most veterans, former boy soldiers and others, said very little about their lives after the war. Veterans were required to list the places where they had lived in the intervening years, but few offered specifics. Most offered only the state and occasionally the county, and even then were often vague about when they had made such a move and almost never said why.

It is only men such as Tyler, whose applications involve two or more presentations to the court, who revealed information about their present circumstances. And among these men, it was the most powerful and cranky who tended to say the most. For Tyler, a successful man who had standing in his community, it was easy to assert himself in front of the court. Samuel Hancock of Virginia, who had served when he was fourteen, did the same thing. He had lost some of the discharge certificates he needed to prove his service, but he had family and neighbors who could testify to it, and, anyway, he noted, "he is known to every member of the Court of which he is now the presiding member." Ebenezer Couch of Connecticut, who had served at ages twelve and thirteen as waiter to his officer-father, was a former state legislator. He confidently told the court that "[i]t was not uncommon in the war of the Revolution that boys from twelve to sixteen years entered the service, not only as musicians and waiters but as soldiers." His poise and slightly aggressive stance won the day.[4]

Other men lacked credentials, wealth, or powerful friends and took a different tone. When the commissioner challenged Jacob Gundy, suspicious about him having served at age eleven, Gundy stayed calm. He simply noted that, "Mr. Edwards is mistaken as to my age." Gundy had in fact been thirteen when he had enlisted and corrected this confusion in an accommodating manner. William Coff, an impoverished free man of color, needed to explain why he was applying for a pension years after he could have. Coff had enlisted in Virginia when he was about fourteen, but now, as he told the court, he was a tenant farmer who had been lame since a broken leg had healed poorly and left him unable to work. He was "poor, old and illiterate and did not learn he was entitled to a pension until long after the law was passed." To compound his problem, he had no proof of his service. He had migrated to Botetourt County, Virginia, nestled between the Blue Ridge and Appalachian Mountains, a long way from people who had known him in his childhood who could testify on his behalf. It took him many months to track down two white former comrades, Daniel Burchel and Richard Pugh, who lived in nearby counties who could give depositions for him. Pugh, who was about six years older than Coff, and Burchel, whose age is not known, had enlisted with Coff in 1780 in the same company of the Continental army. All were poor men who kept their language respectful and communications brief in addressing the court or pension commissioner.[5]

Unless former boy soldiers were, like Coff, Continental veterans applying on the basis of financial need, there is scant information about their economic status. Many boys had served in the militia for multiple short terms and were not eligible for pensions until the legislation of 1832 included them on the basis of service alone. If they had been poor at some point in their lives or were poor in 1832, it was irrelevant, and they said nothing about it. Israel Trask was one of the rare men who mentioned anything about his circumstances. He had lived in Gloucester, Massachusetts, his whole life and had been a prosperous man. He had served as state senator and director of the Gloucester Bank. When Trask applied for a pension in 1845, he told the court he had not applied in 1832 when he was eligible because he was in "easy circumstances." But at age eighty, he had lost money on some investments and was needy. Trask's actions suggest that some veterans saw the pension as a kind of public assistance, but he offered no more financial details.[6]

Financially needy veterans of the Revolutionary War have left only a small footprint in other historical records. The few whose lives are more amply documented reveal how varied were the experiences of this generation of boys who grew to adulthood with the new nation. As the former boy soldiers argued their cases to the pension commissioner, needing to list residences and detail relocations, some provided a glimpse of the demographic shifts occurring.

Some veterans, former boy soldiers and others, headed west, north, or south to start new lives after the Revolutionary War. Continental soldiers had been awarded bounty land grants for their service. Some sold these to solve short-term financial problems. Benjamin Gauss of New York, who enlisted at sixteen, sold his certificate for bounty land for thirty dollars almost as soon as the ink was dry. But others used their land grants to pursue opportunities in Vermont, western New York, Ohio, Tennessee, Kentucky, and other states and territories. Most boys did not earn such bounties. As militiamen, they were not entitled to it. And if they qualified as longer-serving soldiers, the bounty belonged to their fathers. Some fathers may have added their sons' bounties to their own when they moved their families. Cyrus Allen's officer-father probably did this when he moved his whole family from Connecticut to Vermont shortly after the war. Allen had been so young when he served that he was still only about fourteen when the family relocated. It is unlikely he played any role in the decision, but he lived the remainder of his life within about one hundred miles of where his father had settled. Ebenezer Couch also moved from Connecticut to Saratoga, New York, with his father and his family just as he turned twenty-one. There is no record that either father or son received a land bounty or any indication that the decision to migrate was a family one. However, as he was now an adult, by law, Ebenezer had a choice. Whatever his role in that move, Couch spent the rest of his life near Saratoga.[7]

Samuel Aspenwall, also of Connecticut, embarked on two great adventures when he turned twenty-one in 1789: he got married; and he headed off without his family or his new wife to Vermont. Aspenwall did not receive bounty land, but that did not dampen his spirits. He set off for the north with a friend of the same age, Elisha Thayer, whom he had met at the end of the war. They lodged with each other, helped each other plan and build their respective new homes, then brought their wives from Connecticut to join them. They lived as near neighbors for the rest of their lives, raising their families alongside each other. In doing so, Aspenwall and many others participated as adults in a larger migration that was taking place.[8]

Cyprian Parrish, who had first served when he was thirteen, was also part of this migration. Born and raised in Duchess County, New York, on the Connecticut border, Parrish moved after the war to central New York, where he lived for about twenty years. After that, he moved to western New York, living in a variety of small communities near Lake Erie, relocating every six to ten years. When his wife died, he moved in with his son John in Ohio. And when John decided to try his luck in the small village of Flint, Michigan, Parrish went too, embarking on a new life at age seventy-seven.[9]

But some of the boys who had served as part of close networks of friends never ventured far from the towns of their birth. Bishop Tyler and his friends Samuel Branch, Elisha Prentice, Simeon Hewitt, and others from Preston/Griswold, Connecticut, could all be found within the same county fifty years after the war. Similarly, the fifer, John Piatt, who had enlisted at age nine and who was from a closely connected extended family in New Jersey, stayed in the vicinity of his boyhood home his whole life and died only twenty miles away from the place where he had been born.[10]

It was not only boys in the long-settled communities on the East Coast who stayed close to home. Somewhat further inland in the vicinity of Ithaca, New York, boys such as fifer Aaron Day and his fellow musicians Samuel Merriele and William Waddle all stayed in the area and in contact after their service. They had not known each other before enlisting in the Fourth New York Continental Regiment, but they became fast friends and decades later were still well acquainted with each other. They had not moved any great distances in their adult lives. One army musician friend of theirs who had relocated, James Knapp, had only moved about a hundred miles, and he also stayed in touch.[11]

In contrast, many of the boys who served with the backcountry militias were much more mobile. Of the seventy members of the North Carolina patriot forces in the Battle of King's Mountain who enlisted when they were boys, sixty (86 percent) were living in another state when they applied for pensions. And indeed they were sons of mobile families. Their parents had moved to areas such as Rowan, Surry, and Anson Counties around the Yadkin River in North Carolina just before the boys had been born or moved there when they were very young. Abel Pearson, who served many militia terms from the age of fourteen, had relocated to the area with his family from Pennsylvania, near the Maryland border, when he was a young child. John Burchfield, whose family moved to the backcountry from Maryland shortly before he was born, served in the North Carolina militia at around the same age. Both boys seemed to inherit their families' restless spirit.[12]

Pearson's and Burchfield's journeys after the war are representative of the geographic mobility of backcountry boy soldiers. They set out for new opportunities in the decade following their service. From his early twenties onwards, Pearson was on the move. He rarely went far, but he moved multiple times. First he moved to South Carolina, living there twelve years. Then he relocated to Tennessee and thereafter moved every five to seven years to a different county. Pearson zigzagged one or two hundred miles across the central and eastern parts of the state, before finally settling in White County, where he lived when he applied for a pension. Burchfield spread his wings farther. He also moved to western South Carolina for thirteen years, then Warren County, Kentucky for twenty, before settling in southeastern Indiana, within fifty miles of a relative, probably his older brother, who had moved there some years before.[13]

The African American boys, free and slave, for whom enlistment records exist, showed the same diversity in their postwar movements. Peter Brooks Nelson stayed close to home. As a young slave from Lincoln, Massachusetts, he had served both alongside his master and alone. He had been emancipated in 1779 when he was sixteen, two years before all Massachusetts slaves were freed. Nelson immediately changed his last name to Sharon, a rebuke to his master's family, and enlisted again in the army. He fought with the patriots in their victory over the British at Yorktown, and slowly made his way home with his regiment. After the war, he stayed in Lincoln, rented some land, farmed, and probably also worked as a laborer. He died sometime around early 1792, shortly before his thirtieth birthday, long before he was eligible for a pension, but in the postwar years showed no inclination to leave the community he knew well.[14]

Freeborn William Coff, on the other hand, moved well away from his childhood home around Chesterfield, Virginia, not far from the fall line of the James River. He had headed west, first to Franklin County, before going to Botetourt in the mountains. Andrew Ferguson, a former Continental soldier born free in Virginia in 1765, had made his way to Monroe County, Indiana. Perhaps he was driven out of his home state by restrictive regulations passed in Virginia in the early 1790s and at the beginning of the nineteenth century that required free people of color to register with city or county officers. But he offered no explanation. He applied for a pension in 1838, six years after he was eligible. And in 1851 at age eighty-six, living in the bustling town of Bloomington, he applied for a new round of bounty land awards for veterans to "support himself and his aged wife in their old age." He received 160 acres, which he likely promptly sold.[15]

BEYOND THESE ISOLATED cases and aggregated data, the veterans provide limited information about their experiences. However, some allow us to understand something of their lives as they reached maturity and old age. They had been involved in one of the great political transformations in history. They were aware of their role, but, if they were sentimental about it, they rarely stated it and offered few observations about these monumental changes.

Applying for a pension was not simply about receiving a federal benefit. It was also a political act that validated for veterans themselves the role they had played in the founding of the new nation. The act that made pensions generally available was passed in June 1832. In the first months afterward, the occasions when groups of veterans made their way to give their depositions together on court days became days of public festivities in some small towns. When impoverished veterans had applied fourteen years earlier, they too had been celebrated, but news had quickly followed of abuse and corruption in the application process. Now, with a pension system that was efficient, effective, and corruption-resistant, communities again honored their aging veterans. In Delaware County, New York, for example, nestled in the Adirondack Mountains and bordered by the upper reaches of the Delaware River, veterans gathered in the county seat, Delhi, to submit their applications to the county court. The local newspaper, the *Delaware Gazette*, noted that by late morning "the village was literally thronged" with elderly veterans. Some of the young men of the community, "as a token of their respect," improvised a public dinner, and the court adjourned early so that 112 veterans who had gathered in Delhi could be entertained. A fifer and drummer appeared, and the sound of their instruments "seemed to have an electric effect on these veterans of the last age, and revived the sentiments and enthusiasms of bye-gone days." The event recognized the veterans as distinguished elders from a distant time and bound them together as a respected class.[16]

Despite these public celebrations, most veterans (including former boy soldiers) made no reference in their pension applications (or other public documents) to the political issues at stake in the Revolution. Gaius Stebbins could have associated his distinctive first name, that of a famous general and statesman of ancient Rome, with the ideals of the Revolution when recounting how he had enlisted at age fourteen. Instead, he emphasized that he had been of "large stature" for his age. If political ideals were involved, Gaius Stebbins did not claim them. It was his father, a man "uncommonly zealous in the American cause," who had given his consent to his very young son going off to war. Of course, as a minor at the time, the boy might be presumed to have no political opinions, but he felt obliged to attribute his enlistment to his father's consent rather than to his own motivations. Gaius Stebbins never portrayed himself as a political actor.[17]

Similarly, Cyprian Parrish made no reference to the political passions of the Revolutionary era when discussing his military service in his first depositions, but flowery sentiments came to the surface when, as an old man, Parrish again argued for his pension. His original case was clear, and his pension was quickly granted. In subsequent correspondence with the pension office to have his pension routed to a new address, Parrish's letters were similarly matter-of-fact about his service. But for his last relocation to Flint, Michigan, the pension agent in Detroit had erroneously been instructed by the Washington, D.C., pension office to halt his pension. Parrish was outraged and his patriotism offended. After all, he had a right to his pension and to "continue to draw [it for] the short time I have to stay here apon [sic] this earth which is but a few years at most where I must bid a doo [adieu] to that Glorious Independence which I helped to gain." Commissioner Edwards quickly corrected the mistake and reinstated Parrish's pension.[18]

Andrew Ferguson, lobbying for an increase in his pension when his old war wounds incapacitated him, noted that he had suffered at the hands of the "general enemy" rather than saying at the hands of the British or in fighting for liberty. A few others such as Aaron Day referred to fighting against the "common enemy." These phrases were bland, although they united writer and reader in a common understanding of who the enemy was and what the purpose had been. However, that was usually as political as many got.[19]

For a few, applying for a pension began a sequence of events that turned their lives upside down. The public forum of the initial application process and subsequent petitions allowed their communities to know old stories and hear more than a few secrets. A few veterans found that the events of years ago provided an opportunity for neighbors to settle present-day grievances.

Such was the case for Josiah Brandon. As noted in chapter three, when Brandon was a teenager in the North Carolina backcountry, his father had joined the loyalist militia, and Brandon had become a patriot. For a brief period in 1780, Brandon's father had compelled him to go out with the loyalists, and Brandon fought on that side in the Battle of King's Mountain. When Brandon's father was killed in that battle, Brandon immediately rejoined the patriots. In his pension application, Brandon openly acknowledged his brief service with the enemy. His pension was quickly granted; pensions were for service, and he had served for many years with the patriot militia, despite this brief interruption.[20]

Brandon's brief change of sides had never been a secret, and during the war, people had been sympathetic. In many depositions and letters to the commissioners, Brandon and his family and friends testified that his short-lived loyalist affiliation had been well known among them. But when two of Brandon's neighbors complained, and Commissioner Edwards suspended his pension while he investigated the matter further, Brandon was mortified. Now in his seventies and a respected Methodist minister in Lynchburg, Tennessee, Brandon became an object of scorn and the subject of gossip among neighbors and parishioners.[21]

Brandon's friends and family came quickly to his defense—not only had Brandon been a minor child when he was coerced by his father to join the loyalists, they testified, but great shame had also been brought upon him with the suspension of his pension. In petitioning for the pension to be reinstated, Brandon's friend David Eastland argued, he was not writing because Brandon needed the money, but because he wanted "to prevent the stigma from attaching to his character." Brandon's son, Byrd Brandon, a district attorney in Alabama, assigned blame to two men who worked "against my father" for no other reason except "malice against his reputation." The matter was ultimately resolved in Brandon's favor, and his pension was reinstated. But Brandon's spirit had been crushed by the experience.[22]

Drummer John Jenks also had the shame of past transgressions become a subject of public debate in his community in the mid-1820s when he moved his family to another state and reapplied for a pension. Jenks had applied for a need-based pension in 1818 when he was living in Orange County, New York, with his wife and ten children. It was quickly granted. However, when he moved his family about a hundred miles away to Northmoreland, in northeastern Pennsylvania, he had to ask for his pension to be reassigned to a new location. His new neighbors objected to his receiving a pension, because, as an agent for the pension commissioner reported, "his character is not good." Since collecting a pension was a public act involving a visit to the pension agent, and because Jenks was not a man to hide his accomplishments, his neighbors knew he was a Revolutionary War pensioner. But they were suspicious. Asa Keeler wrote to the pension office in 1827 that Jenks could not possibly have been a Revolutionary War soldier, as he was "not far from 55 years I should judge," an age that would have made him an eight-year-old enlistee in 1780. In Jenks's petitions to the courts, he now gave his date of birth as 1768 (he had stated 1770 before). Perhaps his memory was jogged, or perhaps he was responding to the concerns of the pension office. In the Federal Census of 1840, he had lost the extra two years, and was recorded as a seventy-year-old, thus born in 1770. Whatever his age, the much older veterans who had served around him recalled Jenks, in their letters of support, as being unusually small and something of a mascot. They called him "Little Drummer Jenks," and remembered that he had been "one of the Smallest Drummers and beat a very small Blue Drum." His neighbors felt otherwise, and rumors circulated that he had moved to Pennsylvania because he had just completed a sentence for forgery in the recently opened New York state prison at Auburn. Edwards sent an agent to investigate who confirmed that Jenks was a shady character. His pension was suspended. Jenks made no effort to address any accusations about the way he lived his life. Instead, he focused on proving the only thing that legally mattered—that he had been a Revolutionary War soldier.[23]

Jenks launched a vigorous defense. He recounted the childhood circumstances, detailed in chapter three, that resulted in his running away from his master to join the army at the age of ten. He admitted to a variety of jobs after the war. As soon as he had been discharged in 1783, all of thirteen years old, he had traveled to Rhode Island "to support my poor widowed mother!!!" He went to sea, where he would have had to revert to a boy's wages for a number of years, probably a hard adjustment for him. In his early twenties he returned to life on land, became a teacher, married, and settled in New York. Over the next decades, he not only taught, he also did a "course of study" to be a doctor and practiced occasionally. If the stories of his incarceration were correct, he had been a forger, although on this matter he was silent.[24]

Jenks seems to have approached his checkered career with the same verve and enthusiasm as everything else in life. In his 1818 pension application, Jenks claimed to be disabled as a result of a wartime injury—one sustained playing "Wicket Ball." He had been hit by a bat in the abdomen so hard that it resulted in a hernia, leading to "bodily Infirmities!!!!" from which he continued to suffer. Whatever the origin of his disabilities and his work history, his poverty was clear. His possessions totaled only seventeen dollars. His debts amounted to more than seven hundred. However, despite his successes and failures, there is no trace of bitterness in his recollections. His jaunty application recounts his life story, pausing to address the commissioner as "Honorable Sir," or "Noble Sir," with just a hint of sarcasm.[25]

But pensions were not awarded on the basis of virtue. Proof of service was the only requirement. However much Edwards may have been concerned about Jenks's character, his name appeared on all the relevant muster rolls, and Jenks could describe his service in almost mind-numbing detail. The arrears were paid, and regular pension payments continued until Jenks's death in 1843. In as much as we can divine his character from his application, he seems irrepressible. While Josiah Brandon was devastated when his integrity was doubted, and Bishop Tyler was outraged, Jenks just added exclamation points and probably thumbed his nose at his neighbors.

For veteran Samuel Godding the award of a pension also led to emotional upheaval, but his was not induced by any questions from the commissioner but from others who shared his faith and his own religious conscience. Godding had enlisted at about age sixteen in 1777 and served for three years in the New Hampshire Continentals. After the war, he moved to Maine and farmed, but in 1818, he was impoverished and unable to work "by reason of debility and bilious disorder." His wife was also "infirm and feeble," and they struggled to care for two young children (not their own) who lived with them. In the following years, he was unable to find financial stability. Despite this and his indebtedness, he was thought a man of "fair character," and he was promptly awarded a pension when he applied.

Godding's problems began a few years later when he became a Shaker. Shakers were a Protestant evangelical sect, formally known as the United Society of Believers in the Second Coming of Christ, whose members practiced celibacy and lived in communal settlements. They were also pacifists, and, in 1832, Godding renounced his military pension. War was, he observed, "incompatible, and altogether repugnant to the precepts and examples of our Savior." He not only communicated this to the pension office, he paid for a notice in the local paper, the *Eastern Argus*, to make his religious convictions and piety public. But two years later, he wanted his pension back. He claimed that when he had renounced it, he was "under the command or advice" of the Shakers. Now, although still claiming to be a member of the sect, he was no longer living with them. He was again "needy" and felt himself "removed" from such "conscientious scruples." He quickly had his pension reinstated, but took out no notice in the paper to declare this change of heart. For men such as these, pensions provided an important financial safety net and a public acknowledgement of their service, but they also opened the door to public questioning and possibly humiliation. Each former boy soldier had to decide if it was worth it.[26]

AS BOYS, THESE VETERANS had gone off to work and to war. As they matured to adulthood, they married and had their own children as one century ended and another dawned. Just as the colonial and Revolutionary eras were filled with contradictory perceptions of childhood and children, so was the new republic. Attitudes changed toward children's participation in both work and war, influenced by the emerging importance of education. Veterans' recollections hint at these larger transitions and how they were reflected in their own lives.

As legislators and other community leaders agonized over the direction of the infant republic, there was a consensus among them that stability and strength lay in an educated citizenry. The security of the nation, they argued, was at stake. Noah Webster, famous today for writing an early American dictionary of the English language (first published in 1828), thought that education was key to shaping "the characters of individuals." This would in turn form "the general character of a nation." Thus the creation of public schools was an essential matter of state in a country "where government is in the hands of the people." Webster's ideas encouraged enterprising individuals and municipalities. In the decades following the war, private and public schools opened, and many of these new academies admitted girls as well as boys. Benjamin Rush, a signer of the Declaration of Independence, argued that girls needed to be educated too so they could "concur in instructing their sons in the principles of liberty and government." [27]

Infused with these ideas and those of an earlier generation of enlightenment thinkers, families who could afford to do so, kept their children in school for a serious and sustained education. Parents protected their children from economic realities and saw them not as laborers and contributors to the family's welfare but as individuals who required an investment of time and resources. For boys, this was not only about their being able to fulfill their civic duty. It was also partly in response to new work opportunities for youths as clerks and managers in new kinds of industrial business enterprises. With a growing focus on education, there were also many more jobs as teachers, and these were open to both girls and boys. These careers required more sustained training in arithmetic, writing, and grammar than had previously been available to the very young.

Children in poorer families continued to be a critical economic resource. In rural areas, they remained an important asset whose labor was bartered or shared according to the needs of neighbors and kin. In urban areas and in country towns such as Lowell, Massachusetts, that grew up around new factories, there were increasing opportunities for children to contribute to the household economy by working in factories and workshops.[28]

But workplaces of the early nineteenth century differed greatly from the work settings of the colonial period. Then, boys had been apprenticed formally to a master or informally with a male relative who promised to educate them and give them a skill they could use to become independent adults. By the early 1800s, opportunities to become an apprentice and learn a craft declined. Children instead became a source of cheap unskilled labor in industry, working for wages for bosses or masters who had no interest in training them to become more expensive laborers and who had no responsibility to educate them. Children who lived in municipal poorhouses or at home with impoverished parents became part of this new industrial labor force.[29]

Little is known about how former boy soldiers treated their own children. However, there is no indication that their own childhood sufferings or adventures made them especially sympathetic to the problems their children faced. More prosperous veterans rarely mentioned their children. Aged pension applicants of the 1830s—whose children were long gone from the nest—had little reason to refer to them. But impoverished former boy soldiers, applying in 1818, were only middle-aged, and at least a few of their children were still minors. They had mixed views on their obligations to their offspring. Walton Tilman, who enlisted in the Virginia Continentals for three years at age sixteen, made it clear that he needed to support his two sons, aged fifteen and twelve, as they were "not yet free." But others expected their children to work as soon as they were able. Nathan Elwood, a long-serving soldier in the Connecticut Continentals who had enlisted at fifteen, expected his children to contribute to the family economy. Living in central New York, he gave his occupation as farmer, but he was unable to support his family due to severe rheumatism. Elwood told the court that he only wanted a pension to assist himself, his wife, and five-year-old daughter, Hannah. His wife was "weak and infirm," and the little girl was "unable to labor as yet." However, his three older children, aged fourteen, twelve, and nine, he asserted, were in good health and able to support themselves.[30]

John Jenks also expected his ten children to pull their weight as soon as they were able. His two older daughters, Amelia Ann aged twenty and fifteen-year-old Almira Caroline, both had the "occupation [of] housewifery." The older was "weak and infirm," leaving Almira to take care of her asthmatic mother, disabled father, her unmarried older brothers who worked but still lived at home, and her younger siblings, the youngest of whom was two years old. Almira had her work cut out.[31]

This does not mean poorer veterans did not think that education was important. Among Nathan Elwood's meager possessions, a sad list of items of furniture and crockery totaling less than thirty-two dollars, was one Bible, one hymn book, and a "few school books." Together, they made up just over 3 percent of his net worth. John Jenks's assets were about half of Elwood's, and his did not include books. However, Jenks himself could read and write. He had worked as a teacher, and his eighteen-year-old son already held a teaching job. It is likely that his children could read, and even the unlucky Almira may have known how to write, though she would have had little time to develop or enjoy either skill.[32]

Prosperous veterans expected their better-educated descendants to be willing and ready to work. Bishop Tyler's grandson Samuel, despite having had years of schooling by age sixteen, gave insufficient evidence of application. In a will Tyler executed in 1844, he already saw the boy as "profligate and inattentive to business." Tyler bequeathed him $1,000 that he would inherit when he turned twenty-one, but only if "he shall conduct himself with propriety and become steady, industrious and oeconomical." This seemed to be an incentive for Samuel, who received the inheritance when Tyler died five years later. But Tyler's expectation that his grandson would focus his attention on earning a living was clear.[33]

Some veterans, impoverished, did what their own fathers had done and bound their children to another household to work. The system of binding out children was in transition after the war. The practice was only formally continued by the overseers of the poor who placed children out from almshouses up and down the eastern seaboard. However, families in economic distress, and even some administrators of relief for the poor, were now uncomfortable with this kind of indentured servitude. As the national debate raged over slavery—some northern states abolished the institution, others passed legislation for gradual emancipation, and some southern states such as Virginia facilitated manumissions—families and the courts rethought what it meant to be a free child. In a decision in Philadelphia in 1793, the Pennsylvania Supreme Court specifically stated that servitude for otherwise free minors made them "a species of property, holding a middle rank between slaves and freemen." This was a condition that the court found troubling at best and at worst "degrading," especially for white children.[34]

In many places, overseers of the poor still bound out the community's poorest children. Practices varied, determined by local sensibilities and the labor market. In Boston, for example, town officials continued to bind children out but no longer assigned them to potentially rewarding craft training. Instead, most were now sent where labor was needed: to factories, or to farms where boys labored in the fields and girls worked as domestic servants. In Philadelphia, children were also still bound out. The number bound to learn a craft declined, and boys joined girls in becoming waiters or domestic servants. But, following the court's concerns about status, poor white children served short-term contracts to differentiate them from young African Americans living under the gradual emancipation laws of the state, who were bound as indentured servants until they were twenty-eight.[35]

In Savannah, Georgia, and Charleston, South Carolina, town leaders adopted a new and different strategy after the war, creating orphanages or asylums for children whose parents were either dead or unable to support them. These orphanages were flexible. Children at first were not committed or bound for long periods but could go home when the family crisis passed. Education, craft training, and future financial independence remained the goals of the founders. After some formal schooling in their early years, orphans were bound out for vocational training so they could support themselves as adults. The continued focus on education and craft training did not come from nostalgia about the colonial system or from humanitarianism; community leaders had race relations very much in mind. Savannah and Charleston had a significant number of free and enslaved African American craftsmen and women. Poor white children, as adults, had to be able to compete economically in the skilled trades. Orphanages in the postwar period kept the races separate to lessen the risk that poor white and black children would find common cause in their poverty.[36]

While the formal practice of binding out children continued with a different emphasis by city and state institutions, individual families, not so desperate as to need to go to the poorhouse but still in distress, improvised when the family faced difficult circumstances. When Jenks applied for his pension, two of his ten children, fourteen-year-old Moses and twelve-year-old Judge Nelson, had each just returned to the household after being "supported" by friends for several years. Jenks's own childhood experience had not prevented him from seeing the system as an effective strategy for coping with his poverty. Veteran Samuel Dewees, who had been bound out as a very young child by his poor parents, also found himself in his thirties with few options. He had to leave with a militia company to deal with unrest on the Pennsylvania frontier at a time when his wife was weakened by a difficult childbirth and the death of the infant. Consequently, he "broke up housekeeping," stored his household goods with a local barber, and sent his wife and perhaps their two children to her father's. When his wife died some years later, Dewees had a surviving son, possibly about twelve years old, whom he could not look after alone. Dewees bound him out to a tailor so that at least his son would receive craft training. With or without the opportunity to learn a trade, binding out was a strategy that would survive for many years to come.[37]

The circumstances of children's lives in the early years of the nineteenth century were hardly uniform. Some children were protected and sequestered, taught in schools by teachers or at home by tutors and parents; others still enjoyed education and training as part of increasingly rare apprenticeships that had been more common in colonial times; and some labored in factories and new industrial settings where there was little interest in their development.

SOLDIERING WAS INCREASINGLY seen as another kind of work altogether. As the nineteenth century began, while the courts wrestled with the legal status of indentured children, courts and legislators made it harder for boys to serve and less likely for recruiting officers to enlist them. Whether in the small peacetime forces of the United States or its larger armies mobilized for wars against Native peoples and the British, few boys became soldiers.

Ideas were being discussed about age, responsibility, and the duties of citizenship in municipalities, courtrooms, and Congress. James Edwards's views reflected the tension of this debate. Edwards certainly had seen children laboring. By the 1830s, Washington D.C., was a town of just under twenty thousand people, and Edwards could look out his window and see children, slave and free, working all around him. They were everywhere underfoot, working on plantations and farms, in domestic service and trades, and in nearby Baltimore, children labored in textile mills and other factories.[38] However, as noted in the introduction, Edwards's background may provide some reasons for his suspicion of boys serving as soldiers. During his own service as a young officer in the U.S. Army, he would have seen few children and would have been aware of the wartime Congressional debates over eligibility.

Since the end of the Revolution, Congress had slowly developed a military policy, by accident rather than design, of keeping a very small permanent army (in 1784, as few as a hundred men) supplemented in times of crisis by militia and federal volunteers. Since many of these crises, such as frontier wars against Native peoples and domestic insurrections like the Whiskey Rebellion, were short lived, recruits for the supplementary forces enlisted for weeks or months at a time.[39]

The strength of the permanent army prior to the outbreak of war in 1812 was about six thousand men, and certainly soldiers' wives and children were with them. Occasionally, boys were in the ranks. James Summers of Georgia was one of the few. He was eight years old and a mere three feet nine inches when he enlisted for six years in 1808. It is possible that he was alone and impoverished and sought the protection of the army, but it is more likely that he enlisted with his entire family. He may have been formally put on the muster rolls to secure his father's service as a way to offer the family some extra money because there were few tasks such a young child might have done. Still, boys grow up, and by the time Summers was discharged in 1814, he may well have been a sturdy, useful soldier. But he had few companions his age. The soldiers of the peacetime army were a mature bunch. On average they were just over twenty-seven years old.[40]

Following the declaration of war in June 1812, about sixty-two thousand men served in the auxiliary and regular forces until the war ended in February 1815. These new recruits were slightly younger than their peacetime comrades but still mature, with an average age of just below twenty-seven, and more than half of them were over twenty-five when they enlisted. Most joined for only short terms in what turned out to be a brief war, and, with a few exceptions, their families did not travel with them. When recruiting soldiers for this war, officers accepted very few below the minimum age of sixteen. And for the militia, the minimum age was everywhere now eighteen, making it harder for very young substitutes to slip into that branch of the service. A sample of the men whose ages are known, who served between 1798 and the end of the war of 1812 in peacetime and wartime armies, suggests that significantly less than 1 percent were under sixteen at enlistment.[41]

Children were also removed to a great degree from the courtroom for the same reasons. Jury service, as noted earlier, was now only permitted to white male property owners over the age of twenty-one whereas a hundred years earlier even twelve-year-old boys who owned property could serve. In numerous court cases before the Revolution, children—some as young as four—were considered credible witnesses in criminal trials. By the early 1800s, most states deemed fourteen to be the youngest one could be to appreciate what it meant to give evidence under oath and serve as a credible witness.[42]

Courts and legislators reaffirmed that twenty-one was the age at which one had enough understanding to sign contracts. Those made by minors were repeatedly held to be invalid. As Massachusetts jurist Theophilus Parsons asked when he was a young man studying the law during the American Revolution: if an apprentice had signed his indenture when he was a minor, had he really "sealed the deed?" Increasingly courts concluded they had not. If children did not fully have the ability to reason about civic matters until they were twenty-one, then their ability to understand contracts and their implications were similarly impaired.[43]

Military service complicated these lines that were otherwise becoming neatly drawn. No obligation of citizenship was more critical than militia service, but service could by law begin at age eighteen and in the regular army at age sixteen. The Militia Act of 1792, in which Congress set up uniform standards for all the state militias, required all white men between the ages of eighteen and forty-five to serve. There was no debate about this rise in the minimum age from sixteen, and states adjusted their militia laws accordingly. Legislators were likely influenced by discussions in the larger society over who could swear an oath and make a reasoned decision about a commitment to fight. It was probably only the practical need for the service of youths that kept the minimum age below twenty-one.[44]

Thus, minors under twenty-one but over eighteen were required to serve in the militia without a parent's signature. And no one gave any thought as to whether sixteen-year-olds joining the army signed for themselves or not. It was not surprising that Edwards demanded additional proof that young boys had served when, as he told Bishop Tyler, "no law required it," and indeed contract law did not permit them to make the decision alone.[45]

Arguments over enlistment age surfaced again in Congress as soon as the War of 1812 started. There were heated debates over an enlistment bill before the house that provided for a minimum age of service of eighteen, not sixteen. The new age limit attracted no attention. It was the stipulation that boys over eighteen but under twenty-one could enlist without parental consent that outraged Federalist congressmen who were at the time the congressional minority. Federalist Josiah Quincy saw the end of western civilization. He felt that "children were to be seduced from parents," and every recruiting officer would become "an apostle to perfidy." Laban Wheaton accused the Democratic-Republican majority of trying to recruit "boys without discretion," that is, without the ability to reason maturely or act independently. The bill was defeated.[46]

However, by the end of 1814, the army was in much greater need of recruits, and a similar provision was before Congress. Again, the Federalists got hot under the collar. New York congressman Thomas Grosvenor said the proposal would not only undermine the apprenticeship system, it would also jeopardize "the sacred rights of natural affection and all the felicities of domestic life." However, with a compromise that allowed minors a four-day grace period after signing up, during which they could change their minds, the legislation easily passed both houses. The ages under discussion and the terms of the debate indicate how much had changed since the Revolution.[47]

During and after the war, a series of key cases came to higher courts to determine complex issues about age and responsibility in a military setting. In 1813, the New York Supreme Court of Judicature wrestled with a case concerning a young soldier who had deserted. He was under eighteen yet had served as a substitute and signed a contract with a drafted man and regimental officer. The youth's mother and father consented, and each took a share of his pay that was advanced to them by the drafted man. The youth kept the substitution fee he had negotiated. However, the lower and high courts concluded that because he was under eighteen (the mandated age for militia service), the contract was not binding. When the officer charged him with desertion, the court decided the youth had been falsely imprisoned.[48]

In a case after the war involving a minor soldier over eighteen, the Circuit Court for the District of Massachusetts reached a different conclusion. The youth had, with his father's consent, signed his own contract. The court laid out the dilemma that, on the one hand, minors could not make such contracts. On the other, federal militia law and other enlistment bills authorized the enlistment of minors over eighteen, and, in the case of the militia bill, mandated it. In this case, the youth's parents required him to come home before his time was up, which he did, but he was subsequently court-martialed for desertion. The court determined that the needs of the nation in time of war gave it the power to make binding contracts with minors that trumped parental rights. By 1826, a noted legal text, *Commentaries on American Law*, summarized the recent court decisions on pay and bounties for minors noting that, when minors enlist, fathers or guardians were not entitled to bounty payments. These were gifts to the recruit from the state. Only a minor's wages belonged to the father or guardian.[49]

The rights and responsibilities of work and citizenship were clearly associated with mature adults by the time James Edwards was appointed head of the pension office in 1818. But besides these legal changes, Edwards would have known firsthand the conditions of camp life for enlisted men during the War of 1812 from his own military experience. Lash punishment had been abolished since the Revolution but had been replaced by cobbing (paddling), branding, and cropping (chopping ears off). Chronic food shortages plagued the campaigns, and disease continued to take a terrible toll on officers and soldiers alike. It is not surprising that Edwards had difficulty imagining boys in the ranks during the Revolutionary War.

THERE IS NO EVIDENCE that former boy soldiers of the Revolution urged their own young sons to enlist in the War of 1812. Not even John

Jenks, for whom the army had been a haven—having rescued him from homelessness and isolation—pressed his sons to serve. Over the course of the War of 1812, Jenks had three sons who were older than he was when he had enlisted in the Continental army, but only two served, and did so when they were over sixteen.[50]

Yet there were factors other than paternal prompting that might have attracted boys to service in the War of 1812. Boys had been raised in communities that celebrated the military accomplishments of their fathers and grandfathers in the Revolution. And, as in the Revolution, there was celebratory rhetoric about the promise of military glory. On August 20, 1812, a national day of fasting and prayer proclaimed by President Madison early in the War of 1812, troops gathered in several towns to hear local officials and ministers praise their courage. In Plattsburgh, New York, according to the local newspaper, the *Republican*, the Reverend Josiah Lacy Wilson told the soldiers they possessed a "spirit of virtue and patriotism which ought to warm the heart of every American." There were songs to rally martial feelings, most notably by Francis Scott Key, who wrote many songs lauding the soldiers who return "from the battle afar." The substitution system continued in the War of 1812, allowing a drafted man to send another in his place. However, this short war did not bring boys into the military in any noticeable numbers. No long-standing community networks wove boys in. For the few who did serve, the stories behind their enlistment are lost to us. Detailed muster rolls and other bureaucratic records were kept during and after this war; there was no need for veterans to add anything when they applied for pensions.[51]

THE FEW BOYS who served in the War of 1812 found their officers had little patience for their youth and inexperience. The boys were, with one or two exceptions, musicians. Like drummers of an earlier generation, some struggled with the weight of their instruments. Amasa Holden, an eleven-year-old drummer, who was four feet six inches tall at his enlistment, was discharged after three years of his five-year contract on account of his "extreme youth." Given that he was fourteen by this time, it is likely that either he had not grown much or that he was sickly. Another young soldier was also not up to scratch. Virginia-born Fielding Hickman, twelve years old and four feet six inches at his enlistment, signed on for five years in 1814 but was discharged only a few months later when he was "unable to perform the duties of a soldier in consequence of his youth." These discharges may have been arranged by officers sympathetic to boys who had changed their minds; their "extreme youth" was a believable reason for dismissal.[52]

AS THE NATION'S population grew, the few men who had served as boys in the Revolution almost disappeared from view. Indeed, as mid-century approached, many assumed there were no Revolutionary War veterans left. A Whig political campaign broadside from 1844 tried to discredit presidential candidate James K. Polk on the grounds he had voted against a Revolutionary War pension bill. While addressed *To Old Revolutionary Soldiers and their Children and Grandchildren*, it counted on there not being any old soldiers left to read it, reminding voters of the sacrifices their ancestors had made "for Liberty." But Bishop Tyler, Andrew Ferguson, and many other former boy soldiers were still alive. In the towns where they lived, they kept a connection to the Revolution vibrant for subsequent generations as the youngest and hardiest among them lived into the 1840s and 1850s. A few even saw the outbreak of the war that tore the union apart in 1861. Their communities were aware of them, and their service was mentioned in their obituaries as they joined the list of Revolutionary veterans "gone to [their] tomb."[53]

In applying for pensions, these veterans revisited not only their service days, but also the events that had caused them to enlist. Sometimes with anguish, sometimes matter-of-factly, sometimes with pleasure, they recalled their childhoods, their families, and the events that had surrounded their enlistments. For a few, their entrance into the service was smooth and could barely be recollected. For others, it was filled with drama. Boys had struggled with the instability and disruption of disease and war; a few had begged reluctant fathers to let them go; others' hearts had sunk when guardians compelled their service. Some set off with dread; others with restless anticipation. Old grievances with stepparents were felt afresh as memories came flooding back. They had still been minors with years to go to full adulthood. Yet they were eager to make decisions for themselves, so household life could be tense. Service gave young soldiers a chance to feel like grownups but ironically in a military setting in which someone was always telling them what to do.

The army had found tasks for them. Boys marched, sang, grumbled, worked, and fought. They chopped wood, slaughtered meat, stood guard, and did all the countless jobs that keep an army on the move. In short, they worked, and often it was work similar to what they did at home, alongside men and other boys they knew. As they grew older, they probably realized how much their wartime comfort had depended on those around them adjusting to their capacities—troops slowing the pace of a march or officers giving them chores that fit their abilities.[54]

Sometimes boys' service came at a high price. Wounds and sickness could take their toll. Obadiah Benge, serving with North Carolina troops, had been in lifelong pain from the musket ball that had been lodged under his shoulder blade since the Battle of King's Mountain in 1780. He could remember exactly how he had been standing when he was hit and had "ever since been a cripple." Virginian Andrew Ferguson received a musket ball in his leg at the Battle of Camden, a British victory of August 1780; he recovered enough to fight at King's Mountain in October and then was wounded in the head at the Battle of Guilford Courthouse, an important patriot victory in March 1781. That injury laid him low for a month, and both injuries came back to haunt him in later life, causing him "pain and disability" once he was in his seventies.[55] Boys who died submitted no pension requests. They are harder for us to see. Only those who lived to old age entered the pension record. In establishing pensions, the new nation sought reparation for war service. And the pension records that exist for boy soldiers, sparse in quantity and detail, nevertheless remind us that children of varied backgrounds for varied reasons were actors in one of the most tumultuous events of their century, and grew to experience the vivid changes their Revolution had wrought.

Perhaps it was like this:

One hot day in July 1834, sixty-eight-year-old John Piatt, a former fifer in the New Jersey Continentals, was sitting with his wife Jane, their son Daniel, and a relative Eliza, on the porch of their home in Morris County, New Jersey. They were trying to catch whatever breeze was in the air. The porch was on the front of the house allowing them to see who was going along the road and to wave to their neighbors. Soon, a carriage with three men came by, and, to their surprise, turned into their lane. One of the men was a waiter and the other a driver to their guest who was an older "large, fat man" who had "much difficulty" getting out of the carriage. Indeed, he could only do so with the others' assistance. He laboriously walked to the house, climbed the steps, and held out his hand to Piatt saying, "How do you do, John." Piatt had no idea who had just arrived. His guest asked, "Do you not know your own brother William?" Piatt quickly recovered and welcomed the brother he had only seen three times since they had both served with the New Jersey Continentals. The last of those visits had taken place more than twenty years before.

The brothers settled on the porch, caught up on the family news, and compared their lives. Piatt's had been settled. He had served in the early part of the war, beginning his military service at nine and ending it about age fourteen. William, although some years older, had entered the service later waiting for a commission so he could join their father and uncles as an officer, finally becoming a captain before the end of the war. Piatt had married Jane when he was about twenty-five and had four children, three of whom were still alive. They had lost their youngest, Hannah, when she was a month old. He and his remaining children, now mature adults, were comfortably settled. William, on the other hand, had "contracted a roving disposition" during the Revolution. After the war, he joined the regular army and had never left it, serving in the west as quartermaster in a variety of campaigns. William had no family of his own and claimed that with all the traveling, he never had time to marry. Even though infirm, he still enjoyed his work and was now a paymaster on his way to Philadelphia to attend to business there but had decided to take a detour to visit his younger brother.

The two men traded old war stories, with John reverting to calling his brother Captain Billy as he had done years before, to the great delight of all; the relative Eliza would remember William's visit vividly for years to come. The hosts agreed afterwards that their guest had not looked well, and they were not surprised to receive news of his death in Philadelphia barely a month later.

Piatt realized he was slowly becoming the only connection in his neighborhood between the exciting years of the Revolution and the present. At the anniversary celebrations of pivotal moments of the war, community leaders celebrated veterans because the nation they helped create remained as "an imperishable monument of their worth." When they died, the community mourned them because "their example is no longer exhibited to the view of their fellow men," and "their counsel can no longer be imparted." This was a sentiment that Piatt could easily share. He felt the loss of his brother deeply, even though he was in many ways a stranger to him. But he mourned more the loss of the connection to the adventures, wonderful and terrible, of his own wartime childhood.[56]

Notes

Introduction

1. John Piatt, W1473, Revolutionary War Pension Applications (hereafter RWPA), Record Group (RG) 15, National Archives, Washington, D.C. (NAB).

2. John D. Piatt, gravestone, http://www.findagrave.com, accessed February 12, 2014. The pension files for John Piatt, W1473, his brother William Piatt, R8221, and the Daughters of the American Revolution (DAR) register contain confirming genealogical information about the Piatt family.

3. Piatt, W1473, RWPA, RG 15, NAB.

4. Demos, *The Unredeemed Captive*, 17. Numerous scholars have written about the problems and opportunities of using historical imagination. See Bailyn, *On the Teaching and Writing of History*, 71; Spence, *The Death of Woman Wang*, xiv–xv; Lepore, *Book of Ages*; Davis, *The Return of Martin Guerre*, 5; Finlay, "The Refashioning of Martin Guerre," 552–71; Davis, "On the Lame," 572–604. My thanks to Jenny Hale Pulsipher, Kevin Grant, and Lisa Trivedi for many fruitful discussions on this subject.

5. This imaginative account is based on John Piatt, W1473, RWPA, RG 15, NAB; William Piatt, R8221, RWPA, RG 15, NAB, and informed by all the pension files read for this book. Piatt family service is additionally found in http://valley forgemusterroll.org/njl.asp, accessed November 2012, and Wright, *The Sullivan Expedition of 1779*. For a description of a scene of the army in camp, see John H. Hawkins, February 11, 1779, Journal, 1779–81; Historical Society of Pennsylvania, quoted in Mayer, "Wives, Concubines, and Community: Following the Army," 235. General information about conditions on the Quebec expedition, see Roberts, *March to Quebec*. For firsthand accounts of the raging epidemics at Ticonderoga and Lake Champlain in summer of 1776, see Beebe, "Journal of a Physician of the Expedition against Canada, 1776"; Lacey, "Memoirs of Brigadier-General John Lacey of Pennsylvania," 202–4, and David, *A Rhode Island Chaplain in the Revolution*, 26–27.

6. John Piatt, W1473, RWPA, RG 15, NAB.

7. Millet and Maslowski, *For the Common Defense*, 653. For their number of two hundred thousand, Millett and Maslowski draw on the data collected by Howard H. Peckham, et al, William Clements Library, University of Michigan, 1974; Martin and Lender, *A Respectable Army*, xii, 69–77; Papenfuse and Stiverson, "General Smallwood's Recruits"; Lender, "The Social Structure of the New Jersey Brigade"; Neimeyer, *America Goes to War*, xiv–xv; Resch, *Suffering Soldiers*, 10; Royster, *A Revolutionary People at War*, 373–78.

8. See Mintz, *Huck's Raft*; Hawes and Hiner, *American Childhood*; Fass and Mason, *Childhood in America*; Graff, *Growing Up in America*; Heywood, *A History of Childhood*.

9. Kett, *Rites of Passage*, 12–13; Wrigley and Schofield, *The Population History of England, 1541–1871*, 214n.

10. Greene and Harrington, *American Population Before the Federal Census of 1790*, 186–87, 96–97.

11. Francis Baylies, *Eulogy on the Hon. Benjamin Russell*, 12; Samuel Dewees, *A History of the Life and Services of Captain Samuel Dewees*, 2. I am grateful to Justin Clement for directing me to this source. Rebecca Baxter, Indenture, July 1, 1770, Middlesex County Historical Society, in Miller, "Gender, Artisanry, and Craft Tradition in Early New England," 757.

12. Herndon and Murray, *Children Bound to Labor*, 2–7, 86.

13. Diptee, "Imperial Ideas, Colonial Realities," 50; "Royal Africa Company to Cape Coast Castle, June 28, 1709," f.119, quoted in Smallwood, *Saltwater Slavery*, 71; Smallwood, ibid., 71; Eltis and Engerman, "Fluctuations in Sex and Age Ratios in the Transatlantic Slave Trade, 1663–1864," 314. In their own demographic analysis, Eltis and Engerman use age fifteen as a cutoff between adult and child; Donnan, *Documents Illustrative of the Slave Trade*, v. 2, 582, 584.

14. Locke, *Some Thoughts concerning Education*; Rousseau, *Emile, or On Education*; Reinier, *From Virtue to Character*, 1–19; Mintz, *Huck's Raft*, 51.

15. Brewer, *By Birth or Consent*, 140–45, 64–70, 130–40; Lambarde, *Eirenarcha*, 378, quoted ibid., 137.

16. *Journals of the Continental Congress*, 4:63, 4:103–4; George Washington to Edward Hand, October 11, 1776, and Washington, "General Orders," November 10, 1776, in *Papers of George Washington, Revolutionary War Ser.*, 6:536–37.

17. McCarthy, "A Pocket Full of Days," 275–79; Ulrich, *A Midwife's Tale*; Miller, *The Needle's Eye*. See, for example, journals of craftsmen such as Thomas B. Hazard, *Nailer Tom's Diary*.

18. Kiebowicz, *News in the Mail*, 23–25.

19. Wells, *The Population of the British Colonies in North America before 1776*, 268–70. This statistic is for the colonies that became the United States. The number of children in the British Caribbean Islands and Newfoundland was significantly less (ibid., 269). As an example of the way children appear in craftsmen's diaries, see Hazard, *Nailer Tom's Diary*; Russo and Russo, "Responsive Justices," 157, 155.

20. *Records of the Governor and Company of the Massachusetts Bay in New England*, 8–9; Buchan, *Domestic Medicine; or, the Family Physician*; Cadogan, *Essay upon Nursing, and the Management of Children*; Reiner, *From Virtue to Character*, 1–19; Mintz, *Huck's Raft*, 48.

21. Drinker, *The Diary of Elizabeth Drinker*, 1, 422; Fithian, *Journal and Letters of Philip Vickers Fithian*, 41.

22. Eliza Lucas Pinckney, *The Letterbook of Eliza Lucas Pinckney*, 5, 7; John Laurens's letters are in Laurens, *The Papers of Henry Laurens*, see especially volumes 7, 8, and 9.

23. Franklin, *The Autobiography and Other Writings*, 38–39.

24. Barnard, "Autobiography of John Barnard," 179; Lewis, *Morgan Lewis Papers*, New-York Historical Society (NYHS), box 1, folder 3; Smith, *A Narrative of*

the Life and Adventures of Venture, 9–10; Occom, "Short Narrative of My Life."

25. Reach, *Suffering Soldiers*, 203; Schulz, "The Revolutionary War Pension Applications," 104–11; Schulz, "Daughters of Liberty," 139–53.

26. Alfred Young, *Masquerade*; Testimony of Eliza Piatt in William Piatt, R8221, RWPA, RG 15, NAB; Testimony of Mary Truman in Samuel Aspenwall, W20634, RWPA, RG 15, NAB.

27. Martin, *Ordinary Courage*, 28; Depositions of Elizabeth Cain and Abigail Palmer, March 22, 1777, in "British Plundering and Ravishing," 29, 31 in Papers of the Continental Congress, RG 360, M247, NAB.

28. Quarles, *The Negro in the American Revolution*, 19–32, 147, 156–67; Kaplan and Kaplan, *The Black Presence in the Era of the American Revolution*, 71; Frey, *Water from the Rock*, 136–37.

29. John Peters, "A Narrative of John Peters, Lieutenant Colonel of the Queen's Loyal Rangers in Canada, drawn by himself in a letter to a friend in London." John Peters Papers, New-York Historical Society.

30. Bishop Tyler, S17162, RWPA, RG 15, NAB.

31. Ebenezer Couch, W23839, RWPA, RG 15, NAB.

32. John Updike, S22028, RWPA, RG 15, NAB.

33. Brewer, *By Birth or Consent*, 342, for the limits on children's rights and abilities to offer informed consent.

34. Benjamin Peck, S15571, Rufus Beckwith, R698, RWPA, RG 15, NAB.

35. Stagg, "Soldiers in Peace and War," 95, 103; Stagg, "Enlisted Men in the United States Army," 633; John Hallmick, number 2900, volume 11, Amasa Holden, number 254, volume 11, "Enlistments 1798-May 17, 1815," in "Register of Enlistments in the United States Army," 1798–1914," RG 94, M233, NAB.

36. Brewer, *By Birth or Consent*, 34, 132, 141–48, 155–59; "Militia Act 1792," http://www.constitution.org/mil/mil_act_1792.htm; Madison, "Notes on the Constitutional Convention."

37. Resch, *Suffering Soldiers*, 124; Glasson, *Federal Military Pensions in the United States*, 87.

38. Palfrey Downing, S34762, RWPA, RG 15, NAB.

39. John Piatt, W1473, RWPA, RG 15, NAB; Brundage, "No Deed But Memory," 3–4; Furstenberg, *In the Name of the Father*.

40. Young, *The Shoemaker and the Tea Party*, 12.

41. Fass, "Childhood and Memory," 157, 162; Young, *The Shoemaker and the Tea Party*, 10–13; Thelen, "Memory and American History," 117–29.

42. Samuel Younglove, "Record of Samuel Younglove," S14910; Brooks, "Experience of Jonathan Brooks," 74–82.

Chapter 1

1. This imaginative account is based on the pension application of George Hofstalar, S15176, RWPA, RG 15, NAB. For detailed information about the battle of Briar Creek, see Howard, "Things Here Wear a Melancholy Appearance."

The battle lasted only minutes. The British lost six men. The patriots lost between 150 and 200 killed or drowned, with another more than 250 taken prisoner or missing (ibid., 496). Ervin, "A Colonial History of Rowan County, North Carolina," see chapters three and seven.

2. Malcolm, *Peter's War*, 127–130; Washington to John Hancock, September 25, 1776, in *Papers of George Washington, Revolutionary War Ser.*, 6:396; Martin, *Ordinary Courage*, 33.

3. Cox, *A Proper Sense of Honor*, 120; Anderson, *A People's Army*, 99, 101; Selesky, *War and Society in Colonial Connecticut*, 190–91; Greven, *Four Generations*, fn 16, 196–97; Anderson *Crucible of War*, 500–501. Boston's mortality rate averaged between roughly 31 and 46 per thousand from the beginning of the century until the Revolution. Andover's annual mortality rates were usually below about 21 per thousand, but with a high of 71 per thousand during a "throat distemper" (probably diphtheria) epidemic. In contrast, death rates for different units of Massachusetts provincials varied widely but ranged as high as 137.5 per thousand for a period of much less than a year. Connecticut troops in Havana experienced a mortality rate of 193 per thousand for a similarly short period. Data from the works cited; Clodfelter, *Warfare and Armed Conflicts*, 1:198.

4. Demos, *Unredeemed Captive*, 38–39. Demos shows that all twenty-one teenagers captured from Deerfield, Massachusetts, by French and Native raiders in 1704 survived the arduous journey to Canada. They were the only age/set category in which everyone survived; Simeon Hewitt, W25766, RWPA, RG15, NAB. Since almost no complete data exists on soldiers in this era, it is impossible to parse disease mortality statistics by age. However, modern epidemiology indicates that some populations are more vulnerable than others depending on the virus. For example, most influenza viruses see the greatest mortality among very young children and the elderly. However, teenagers and young adults were particularly vulnerable to the virus of the great influenza pandemic of 1918–1919. Barry, *The Great Influenza*, 4.

5. "A Scheme for the Immediate Levying of Ten Thousand Men, 1756," Barrington Papers, British Library; Lord Barrington to General Thomas Gage, January 4, 1775, WO 4/273, National Archives, Kew, Great Britain; Washington to Edward Hand, October 11, 1776, in *Papers of George Washington, Revolutionary War Ser.*, 6:536–37; General Arthur St. Clair to James Bowdoin, July 9, 1777, in *Writings of George Washington*, 5:485, fn. Bowdoin was president of the Massachusetts Provincial Congress and the de facto governor of Massachusetts. While St. Clair was criticized at the time for his actions, a court-martial later exonerated him, and modern historians have also defended his decision to abandon the fort. Boatner, *Encyclopedia of the American Revolution*, s.v. St. Clair.

6. Samuel Branch, referring to himself in his deposition in support of the claim of David Avery, S12022; testimony of Simeon Hewitt and David Avery in Bishop Tyler, S17162; Robert Gale, S31053, Nathaniel Warner, S23990, RWPA, RG 15, NAB.

7. Shakespeare, *Henry V*, Act IV, Scene viii; Laqueur, "Naming and Memory in the Great War," 150–52. We know more about the ages of soldiers in the ancient European world, and there no young boys appeared in the phalanxes.

Ancient Greek warriors carried as much as fifty pounds of protective clothing, a shield weighing another twenty, and a spear between seven to nine feet in length. Even in a warrior society such as Sparta, where boys were taken from home at age seven and trained to fight, they were age twenty before they were formally brought into a military cohort. In ancient Rome, the army enlisted soldiers from age eighteen to twenty-one, and a special recruiting board had to approve all of them. When the state needed more soldiers, it raised the age to include men up to thirty. And the same minimum and approval were required when the empire started enlisting soldiers in the regions it controlled. Hodkinson, "Was Classical Sparta a Military Society?," 138–39; Cartledge, *The Spartans*, 69–71; Kennell, *The Gymnasium of Virtue*, 31–38. Southern, *The Roman Army*, 131–33; Le Bohec, *The Imperial Roman Army*, 68–82; Grossman, *On Killing*, 13.

8. Curry, *Agincourt*, Appendix C, 276–79.

9. Goldberg, "What Was a Servant?" in Curry and Matthew, eds., *Concepts and Patterns of Service in the Later Middle Ages*, 1–20; David Morgan, "The Household Retinue of Henry V and the Ethos of English Public Life," ibid., 64–79.

10. Bell, *War and the Soldier in the Fourteenth Century*, 88; Bell, "The Soldier, 'hadde he riden, no man ferre,'" in *The Soldier Experience in the Fourteenth Century*, 213; Nicholson, *Medieval Warfare*, 63.

11. *Medieval Warfare*, 183; Brewer, *By Birth or Consent*, 37.

12. Richter, *Ordeal of the Longhouse*, 36; Trigger, *Children of Aataentsic*, 48–50.

13. Morillo, et al., *War in World History*, 314, 321. The matchlock firing mechanism required a burning wick to be introduced to a pan of gunpowder just as the trigger was pulled. This flash in the pan detonated another larger charge in the barrel that launched the projectile. This was not only risky to the person using it but also the men next to him. Royal Armouries, National Museum of Arms and Armour, Leeds England, www.royalarmouries.org/english-civil-wars-muskets, accessed February 21, 2014. Markham, "The Muster Master," 69. The extant copy is handwritten and was never published, but numerous references to it exist in other works indicating that it may have circulated, and certainly its ideas did. Hamilton, *Camden Miscellany*, 49–53.

14. Games, *Migration and the Origins of the English Atlantic World*, 19–21, 25; London Port Register, 1634–1635, "Licenses to Pass Beyond the Seas," National Archives, Kew, Great Britain.

15. Donagan, *War in England*, 215–24. See Muster Roll, Harleian MSS 427, British Library; Colonel Willonbys Regmt for ye Citty of Coventry, 30 October 1645 and Coventry Forces Mustered the 13th of September 1645, SP28/136/53a and b, National Archives, Kew, Great Britain; Pafford, ed., *Accounts of the Parliamentary Garrisons of Great Chalfield and Malmesbury, 1645–1646*, 94–95.

16. Donagan, *War in England*, 220–21; Robert, 3rd Earl of Essex, quoted ibid., 220; John Pym, member of Parliament, quoted ibid., 220; Green, ed., *Calendar of the Proceedings of the Committee for Compounding & C., 1643–1660*, 1098. The Committee for Compounding was a parliamentary committee set up to confiscate the estates of royalists. Cundy's fine was later remitted. Carlton, *Going to the Wars*, 67, 363 n3.

17. Smith, "Almost Revolutionaries," 313–28.

18. Mayer, *Belonging to the Army*, 8–10; Duffy, *The Army of Frederick the Great*, 60, 54–68.

19. Schwoerer, "No Standing Armies!," 139–42, 146; Martin and Lender, *A Respectable Army*, 6–9 and Royster, *A Revolutionary People at War*, 35–38.

20. Mayer, *Belonging to the Army*, 129; Colonel John Lamb's Orderly Books, 2nd Regiment, Continental Artillery, August 19, 1781, Collection of Early American Orderly Books, New-York Historical Society, quoted ibid., 129; Patrick Cronkhite, W16932, RWPA, RG 15, NAB.

21. Mayer, *Belonging to the Army*, 10, 7, 126.

22. Fann, "On the Infantryman's Age in Eighteenth Century Prussia," 166–67; Duffy, *The Army of Frederick the Great*, 60. There was no plan for what should happen to the girls when they turned sixteen. Cuthbertson, *System*, 14–16.

23. Morillo, et al., *War in World History*, 321; "Brown Bess Musket," Smithsonian, National Museum of American History: Behring Center. "Brown Bess Musket," http://amhistory.si.edu/militaryhistory/collection/, accessed February 20, 2014.

24. Reuben Woodworth, W26118, RWPA, RG 15, NAB.

25. For the following paragraphs on music, see Monelle, *The Musical Topic*, 113–18 and Blades, *Percussion Instruments and Their History*, 210–17; Markham, *Five Decades of Epistles of Warre*, 57–58.

26. "A Scheme for the Immediate Levying of Ten Thousand Men, 1756," Barrington Papers, British Library; Lord Barrington to General Thomas Gage, January 4, 1775, WO 4/273, National Archives, Kew, Great Britain.

27. Cuthbertson, *System*, 14–16.

28. Corvisier, *L'Armée Française de la Fin du XVIIe Siècle au Ministère de Choiseul*, 1:476–78; Lynn, *The Bayonets of the Republic*, 45–49; Scott, *The Response of the Royal*, 4–9. Fann, "On the Infantryman's Age in Eighteenth Century Prussia," 166–67; Duffy, *The Army of Frederick the Great*, 60, 54–68; Brumwell, *Redcoats*, 77–78, 316. There were some aristocratic boys in every European army who were there either as officer cadets or having regular officers' commissions. They were learning how to command and did not do physical labor. Ibid.

29. *George Washington Papers*, Series 4, "Size Rolls"; Titus, *The Old Dominion at War*, 82; "Muster Rolls of the New York Provincial Troops, 1755–1764," *Collections of the New-York Historical Society* 24 (1891), all. Two young boys are listed as being ten inches and twelve inches respectively, but these seem to be transcription errors as they are identified as craftsmen, a "baker" and a "mason." They are Samuel Waller (70) and Joseph Wood (180); Waller is listed as five-feet, four-inches tall and passes without mention directly above the sixteen-year-old specifically identified as a "boy" (70). There is also one ten year-old, David Reeves, a laborer, whose age also appears to be erroneous. (204).

30. Cuthbertson, *System*, 14.

31. Meyers, *Ten Years in the Ranks of the U.S. Army*, 2, 6. Meyers enlisted in 1854.

32. Rees, "'The Music of the Army,'" 2–12; Fann, "On the Infantryman's Age in Eighteenth Century Prussia," 167–68.

33. Lewis, *The Orderly Book*, 6–7, 27; Meyers, *Ten Years in the Ranks*, 11.

34. Weedon, *Valley Forge Orderly Book*, 224–25; *Major Moses Ashley's Orderly Book*, 1780, John Carter Brown Library (PRJCB hereafter).

35. General Return, Royal Welch Fusiliers, Chatham, September 24, 1757, WO 27/5; General Return, 3rd Regiment Dragoon Guards, June 1758, WO 27/5; National Archives, Kew; Cuthbertson, *System*, 14–15; Lynn *Battle*, 114–18.

36. Childs, *Armies and Warfare in Europe*, 68; Brereton, *The British Soldier*, 28–29; Gilbert, "Changing Face of British Military Justice," 81; Cox, *A Proper Sense of Honor*, 88.

37. Kirkwood, "Journal and Order Book," 95.

38. Fisk Durand, S12807, William Durand, W25552, Aaron Day, S43462, John Vaughan, S42570, RWPA, RG 15, NAB.

39. Krebs, "Usable Enemies," chapter three of the unpublished manuscript. My thanks to Dr. Krebs of the University of Louisville, KY, for making this available to me. Hick, "Soldaten gegen Nordamerika." Many thanks to Dr. Hick for providing me with a copy of the relevant chapters of his work. Scott, *The Response of the Royal Army to the French Revolution*, 7–8; Frey, *The British Soldier in America*, 23–26; C. Jenkinson to Lt. Col. Fraser of the Royals, May 1779, WO 4/966; Returns from First Regiment of Dragoon Guards, May 1775, WO/33, 31st Regiment of Foot, 1782, 28/10. Brunswick Regiment, 1783, WO 28/10, Loyal Rangers, December 1781, WO 28/10, National Archives, Kew.

40. Sargent, "The Massachusetts Rank and File of 1777," 57–58; Moss, *Patriots at King's Mountain*. One complete size roll from Maryland in 1782 shows only just over 1 percent as under sixteen. A few sixteen-year-olds, listed at only five feet tall or just over, may have been younger. Unfortunately, there are only a few men on the roster who applied for a pension, others either not surviving to do so, not inclined to, or unaware of the benefit. Some of the older youths who left pension applications first enlisted at a younger age; for example, Thomas Craig (W5255), appearing as a twenty-year-old on the roll, first enlisted as a fifteen-year-old in 1776, and Robert Deane (S34742), seventeen on the roster but who was either fifteen or sixteen when he first enlisted in 1782. "Roster of General Smallwood's Recruits, September 1782," Maryland Historical Society (MHS); Papenfuse and Stiverson, "General Smallwood's Recruits," 129–31.

41. Israel Trask, S30171, RWPA, RG 15, NAB; Fitch, *The New York Diary*, 59.

42. Timothy Blackmore, S2378; Jacob Diefendorff, S10567, RWPQ, RG 15, NAB; Adlum, *Memoirs of the Life of John Adlum*, 24–36.

43. Samuel Aspenwall, W20634; Reuben Blankenship, S32120; Stephen Hammond, S10800; William Guest, W21239, RWPA, RG 15, NAB.

44. Ebenezer Atwood, W23469, Jacob Gundy, S32284, Gaines Hitchcock, S19339, Nathaniel Warner, S23990, James P. Collins, R2173; Henry Eckler, S10605; William Coff, S39347, Isaac Bedell, S15322, RWPA, RG 15, NAB.

45. Samuel Younglove, S14910, William Addison, W5599, George Paul, W5741, RWPA, RG 15, NAB.

46. Fox, "The Adventures of Ebenezer Fox," 34–36.

47. Elijah Lacy, W10189, Adam Gerlock, R3917, David McCance, S16464, Samuel Hancock, W——(no number given). Some of this information is in

the file of Jacob Moon, W4691. (Hancock's widow, Ann, later married Moon, another Revolutionary War veteran); Richard Frost, W13212, RWPA, RG 15, NAB.

48. Ramsey, *History of the Revolution in South Carolina*, 1:272–73.

49. Samuel Aspenwall, W20634, Doctor Bostwick, S2384, Thomas Groves, W4211, John Meany, W9948, Samuel Boyd, W9737, RWPA, RG 15, NAB.

50. Moses King, W24672, RWPA, RG 15, NAB.

51. Henry Knox to John Lamb, April 13, 1777 and Captain Jacob Reed to Lamb, October 8, 1778, John Lamb Papers, NYHS, Microfilm Reel 1; General Edward Hand to Brigadier General John Patterson, May 21, 1781, and Hand to Colonel Walter Steward, July 17, 1782, Numbered Record Books, M853, roll 17, volume 162; Mayer, *Belonging to the Army*, 57–58.

52. John Piatt, W1473, RWPA, RG 15, NAB.

53. John Burchfield, W8175, Benjamin Peck, S5571, John Piatt, W1473, RWPA, RG 15, NAB.

Chapter 2

1. Samuel Aspenwall, W20634, RWPA, RG 15, NAB.

2. Ibid.; Painter, *Autobiography of Thomas Painter*, 9.

3. This imaginative account is based on Samuel Aspenwall, W20634, RWPA, RG 15, NAB; Buel, *Dear Liberty*, 36, 272–74; Harris, *The Battle of Groton Heights*; Martin, *Ordinary Courage*, 4–6.

4. Painter, *Autobiography of Thomas Painter*, 9; Martin, *Ordinary Courage*, 11; Bishop Tyler, S17162, RWPA, RG 15, NAB.

5. This subject encompasses a vast body of scholarship. A sampling of recent works is Broyles, "Why Men Love War," 61, 56. Broyles has written of his own experiences as a young soldier in Vietnam in *Brothers in Arms: A Veteran Returns to Vietnam in Search of His Enemy and Himself* ; Lee, *Barbarians and Brothers*; Hedges, *War Is a Force That Gives Us Meaning*; Maldonado-Torres, *Against War: Views from the Underside of Modernity*.

6. Wilson, *Ye Heart of a Man*, 2–4; Brown, *Good Wives, Nasty Wenches, and Anxious Patriarchs*, 321.

7. Brown, *Good Wives, Nasty Wenches, and Anxious Patriarchs*, 322.

8. Anne S. Lombard, *Making Manhood*, 120–24, 135; *Blanchard v. Shepherd*, Middlesex Folio Collection, ff. 183–185, September 1679, Massachusetts State Archives, quoted ibid., 120.

9. Levi Beardsley, "Reminiscences," 43; Calvert, *Children in the House*, 49; Charlevoix, *Voyage to North America*, 114–15; King, *Stolen Childhood*, 44–47.

10. Little, *Abraham in Arms*, 10, 167–69; Nowell, *Abraham in Arms*, 3, 12.

11. Boulware, "'We are MEN,'" 52; Ruggles, *The Usefulness and Expedience of Souldiers as Discovered by Reason and Experience . . .* , 6, 9; Lidenius, *The Lawfulness of Defensive War*, 3, 7.

12. Boulware, "'We are MEN,'" 52; Davies, *The Curse of Cowardice*, 15. There were many editions of this sermon published in North America and Britain.

13. Nancy Shoemaker, "An Alliance between Men," 254–55; Little, *Abraham in Arms*, 2–3; Boulware, "'We are MEN,'" 55; James Grant of Ballandich Papers, Reel 32, quoted in Boulware, "'We are MEN,'" 63; *Pennsylvania Gazette*, August 7, 1760; Little, *Abraham in Arms*, 173–175.

14. John Hurt, *The Love of Our Country*, 21; Willard, *The Duty of the Good and Faithful Soldier*, 1.

15. Buechner, *Yankee Singing Schools*, 16–27; Walter, *Grounds and Rules of Musick Explained*; Bayley, *A New and Compleat Introduction to the Grounds and Rules of Musick*; Sewall, *Diary*, March 15 and 16, 1721, 2:976; Mather, "Diary of Cotton Mather," 608.

16. *Boston Evening Post*, May 9, 1774; Camus, "Military Music of Colonial Boston," 90.

17. "The Soldier's Adieu," in Lieutenant George Bush Journal, Historical Society of Delaware; "Soldier, Soldier, won't you marry me" in Wright, *The American Musical Miscellany*.

18. Bishop Tyler, S17162, RWPA, RG 15, NAB.

19. Orme, *Medieval Children*, 181–82.

20. Peter Johnson, *Toy Armies*, 17–18.

21. Calvert, *Children in the House*, 50–51; Chudacoff, *Children at Play*, 24–27; "Washington Invoices and Letters, Mount Vernon Ladies Association," quoted in "Toys Acquired by Children in the Washington Family," memorandum, April and May 2001, Mary V. Thompson, Mount Vernon Estate and Gardens. My thanks to Mary Thompson for sharing this unpublished memorandum with me.

22. Calvert, *Children in the House*, 49–52; Chudacoff, *Children at Play*, 19–38; Locke, *Some Thoughts concerning Education*, 29.

23. Charlevoix, *Voyage to North America*, v. 2, 114–15; Bell, "How to Play Tip-Cat," http://boston1775.blogspot.com/2007/07how-to-play-tip-cat.html, accessed August 12, 2012; Beardsley, "Reminiscences," 37.

24. King, *Stolen Childhood*, 44–47.

25. Fox, "The Adventures of Ebenezer Fox," 10.

26. Adams, *Diary and Autobiography of John Adams*, 1:341; Schrader, "Songs to Cultivate the Sensations of Freedom," 105, 108; "British Lamentation," Printer, Wm. Mack, no city given, Connecticut Historical Society (CHS); Jehu Grant, R4197, RWPA, RG 15, NAB.

27. Dickinson, *The Farmer's and Monitor's Letters*. The song appeared in the *New York Gazette*, July 4, 1768 and the *Boston Gazette*, July 18, 1768. "A New Liberty Song—To the Tune of the 'British Grenadiers,'" CHS; Schrader, "Songs to Cultivate the Sensations of Freedom," 105–8, 115.

28. See Billings, *New Grove Dictionary of Music and Musicians*.

29. Charlevoix, *Voyage to North America*, 2, 114–15.

30. Beales and Green, "Libraries and Their Users," 402–3; Alter, *The Pleasures of Reading*, 238; Davis, *A Colonial Southern Bookshelf*, 3; "Washington Invoices and Letters, Mount Vernon Ladies Association," quoted in "Toys Acquired by Children in the Washington Family," memorandum, April and May 2001, Mary V. Thompson, Mount Vernon Estate and Gardens. My thanks to Mary Thompson

for sharing this unpublished memorandum with me. *Papers of Washington, Col. Ser.*, 7:336; Neuberg, "Chapbooks in America," 81–82; Felton, "The Life or Biography of Silas Felton Written by Himself," 126–27.

31. Mott, *Golden Multitudes*, 26–34.

32. Grenby, *The Child Reader*, 2–5; *The Renowned History of Giles Gingerbread; The History of Sir Richard Wittington; A True Tale of Robin Hood*, 5, 17.

33. *The Dying Words of Captain Kid*; Andrews, *The Last Dying Speech and Confession of Joseph Andrews*; Johnson, *A General History of the Lives and Adventures of the Most Famous Highwaymen, Murderers, Street Robbers*.

34. Kropf, "The Availability of Literature to Eighteenth Century Georgia Readers," 356–57; Fliegelman, *Prodigals and Pilgrims*, 5, 55–57, 67–83.

35. Paine, *Common Sense*; Hopkins, *A Pretty Story*, 22.

36. *Boston Chronicle*, August 15–22, 1768.

37. Avery, *Behold the Child*, 61–62; Goodrich, *Reflections of a Lifetime*, 164–66.

38. *The New-Year Verses*; Kars, *Breaking Loose Together*, 95, 99.

39. Thornton, *Handwriting in America*, 4–5; Cressy, *Literacy and the Social Order*, 2–3, 134–37.

40. Monaghan, "Literacy Instruction and Gender in Colonial New England," 54–59; Sewall, *Diary*, 277; Barnard, "Autobiography," 178; *Pennsylvania Packet*, August 1, 1774.

41. Cressy, *Literacy and the Social Order*, 2–3, 11–12, 41, 183; Lepore, "Literacy and Reading in Puritan New England," 42; Lockridge, *Literacy in Colonial New England*, 13, 28; Main, "An Inquiry into When and Why Women Learned to Read and Write in Colonial New England," 580; Auwers, "Reading the Marks of the Past," 204–5; Tully, "Literacy Levels and Educational Development," 301–12; Beales and Monaghan, "Literacy and Schoolbooks," 380–81; Cressy, *Literacy and the Social Order*, 177–89.

42. Russo and Russo, "Responsive Justice," 161–62.

43. Malcolm, *Peter's War*, 18–19; Winch, *A Gentleman of Color*, 8–27. As a sailmaker, the young Forten also had to learn to write and become numerate, which were essential skills for his trade (ibid.). Stephen Gloucester on Margaret Forten, quoted ibid., 12; Pinckney, *Letterbook*, 12; *New York Mercury*, August 11 and September 15, 1760.

44. Szasz, *Indian Education*, 184, 199–201; Zeisberger, *The Moravian Mission Diaries of David Zeisberger*, for example 118, 128, 179, 292, 355.

45. *New England Primer*. The second edition published in 1690 is the earliest extant copy of this ubiquitous eighteenth-century primer (Beales and Monaghan, "Literacy and School Books," 384). Dyche, *A Guide to the English Tongue*; Lepore, "Literacy and Reading in Puritan New England," 42.

46. Burroughs, *Memoirs*, 2–9. I am grateful to Larry Cebula for directing me to the colorful character of Stephen Burroughs in our conversation and his blog, http://northwesthistory.blogspot.com/2008/07/bring-me-head-of-stephen-burroughs.html, accessed March 4, 2014.

47. Bishop Tyler, S17162, RWPA, RG 15, NAB; Benjamin Peck, S15571, RWPA, RG 15, NAB; John Romer, interviewed November 8, 1848, in "Interviews with

eyewitnesses to the American Revolution, done between 1845–1849," collected by John McDonald, 1849, 3:833 (hereafter McDonald Interviews), New-York Historical Society (hereafter NYHS); Gaius Stebbins, S7597, RWPA, RG 15, NAB.

48. John Tileston, "Extracts from the Diary of Mr. John Tileston," 11; Colesworthy, *John Tileston's School*, 33.

49. See Seymour, *Documentary Life of Nathan Hale*; *Connecticut Journal*, September 10, 1773; *New London Gazette* (later *Connecticut Gazette*), March 14, 1777. My thanks to Virginia Anderson for reminding me of the Nathan Hale connection.

50. Bishop Tyler, S17162, RWPA, RG 15, NAB; Perkins, *A Sermon Preached to the Soldiers*.

51. Denson, "Diversity Religion," 39; Hugh McAdam, "Journal," quoted in Foote, *Sketches of North Carolina*, 324–25; Kars, *Breaking Loose Together*, 5–6, 81, 95; Andrews, "Religion in the American Revolution," 977–84; Andrews, *The Methodists and Revolutionary America*; Foote, *Sketches of North Carolina*, 324–25.

52. J. L. Bell, "From Saucy Boys to Sons of Liberty," 205.

53. Alexander Gordon, "Gordon, William (1727/8–1807)"; William Gordon, *History of the Rise, Progress, and Establishment of the United States*, 277.

54. Bell, "From Saucy Boys to Sons of Liberty," 211; *Boston Evening Post*, February 26, 1770; John Boyle, "Journal," 263; Gordon, *History of the Rise, Progress, and Establishment of the United States*, 276.

55. Perkins, "To My Children, July 18, 1846," 5–6, Thomas Perkins Papers, quoted in Bell, "From Saucy Boys to Sons of Liberty," 207; Loring, *The Hundred Boston Orators*, 1:22–23.

56. Lee, *Crowds and Soldiers in Revolutionary North Carolina*, 46–49; Selesky, "Regulators," 2:976–77.

57. Robert Burns, "Tam O'Shanter," *Selected Poems*, 12–18. In the poem, Tam's wife sits at home while he is out drinking, "Gathering her brows like gathering storm/Nursing her wrath to keep it warm."

58. Samuel Boyd, W9737, RWPA, RG 15, NAB.

59. Greenwood, *A Young Patriot in the American Revolution*, 41; Bishop Tyler, S17162, RWPA, RG 15, NAB; v. 4, 997, NYHS; Jonathan Keeler, interview, September 29, 1845, McDonald Interviews, 1:173; Abraham Weeks, interview, ibid., October 19, 1848, 3:721; Josiah Quimby, interview, October 25, 1848, ibid., 3:737.

Chapter 3

1. John Jenks, S39775, RWPA, RG 15, NAB.

2. Ibid.; Federal Census, 1840. A letter of complaint from Asa Keeler is in Jenks's file as are affidavits of support from Ebenezer Bartlett and Isaiah Adkins. Jenks also refers to an affidavit from Israel Harding. There is no pension application for Bartlett, though his affidavit makes his service clear. Adkins and Harding were both long-serving soldiers in the Connecticut Line of the Continental army. They were respectively nine and thirteen years older than Jenks. Isaiah Adkins, S49292, and Israel Harding, W2791, RWPA, RG 15, NAB.

3. John Jenks, S39775, RWPA, RG 15, NAB. Jenks does not specify when he learned to read, but he probably learned to do so before his father died, although he may have learned in the army. From what Jenks tells us of Samuel Whipple, it is unlikely that he made any investment in Jenks's education. The boy could read and write when he became a teacher ten years later. Herndon and Murray, eds., *Children Bound to Labor*; Maryland Reading Study.

4. Herndon and Murray, eds., *Children Bound to Labor*, 1–18.

5. Purcell, *Sealed With Blood*, 1–3; Young, *The Shoemaker and the Tea Party*, 132–42. For important discussions on the use of the war in public rhetoric in the early republic, see Waldstreicher, *In the Midst of Perpetual Fetes* and Resch, *Suffering Soldiers*.

6. Haswell, *An Oration delivered at Bennington, Vermont, August 16, 1799*, 24; Plumb, *The Death of the Past*, 17.

7. See Mintz, "Rise of Democratic Politics"; Keyssar, *The Right to Vote*, xx–xxi, 53, 75, Appendix A.1 and A.2; Baldino and Kreider, *Of the People, By the People, For the People*.

8. Purcell, *Sealed with Blood*, 188; Resch, *Suffering Soldiers*, 3–5; Young, *The Shoemaker and the Tea Party*, 132–36. For public toasts see, for example, *Baltimore Patriot*, July 8, 1826, 2.

9. Forrest, *Oration Delivered by Edwin Forrest*, 3.

10. Reiner, *From Virtue to Character*, 62, 265, n65; See Haines, "Fertility and Mortality in the United States."

11. See Janeway, *A Token Children*; *The Friendly Instructor*, 36; Houlbrooke, *Death, Religion, and the Family in England, 1480–1750*, 191–203; Demos, "From this World to the Next," 160–65.

12. Stannard, "Death and the Puritan Child," 465; Smith, "Mortality and Family in the Colonial Chesapeake," 411–13; Schulz, "Children and Childhood in the Eighteenth Century," 67–69; Muhlenberg, *The Journals of Henry Melchior Muhlenberg*, 1:656–63. Child mortality, before the twentieth century, was remarkably consistent over the course of human history, with some variations depending on place, period, and culture. Average infant mortality was 27 percent, and child mortality was about 48 percent (Anthony Volk, "The Evolution of Childhood," 475–77).

13. Colesworthy, *John Tileston's School*; Dewees, *A History of the Life and Services of Captain Samuel Dewees*, 84.

14. King, *Stolen Childhood*, 1–19; Malcolm, *Peter's War*, 3–7. Peter sometimes used the last name Brooks, the name of his father's owners; and sometimes Nelson, the name of his own master and mistress. Ibid.

15. Joyner, *Down by the Riverside*, 37, 137.

16. Painter, *Autobiography of Thomas Painter*, 8; William Conner, S30955, RWPA, RG 15, NAB.

17. See Smith, *Memoirs*.

18. Laurens, *The Papers of Henry Laurens*, volumes 3–9; Martha Laurens Ramsay, *Memoirs of the Life of Martha Laurens Ramsay*, 13, 25.

19. Hemphill, "Sibling Relations in Early American Childhoods," 83; Smith, *Inside the Great House*, chapter 5.

20. Ramsay, *Memoirs*, 13, 25.

21. Younglove, "Record of Samuel Younglove," 38–39; Samuel Younglove, S14910, RWPA, RG 15, NAB.

22. Jonathan Burrows, April 16, 1782, in *Dubrose Times: Selected Depositions of Maine Revolutionary War Veterans*, by Sylvia J. Sherman, (Augusta: Maine State Archives, 1975), 9. Burrows was in is twenties when he served in the Revolutionary War. Jonathan Burrows, Pension File W15615, NAB; King James Bible, "Book of Samuel," 18:1–4; Painter, *Autobiography*, 6.

23. Dewees, *A History of the Life and Services of Captain Samuel Dewees*, 31; John Jenks, S39775, RWPA, RG 15, NAB.

24. Herndon and Murray, eds., *Children Bound to Labor*, 2.

25. George Whitefield, *A Collection of Papers, Lately Printed on the Daily Adviser No. 7*, (London, 1740), 42 and 44; and George Whitefield, *An Account of Money Received and Disbursed for the Orphanage House in Georgia* (London, 1741), quoted in Sundue, *Industrious in Their Stations*, 135–37; Sundue, *Industrious in Their Stations*, 137–62; Hindle and Herndon, "Recreating Proper Families in England and North America," 35.

26. Perry, "Life of David Perry," 7; Drinker, *Diary*, 1, 511, 533, 535, 631.

27. Painter, *Autobiography*, 9. Painter surely meant "shift for myself"; Fox, "The Adventures of Ebenezer Fox," 9–10.

28. Thwaites, *Jesuit Relations and Allied Documents*, 57:45; Szasz, *Indian Education*, 18–22; Zeisberger, *David Zeisberger's History of the Northern American Indians*, 81.

29. Levy, "'Tender Plants,'" 116; Chester Monthly Meeting, quoted ibid, 124–25.

30. Calvert, *Children in the House*, 12.

31. "Paul Revere," http://www.paulreverehouse.org/bio/father.html.

32. Sewall, *Diary of Samuel Sewall*, 300; Esther Burr to Sally Prince, February 28, 1755, in Karlsen and Crumpacker, eds., *The Journal of Esther Edwards Burr*, 95. Esther Burr wrote a journal but addressed it to her friend Sarah Prince in Boston. Periodically Burr bundled up her journal and sent it to Prince who did the same in reverse. Prince's journal (letters) has not survived. Ibid.

33. Heywood, *A History of Childhood*, 100; King, *Stolen Childhood*, 93–95.

34. Cox, *A Proper Sense of Honor*, 98–100.

35. *Records of the Quarterly Courts of Essex County*, 8:302–3; *Cases of the Mayor's Court of New York City*, 185, quoted in Robert Bremmer, ed., *Children and Youth in America*, 1:126.

36. David Granger, S17452, RWPA, RG 15, NAB; Granger, "A Boy Soldier under Washington," 540; Dewees, *A History of the Life and Services of Captain Samuel Dewees*, 40.

37. "Records of the South Carolina Line," 89, quoted in Cox, *A Proper Sense of Honor*, 102. No veteran admitted in his pension application to having been punished by a court-martial, although some particularly remembered witnessing such punishments inflicted on others.

38. Barnard, "Autobiography," 180; Beales, "The Child in Seventeenth-Century America," in Hawes and Hiner, *American Childhood*, 29.

39. Joseph Illick, *American Childhoods*, 29; Lewis, *The Pursuit of Happiness*, 30–39; Reinier, *From Virtue to Character*, 22; Fithian, *Journal*. See, for example, 64, 66, 86, 104, 154.

40. Hill, "Journal of Hiram Hill and His Ancestors," 1812–1856.

41. Burroughs, *Memoirs*, 8. My thanks to Larry Cebula for introducing me to Stephen Burroughs.

42. See *New England Primer*.

43. Benjamin Walker to lieutenant colonel Francis Barber, January 21, 1783, George Washington Papers, Series 3b, Varick Transcripts; Eli Jacobs, W1193 and George Blackmore, RWPA, RG 15, NAB.

44. Obadiah Benge, R743, RWPA, RG 15, NAB; James Ayres, R334, RWPA, RG 15, NAB. The account of the dissent in the Ayres household is from the deposition in Ayres's file from Benjamin O'Bannon, a near neighbor, who had known James since his early childhood. "Molecatchers: A Brief History," http://www.the-mole-catcher.co.uk/molecatchers.html; "We don't make a mountain out of a molehill," "British Traditional Mole Catchers' Register," http://www.britishmolecatchers.co.uk.

45. Cyrus Allen, W8094, RWPA, RG 15, NAB; David Carpenter's deposition in Allen's file. His own service is detailed in W16892, RWPA, RG 15, NAB.

46. John Piatt, W1473, RWPA, RG 15, NAB.

47. Malcolm, *Peter's War*, 75–76. Peter did not live long enough to apply for a pension so there is no account of these years from him. In her wonderful biography of Peter, Joyce Lee Malcolm believes he must have been eager to go, overcoming the resistance of his master and mistress who would have thought it too risky. I think Peter may well have been eager, but that his master would have needed persuading. Indeed Josiah Nelson may even have suggested it (ibid., 76).

48. Quarles, *The Negro in the American Revolution*, 54; Malcolm, *Peter's War*, 192–93. The preamble to the Massachusetts state constitution of 1780 declared that, "All men are born free and equal." In April of the following year, a slave, Quok Walker, brought a lawsuit that resulted in the Massachusetts Supreme Judicial Court asserting that the phrase "born free" was literal. It was the death knell to an already dying institution in the state. Quarles, *The Negro in the American Revolution*, 47–48.

49. Patrick Cronkhite, W16932, RWPA, RG 15, NAB. Patrick Cronkhite was John Cronkhite's father. The family story is in depositions on behalf of Patrick Cronkhite's widow, Maria. See also muster rolls for Captain John Wendell's Company, Colonel Goose Van Scheick's New York Continentals, 391–99.

50. Gaines Hitchcock, S19339, Thomas Price, W1066, William Price, W1072, RWPA, RG 15, NAB.

51. Mayer, "Wives, Concubines, and Community," 249, 250–51. Theotist Paulin gave her testimony under her married name, Theotist Blow. She was being deposed in support of her mother's pension application. Alexander Ferriol, S43551, RWPA, RG 15, NAB. My thanks to Holly Mayer for introducing me to the French Canadian refugees and for many fruitful conversations about their experiences.

52. Josiah Brandon, W355, RWPA, RG 15, NAB; Lee, *Crowds and Soldiers in Revolutionary North Carolina*, 46–49; Selesky, "Regulators," *Encyclopedia of the American Revolution*, 2:976–76.

53. Josiah Brandon, W355, RWPA, RG 15, NAB.

54. Ibid.

55. Martin, *Ordinary Courage*, 47, 53; Walton, William Jr., S17184, RWPA, RG 15, NAB.

56. Henry Eckler, S10605, and Adam Gerlock, R3917, RWPA, RG 15, NAB.

57. For Baker's rejection, see Muster Rolls of the Revolutionary War, 35:201, Massachusetts State Archives; Benoni Baker, W14237 and Andrew Ferguson, S32243, RWPA, RG 15, NAB. My thanks to Judith Van Buskirk for introducing me to Benoni Baker.

58. Martin, *Ordinary Courage*, 160; William Creamer, W17692, Thomas Craig, W5255, Samuel Morrow, W21825, and John Jenks, S39775, RWPA, RG 15, NAB; Mayer, "Wives, Concubines, and Community," 250.

Chapter 4

1. Cyril Eaton, S32227, RWPA, RG 15, NAB.

2. This imaginative account is based on the details provided in Cyril Eaton, S32227, Stephen Eaton, S23209, RWPA, RG 15, NAB, and Martin, *Ordinary Courage*, 12–13. It is also informed by the hundreds of pension applications read for this study.

3. Meshack Burchfield, S16668, William Conner, S30955, RWPA, RG 15, NAB; Recruiting Broadsheet for the Continental Army, Philadelphia, s.n., 1776.

4. Daniel Granger, S17452, RWPA, RG 15, NAB; Granger, "A Boy Soldier under Washington," 539–40.

5. John Burgess, S30302, RWPA, RG 15, NAB.

6. Henry Yeager, R11929, RWPA, RG 15, NAB. There is no pension application for George Lechler. His story is in Yeager's application.

7. Mintz, *Huck's Raft*, 34–35; Zeisberger, *David Zeisberger's History of the North American Indians*, 16; Weed, *The Autobiography of Thurlow Weed*, 2–3.

8. Blackstone, *Commentaries*, 1:281–85, 289.

9. Ibid.; Rorabaugh, *The Craft Apprentice*, 4. See the English Statute of Artificers of 1563 that required parents to find some appropriate vocation for their sons in the craft shop or on the land. This was bolstered by the 1601 Poor Law requiring the courts to bind children out if their parents were too poor or feckless to arrange it themselves (ibid.). Levy, *Town Born*.

10. Blackstone, *Commentaries*, 1:281–85, 289; ibid., 1:284; Mason, *From Father's Property to Children's Rights*, 47.

11. Franklin, *The Autobiography*, 25–26; Hill, "Journal of Hiram Hill"; Perry, "Life of David Perry," 7.

12. Franklin, *The Autobiography*, 25–26; Painter, *Autobiography*, 8–9.

13. Adams, *The Earliest Diary of John Adams*, 71.

14. Sewall, *Diary*, I, 167, 321–22, 348.

15. Fox, "The Adventures of Ebenezer Fox," 29–30.

16. Henry Laurens to John Lewis Gervais, April 18, 1766, *The Papers of Henry Laurens*, 104; Winslow, *Diary of Anna Green Winslow*, 7, 5, 20.

17. Shammas, "Child Labor and Schooling in Late Eighteenth-Century New England," 539, 540, 547–48, 545, 547; Sundue, *Industrious in Their Stations*, 28–29. "Quincy Thaxter His Journal, 1774," is in the Thaxter Family Papers, Massachusetts Historical Society. It is studied by Shammas (ibid.) and Sundue (ibid.).

18. Dewees, *A History of the Life and Services of Captain Samuel Dewees*, 1844, 2; Vickers, *Farmers and Fishermen*, 221; Hill, "Journal of Hiram Hill"; Franklin, *The Autobiography*, 23.

19. George, "An Account of the Life,"473; Smith, "Narrative," 12; Washington, schedule of slaves held, June 1799, *Papers of George Washington, Retirement Series*, 4: 527–37; Washington, "List of Dower Slaves," Appendix F, *Papers of George Washington, Colonial Series*, 6: 311–13; Jefferson, *Thomas Jefferson's Farm Book*, 6–12.

20. Vickers, *Farmers and Fishermen*, 221.

21. Dye, "Early American Merchant Seafarers," 337–39. Dye analyzed the records in the National Archives generated by the federal legislation of 1796, "An Act for the Relief and Protection of Seamen." One of the results of this act was that some cities such as Philadelphia, offered a "seamen's protection certificate." In order to apply for one, a mariner needed to provide personal information, including his age when he first went to sea (ibid., 331–32). For Benjamin Salter's story, see Vickers, *Farmers and Fishermen*, 173, and Walsh, "Young Men and the Sea," 25–26; Rediker, *Between the Devil and the Deep Blue Sea*, 299. Both Vickers and Rediker draw on Dye's study. Simon Newman's study of tattooed sailors, which also draws on the protection certificates, found similar results (Newman, "Reading the Bodies," 63).

22. Kilby, "Narrative of John Kilby," 25, 29; Dye, "Early American Merchant Seafarers," 335–36; Vickers, *Farmers and Fishermen*, 182–85.

23. John Peck, W6857, Israel Trask, S30177, RWPA, RG 15, NAB. Trask's pension deposition is also in Dann, *The Revolution Remembered*, 406–14.

24. Vickers, *Farmers and Fishermen*, 173; John Peck, W6857, Israel Trask, S30177, RWPA RG 15, NAB.

25. John Peck, W6857, RWPA, RG 15, NAB; Winch, *A Gentleman of Color*, 38; Fox, "The Adventures of Ebenezer Fox," 20; Main, "Gender, Work, and Wages in Colonial New England, 43, 48; Selesky, *War and Society in Colonial Connecticut*, 151; Anderson, *A People's Army*, 225. Selesky shows Connecticut troops in the Seven Years' War making £1.6s.8d in 1755 rising to £2 by the war's end. Anderson shows similar soldiers' pay at similar levels in Massachusetts in 1755 rising to £1.16s by 1762. Army pay was that of the community's lowest paid workers (Selesky, 151).

26. Cyrus Allen, W8094, Ebenezer Atwood, W23469, Moses Hall, S43—— (index card torn), RWPA, RG 15, NAB. Note, as neither the state in which Hall served nor his index number is legible, the digitized versions of the pension records have him listed under "blank."

27. Jeremiah Parrish, S11215, Samuel Dewees, W9405, RWPA, RG 15, NAB.

28. Israel Trask, S30177, Samuel Dewees, W9405, RWPA, RG 15, NAB.

29. Brewer, *By Birth or Consent*, 279–82; Schmidt, *Industrial Violence*, 122–24.

30. King, *Two Tracts*, 31; Dalrymple, *A Military Essay*, 8.

31. Houlding, *Fit For Service*, 117–21; Bowen, *War and British Society*, 15; Frey, *The British Soldier in America*, 6–16; Childs, *Armies and Warfare in Europe*, 61–63; Brumwell, *Redcoats*, 319; Way, "Rebellion of the Regulars," 769–71; Elliot, "The Last and True Speech of Archibald Elliot"; Kirk, *Memoirs and Adventures of Robert Kirk*, 1.

32. *George Washington Papers*, Series 4, "Size Rolls"; Titus, *The Old Dominion at War*, 82; "Muster Rolls of the New York Provincial Troops, 1755–1764," all. Selesky, *War and Society in Colonial Connecticut*, 151–52. In Connecticut, soldiers' wages went from £1.6s.8d in 1755 to £2 in 1762, an increase of 46.6 percent. Bounty payments rose from £3 to £8.15s in the same period, an increase of 191 percent (data, ibid.). Davies, *The Curse of Cowardice*, 16–17.

33. Davies, *The Curse of Cowardice*, 29–30.

34. Titus, *The Old Dominion at War*, ix, 121–22; Selesky, *War and Society*, 149–50; George Washington to Thomas Waggener, April 25, 1758, *Papers of George Washington, Colonial Series*, 5:145.

35. Baylies, "Eulogy on the Hon. Benjamin Russell." This eulogy included a brief memoir Russell had written prior to his death. Benjamin Russell, S30685, RWPA, RG 15, NAB.

36. Welles, March 25, 1783, *The Revolutionary War Letters*.

37. Burroughs, *Memoirs*, 14–20 (pages refer to 1835 edition). Burroughs reproduced the letter he claimed his father, Eden Burroughs, had written to Washington dated December 24, 1779 (ibid.).

38. Ditz, *Property and Kinship*, 117.

39. Daniel Granger, S17452, RWPA, RG 15, NAB.

40. Martin, *Ordinary Courage*, 12–13; Austin Wells, S32054, Joshua Davies, S38656, Moses Piper, S33474, RWPA, RG 15, NAB.

41. Peter Fulp, W5278, Michael Fulp, W10043, Elijah Freeman, W24240, Stephen Freeman, S43575, RWPA, RG 15, NAB.

42. David Lockwood, W26223, RWPA, RG 15, NAB.

43. Obadiah Benge, R743, Enoch Berry, W8128, RWPA, RG 15, NAB.

44. Israel Trask, S30177, Samuel Dewees, W9405, RWPA, RG 15, NAB; Jabez Fitch, "Diary," 48–50.

45. Frederick Vaughn, S32565, RWPA, RG 15, NAB.

46. Jacob Meech, S15524, Simeon Jones, S16894, Elisha Prentice, S15563, Simeon Hewitt, W2576, Bishop Tyler, S11162, Samuel Branch, W3717, David Avery, S12022, RWPA, RG 15, NAB.

47. David Avery, S12022, Bishop Tyler, S11162, Simeon Hewitt, W2576, RWPA, RG 15, NAB.

48. Nicholson, *Medieval Warfare*, 41.

49. Ibid., 41–42.

50. Shy, "New Look at Colonial Militia," 182.

51. Governor George Clinton, New York State, Broadside (Poughkeepsie, New York: John Holt, 1780); *Berks County, Pennsylvania, Board of Commissioners, July 19, 1781* (Reading, Penn.: s.n., 1781).

52. Bell, *The Rise and Continuance.*

53. *Journals of the Continental Congress,* 7:262; Bell, *The Rise and Continuance.*

54. Bell, *The Rise and Continuance.*

55. William Addison, W5599, Joseph Brown, W5744, Daniel Bennett, R752, Isaac Bedell, S15322, RWPA, RG 15, NAB. Some of Bedell's story is pieced together from depositions he gave to support other men's claims. See especially Daniel Doty, W243 and Joseph Sutton, W872, RWPA, RG 15, NAB.

56. Peter DeWolf, S18377, Joseph DeWolf, S3280, Nathan (sometimes Nathaniel) Gillet, S42744, RWPA, RG 15, NAB.

57. This relative absence may also be skewed by my sample of pensions and pension process. African American applicants deposed in 1818 for need-based pensions found the pension office accommodating and had little difficulty making a case for either their long service or their poverty. Only about 3 percent were rejected versus 8 percent of whites. In the harsher racial climate of 1832, when pensions were offered on the basis of short service alone, when most of the former boy soldiers applied, African American veterans were more commonly challenged for having been only waiters or teamsters. The pension office was less inclined to believe their claims that they had also carried a musket or stood on guard duty. Their rejection rate was now 31 percent as opposed to 13 percent for white veterans. (Van Buskirk, "Claiming Their Due," 133, 142–45.) For this reason, some more prosperous black veterans may have avoided applying at all. Additionally, while no good data on life expectancy for black men exist for this time, a shorter life expectancy might also explain their absence from the pension pool.

58. Andrew Ferguson, S32243, RWPA, RG 15, NAB; Malcolm, *Peter's War,* 76; Winch, *A Gentleman of Color,* 37–38.

59. Tim Jones, S18063, London Hazard, S17463, RWPA, RG 15, NAB; Van Buskirk, "Claiming Their Due," 135.

60. Thomas Fox, S37930, John Collins, W6735, RWPA, RG 15, NAB. Slaves also left little indication of feeling exploited. As free men applying for pensions, they would be unlikely to express that sentiment if it was felt. Even Tim Jones, who through his service earned his freedom but lost a leg at the Battle of Yorktown in 1781, gave no indication as to how he felt about this trade-off (Jones, S18063).

61. Fox, "The Adventures of Ebenezer Fox," 31–38.

62. Obadiah Benge, R743, RWPA, RG 15, NAB.

Chapter 5

1. Bishop Tyler, S17162, RWPA, RG 15, NAB.

2. Ibid.

3. This is an imaginative account based on Bishop Tyler, S17162, RWPA, RG 15, NAB and a variety of other sources. These include David Lawrence, W26196,

RWPA, RG 15, NAB; *The Courier*, September 17, 1817, February 10, 1819, November 17, 1824, March 22, 1826, "Obituary Notices of Pennsylvania Soldiers," 447; *United States Census Records, 1800–1840*, NAB; Brigham, *The Tyler Genealogy*, 1:174, 346, 351 and 2:587–88; *Delaware Gazette*, October 10, 1832, in Houck, Garti, and Ridell, eds., *Delaware County's War Papers*. This New York newspaper has a detailed account of the festive first application day for veterans in 1832. This short-lived newspaper is not available on databases of United States newspapers from the era.

4. Bishop Tyler, S17162, Samuel Hancock, W——. Hancock had married Ann (Nancy) Moon, the widow of Revolutionary War veteran Jacob Moon. Since Nancy Moon ultimately received widows' pensions from both Jacob Moon and Samuel Hancock, all the records are held in the file for Jacob Moon, W4691. Ebenezer Couch, W23839, RWPA, RG 15, NAB.

5. Jacob Gundy, S32284, William Coff, S39347, Richard Pugh, S38319, Daniel Burchel, S39261, RWPA, RG 15, NAB. Pugh lived in Franklin County, just to the south of Botetourt County, and Burchel lived in Henry County, on the North Carolina border. Both men were living within one hundred miles of Coff when he tracked them down, and both had filed need-based pension applications.

6. Israel Trask, S30177, RWPA, RG 15, NAB; *Salem Gazette*, June 19, 1827, October 16, 1827.

7. Benjamin Gauss, S13125, Cyrus Allen, W8094, RWPA, RG 15, NAB.

8. Samuel Aspenwall, W20634, RWPA, RG 15, NAB.

9. Cyprian Parrish, S29363, RWPA, RG 15, NAB.

10. Bishop Tyler, S17162, Samuel Branch, W3717, Elisha Prentice, S15563, Simeon Hewitt, W2576, John Piatt, W1473, RWPA, RG 15, NAB.

11. Aaron Day, S43462, RWPA, RG 15, NAB.

12. Abel Pearson, S3661, John Burchfield, W8175, RWPA, RG 15, NAB.

13. John Burchfield, W8175, Robert Burchfield, R1444, RWPA, RG 15, NAB. Neither man ever specifies their relationship, yet their early life-courses track each other. Robert was six years older than John, and John later testified on behalf of Robert's widow that he had been present at her marriage. Far Western North Carolina became the new state of Tennessee following the war. During the war, the boys all lived in counties that stayed well within North Carolina after this postwar division. Those who applied for pensions from Tennessee, twenty (28 percent), had moved some distance from their childhood homes and, like the others, had often moved multiple times.

14. Malcolm, *Peter's War*, 193, 234.

15. William Coff, S39347, Andrew Ferguson, S32243, RWPA, RG 15, NAB. In 1851, Ferguson describes himself as being over ninety, but in his depositions he specified his birth year as 1765, making him only in his eighties.

16. Resch, *Suffering Soldiers*, 119–21; *Delaware Gazette*, October 10, 1832, in Houck, Garti, and Ridell, *Delaware County's War Papers*.

17. Gaius Stebbins, S7597, RWPA, RG 15, NAB.

18. Cyprian Parrish, S29363, RWPA, RG 15, NAB.

19. Andrew Ferguson, S32243, RWPA, RG 15, NAB.

20. Josiah Brandon, W355, RWPA, RG 15, NAB.

21. Ibid.

22. Ibid.

23. John Jenks, S39775, RWPA, RG 15, NAB; Rothman, *The Discovery of the Asylum*, 79.

24. John Jenks, S39775, RWPA, RG 15, NAB.

25. Ibid.

26. Samuel Godding, S35340, RWPA, RG 15, NAB; *Eastern Argus*, May 22, 1832; "Shaker Heritage Society of Albany, New York."

27. Mintz, *Huck's Raft*, 75–77; Reinier, *From Virtue to Character*, 43–44; Webster, "On the Education of Youth in America," 44, 66; Rush, "Thoughts upon the State of Female Education, 27–30, 32.

28. Reinier, *From Virtue to Character*, 125.

29. Ibid.

30. Walton Tilman, W4373, Nathan Elwood, W15765, RWPA, RG 15, NAB.

31. John Jenks, S39775, RWPA, RG 15, NAB.

32. Nathan Elwood, W15765, John Jenks, S39775, RWPA, RG 15, NAB.

33. Bishop Tyler, S17162, RWPA, RG 15, NAB.

34. *Respublica v. Keppele*, 2 Dallas 197 (Pennsylvania 1793) quoted in Sundue, "Class Stratification and Children's Work," 198–99; Brewer, *By Birth or Consent*, 279.

35. Sundue, "Class Stratification and Children's Work," 200–202, 208–9; Herndon, *Children Bound to Labor*, 15.

36. Lockley, "To Train Them to Habits of Industry and Usefulness," 136; Murray, "Mothers and Children in the Charleston Orphan House," 111; Sundue, "Class Stratification and Children's Work," 206.

37. John Jenks, S39775, RWPA, RG 15, NAB; Dewees, *A History of the Life and Services of Captain Samuel Dewees*, 65, 83.

38. *United States Census 1830*; Rockman, *Scraping By*, 24; *The Farmers' Cabinet*, November 27, 1830. Edwards's early life has been difficult to trace. However, since he joined the marines in 1811 and then was commissioner of pensions until 1850, he probably was born between 1785 and 1795.

39. Cox, *A Proper Sense of Honor*, 246–47; Hickey, *The War of 1812*, 303; Hare, "Military Punishments in the War of 1812," 225–39.

40. Millett and Maslowski, *For the Common Defense*, 91–103.

41. Ibid., 91–103, 654–55; James Summers, number 4442, volume 23, "Enlistments 1798–May 17, 1815," in "Register of Enlistments in the United States Army, 1798–1914," RG 94, M233, NAB. Note: While the information on soldiers is organized into volumes by the first initial of their last names, the soldiers' names are not alphabetical within each volume. But the clerk gave each man in the volume a sequential number, provided here. This can be used to locate the veteran on the microfilm, which has not been digitized.

42. Brewer, *By Birth or Consent*, 34; Madison, "Notes on the Constitutional Convention," http://avalon.law.yale.edu/subject_menus/debcont.asp.

43. Brewer, *By Birth or Consent*, 132, 141–48, 155–59.

44. Parsons, "Precedents Book of Massachusetts Law, 1775," Harvard University Law Library, Cambridge, Mass., quoted in Brewer, *By Birth or Consent*, 280; see also, Brewer, 279–82.

45. Brewer, *By Birth or Consent*, 138–39.

46. Hickey, *War of 1812*, 243–44; "Speech of Josiah Quincy," 169, 173; *Annals of the Congress of the United States*, Twelfth Congress, Second Session, v. 25, 167–69, 178.

47. *Annals of the Congress of the United States*, Thirteenth Congress, Third Session, v. 28, 733.

48. *Grace v. Wilbur*, 10 Johns, 453 (N.Y. Sup. Ct. 1813). (The Supreme Court of Judicature in New York is the predecessor of the New York Supreme Court.)

49. *United States v. Bainbridge*, 24F. Cas. 946 (C.C.D. Mass. 1816) No. 14,497. (The Circuit Court for the District of Massachusetts is the predecessor to today's federal district courts). Kent, "Lecture XXIX: On the Rights of Persons," 193.

50. John Jenks, S39775, RWPA, RG 15, NAB.

51. *Republican*, August 21, 1812; Hildebrand, Keller, and Keller, "Music of the War of 1812," http://www.1812music.org. Hildebrand and the Kellers record and perform music from the era on period instruments.

52. Amasa Holden, number 254, and Fielding Hickman, number 48, volume 11, "Enlistments 1798-May 17, 1815," in "Register of Enlistments in the United States Army, 1798–1914," RG 94, M233, NAB.

53. Obadiah Benge, R743, Andrew Ferguson, S32243, RWPA, RG 15, NAB.

54. This paragraph and the one preceding it are based on many pension applications, letters, and memoirs.

55. Obadiah Benge, R743, Andrew Ferguson, S32243, RWPA, RG 15, NAB; *New England Chronicle*, November 7, 1776. Soldiers were paid just under seven dollars a month, about the same low rate as unskilled day laborers, but their income was regular (at least in theory).

56. This imaginative account is based on the pension application of John Piatt, W1473, and William Piatt, R8221, RWPA, RG 15, NAB. William Piatt's application was filed by John Piatt's son Daniel in 1855. Eliza Piatt was probably Daniel's wife and thus John's daughter-in-law, but she may have been a niece. William Piatt died without heirs. After John Piatt's death, Daniel hoped that William's estate, including his pension rights, might pass to the next generation. This position was rejected by the pension office.

Bibliography

Websites

http://www.royalarmouries.org/home
http://valleyforgemusterroll.org/regiments/nj1.asp

Archival Sources

British Library (BL)
  Barrington Papers
  Blenheim Papers
John Carter Brown Library (PRJCB)
  Major Moses Ashley's Orderly Book, 1780
Historical Society of Delaware, Wilmington
  Lieutenant George Bush, Journal
  Papers of the Historical Society of Delaware
Historical Society of Western Pennsylvania (HSWP), Pittsburgh
  Denny O'Hara Papers
Huntington Library, San Marino, California (HL)
Library of Congress (LC)
  George Washington Papers
Maryland Historical Society (MHS), Baltimore
  Muster Rolls and Other records of the Maryland Troops in the American
    Revolution, 1775–1783
Massachusetts Historical Society, Boston
  Thomas H. Perkins Papers
  Thaxter Family Papers
Massachusetts State Archives, Boston
  Muster Rolls of the Revolutionary War
  Middlesex Folio Collection
Morris County Historical Society, Morristown, New Jersey
  Morris County Revolutionary Soldiers
Mount Vernon Estate and Gardens, Mount Vernon, Virginia
  Unpublished memoranda—Washington
National Archives, Kew, England
  War Office Records (WO)
  Treasury (T)
  London Port Register, 1634–1635, "Licenses to Pass Beyond the Seas."
National Archives, Washington, D.C. (NAB)
  Papers of the Continental Congress

"Records of Men Enlisted in the U.S. Army Prior to the Peace Establishment, May 17, 1815," RG 94
Revolutionary War Pension Applications, RG 15
United States Census Records, 1800–1840
New-York Historical Society (NYHS), New York
Giles Family Papers
John Lamb Papers
Morgan Lewis Papers
John Peter Papers
Richard Varick Papers
John McDonald Interviews, 1845–49, originals in Westchester County Historical Society, Elmsford, New York
Muster Rolls of the New York Provincial Troops, 1755–1764
Rhode Island Historical Society (RIHS), Providence
Hiram Hill, Journal, 1812–1856

Newspapers

Baltimore Patriot	Enquirer	New York Gazette
Boston Chronicle	Evening Post	New York Mercury
Boston Evening Post	Farmers' Cabinet	Norwich Gazette
Boston Gazette	Georgia Gazette	Pennsylvania Gazette
Boston Post-Boy	Middlesex Gazette	Pennsylvania Packet
Connecticut Journal	New England Chronicle	Republican
The Courier	New London Gazette (later	Salem Gazette
Eastern Argus	Connecticut Gazette)	

Government Documents

Annals of the Congress of the United States. 42 vols. Washington: Gales and Seaton, 1834–56.
Board of Commissioners, Berks County, Pennsylvania, July 19, 1781, Broadside. Reading, Penn.: s.n., 1781.
Calendar of the Proceedings of the Committee for Compounding, 1643–1660. Edited by M. A. E. Green. London: Eyre and Spottiswoode for Her Majesty's Stationary Office, 1890.
Journals of the Continental Congress, 1774–1789. 34 vols. Edited by Worthington Chauncey Ford. Washington, D.C.: Government Printing Office, 1907.
Records and Files of the Quarterly Courts of Essex County, Massachusetts. 9 vols. Salem: Essex Institute, 1921.
Records the Governor and Company and of the Massachusetts Bay in New England. Volume 2. Edited by Nathaniel Shurtleff. Boston: William White, 1853.
"Muster Rolls of the New York Provincial Troops, 1755–1764." Collections of the New-York Historical Society 24 (1891).

Published Primary Sources

Accounts of the Parliamentary Garrisons of Great Chalfield and Malmesbury 1645–1646. Edited by J. H. P. Pafford. *Wiltshire Archaeological and Natural History Society, Records Branch*, vol. 2. Devizes, 1966.

Adams, John. *Diary and Autobiography of John Adams.* 4 vols. Edited by L. H. Butterfield. Cambridge: Harvard University Press, 1961.

———. *The Earliest Diary of John Adams.* Edited by L. H. Butterfield. Cambridge: Harvard University Press, 1966, original work ca. 1758.

Adlum, John. *Memoirs of the Life of John Adlum in the Revolutionary War.* Edited by Howard Peckham. Chicago: William L. Clemens Library Associates, 1968.

Andrews, Joseph. *The Last Dying Speech and Confession of Joseph Andrews, who was executed at New York on Tuesday the 23rd May, 1769 for Piracy and Murder.* New York: Lawrence Sweeney, 1769.

Barnard, John. "Autobiography of John Barnard." *Collections of the Massachusetts Historical Society* 5 (1836): 177–243.

Bayley, Daniel. *A New and Compleat Introduction to the Grounds and Rules of Musick.* Boston: Thomas Johnston, 1766.

Baylies, Francis. "Eulogy on the Hon. Benjamin Russell, delivered before the Grand Lodge of Free and Accepted masons of the State of Massachusetts, March 10, 1845." Boston: *Boston Freemason's Magazine*, 1845.

Beardsley, Levi. "Reminiscences." In *Growing Up in Cooper Country: Boyhood Recollections of the New York Frontier*, edited by Louis C. Jones, 29–89. Syracuse: Syracuse University Press, 1965.

Beebe, Doctor Lewis. "Journal of a Physician on the Expedition against Canada, 1776." *Pennsylvania Magazine of History and Biography* 59 (1935): 321–61.

Bell, Robert, et al. *The Rise and Continuance of the Substitutes in the Continental Army.* Philadelphia: Robert Bell, 1777.

Bickham, George, engraver. *The Universal Penman.* London: H. Overton, 1743.

Blackstone, Sir William. *Commentaries on the Laws of England.* Edited by William Carey Jones. San Francisco: Bancroft-Whitney Company, 1915–1916.

Boyle, John. "Journal." *New England Historical and Genealogical Register* 84 and 85 (1930 and 31).

Bremmer, Robert, ed. *Children and Youth in America: A Documentary History.* Cambridge: Harvard University Press, 1970.

Brooks, Jonathan. "Experience of Jonathan Brooks." In *The Battle of Groton Heights: A Collection of Narratives, Official Reports, Records, etc., of the Storming of Fort Griswold*, edited by William W. Harris, 74–82. New London: Charles Allyn, 1882.

Buchan, William. *Domestic Medicine or The Family Physician.* Philadelphia: Dunlap, 1772.

Burroughs, Stephen. *Memoirs of the Notorious Stephen Burroughs of New Hampshire.* Hanover: Benjamin True, 1798.

Cadogan, William. *An Essay upon Nursing and the Management of Children from their Birth to Three Years of Age.* Boston: Cox and Berry, 1772.

Charlevoix, Pierre-Francois-Xavier. *Voyage to North America, undertaken by Order of the French King*. London: R. Dudsley, 1761.

Clinton, Governor George. *New York State, Broadside*. Poughkeepsie: John Holt, 1780.

Cuthbertson, Bennett. *Cuthbertson's System for the Compleat Interior Management and Oeconomy of a Battalion of Infantry*. Dublin: Boulter Grierson, 1768.

Dalrymple, Campbell. *A Military Essay, containing Reflections on the Raising, Arming, Cloathing, and Discipline of the British Infantry and Cavalry*. London: D. Wilson, 1761.

Dann, John C. *The Revolution Remembered: Eyewitness Accounts of the War for Independence*. Chicago: University of Chicago Press, 1999.

David, Ebenezer. *A Rhode Island Chaplain in the Revolution: Letters of Ebenezer David to Nicholas Brown*. New York: Kennikat Press, 1949.

Davies, Samuel. *The Curse of Cowardice: A Sermon Preached to the Militia of Hanover County in Virginia at General Muster, May 8, 1758, with a View to Raise a Company for Captain Samuel Meredith*. Boston: J. Buckland, 1758.

Dewees, Samuel. *A History of the Life and Services of Captain Samuel Dewees, A Native of Pennsylvania, and a Soldier of the Revolutionary and Last Wars*. Baltimore: Robert Nielson, 1844.

Dickinson, John. *The Farmer's and Monitor's Letters*. Williamsburg: William Rind, 1796.

Donnan, Elizabeth. *Documents Illustrative of the History of the Slave Trade*. Washington, D.C.: Carnegie Institute of Washington, 1930–35.

Drinker, Elizabeth. *The Diary of Elizabeth Drinker*. Edited by Elaine Forman Crane. Boston: Northeastern University Press, 1991.

Dyche, Thomas. *A Guide to the English Tongue*. London: Richard Ware, 1727.

The Dying Words of Captain Kid, a noted Pirate who was hanged at Execution-Dock in England. Boston: Thomas Fleet, 1780.

Elliot, Archibald. "The last and True Speech of Archibald Elliot, Dragoon in Collonel Montgomerie's Troop . . . who was executed at Hamilton the 11th Day of April, 1723." *CUP* 21 (1723): 33–42.

Felton, Silas. "The Life or Biography of Silas Felton Written by Himself." *Proceedings of the American Antiquarian Society* 69 (1959): 119–54.

Fisher, George. *The American Instructor of the Young Man's Best Companion*. Philadelphia: B. Franklin, 1748.

Fitch, Jabez. *The New York Diary of Lieutenant Jabez Fitch of the 17th (Connecticut) Regiment from August 22, 1776 to December 15, 1777*. Edited by W. H. W. Sabine. New York: Privately published, 1954.

Fithian, Philip Vickers. *Journal & Letters of Philip Vickers Fithian, 1773–1774: A Plantation Tutor of the Old Dominion*. Edited by Hunter Dickinson Farish. Williamsburg: Colonial Williamsburg, 1943.

Foote, William Henry. *Sketches of North Carolina, Historical and Biographical*. New York: Robert Carter, 1846.

Forrest, Edwin. *Oration Delivered by Edwin Forrest, New York, 1838*. Philadelphia: John Ferral, 1838.

Fox, Ebenezer. "The Adventures of Ebenezer Fox." In *Narratives of the American Revolution*, edited by Hugh F. Rankin, 1–164. Chicago: R. R. Donnelly & Sons Company, 1776.

Franklin, Benjamin. *Benjamin Franklin, The Autobiography and Other Writings.* Edited by L. Jesse Lemisch. New York: New American Library, 1961.

The Friendly Instructor: or a Companion for Young Ladies and Gentlemen. New York: J. Holt, 1769.

George, David. "An Account of the Life of Mr. David George from Sierra Leone in Africa," *Baptist Annual Register for 1790, 1791, 1792 and part of 1793.* Edited by John Rippon. London, 1793: 473–84.

Goodrich, Samuel. *Reflections of a Lifetime: Or Man and Things I Have Seen in a Series of Familiar Letters to a Friend.* New York: Miller, Orton, and Mulligan, 1857.

Gordon, William. *History of the Rise, Progress, and Establishment of the Independence of the United States of America.* London: Charles Dilly, 1788.

Granger, David. "A Boy Soldier under Washington: The Memoir of David Granger." *Mississippi Valley Historical Review* 16 (1930): 538–60.

Greenwood, John. *A Young Patriot in the American Revolution, 1775–1783.* Edited by Isaac J. Greenwood. Tyrone, Pa.: Westvaco, 1981.

Harris, William W., ed. *The Battle of Groton Heights: A Collection of Narratives, Official Reports, Records, etc., of the Storming of Fort Griswold.* New London: Charles Allyn, 1882.

Haswell, Anthony. *An Oration delivered at Bennington, Vermont August 16, 1799: in Commemoration of the Battle of Bennington.* Bennington: Anthony Haswell, 1799.

Hayward, John. *The New England Gazetteer; Containing Descriptions of all the Counties and Towns in New England.* Concord: John Hayward—Boyd & White, 1839.

Hazard, Thomas B. *Nailer Tom's Diary, Otherwise the Journal of Thomas B. Hazard of Kingstown, Rhode Island, 1778–1840.* Edited by Caroline Hazard. Boston: Merrymount Press, 1930.

The History of Sir Richard Whittington: Three Times Lord Mayor of London. Boston: T. and J. Fleet, 1770.

Hopkinson, Francis. *A Pretty Story Written in the Year of Our Lord 1774 by Peter Grievous, Esq.* Philadelphia: John Dunlap, 1774.

Houck, Shirley, Anne Marie Garti, and Hugh Ridell. *Delaware County's War Papers: Abstracts of Revolutionary War Pension Applications, Pension Laws, and Relevant Contemporary Events in Delaware County.* Walton: Board of Supervisors, Delaware County and Delaware County Historical Society, 1978, and digitized in 2011.

Hurt, John. *The Love of Our Country: A Sermon Preached Before the Virginia Troops in New-Jersey.* Philadelphia: Styner and Cist, 1777.

Janeway, James. *A Token Children: An Exact Account of the Conversion, Holy and Exemplary Lives and Joyful Deaths of Several Young Children.* Boston: Nicholas Boone, 1700.

Jefferson, Thomas. *Thomas Jefferson's Farm Book, with Commentary and Relevant Extracts from Other Writings.* Edited by Edwin Morris Betts. Princeton: Princeton University Press, 1953.

Johnson, Charles. *A General History of the Lives and Adventures of the Most Famous Highwaymen, Murderers, Street Robbers, & C . . . To which is added a genuine account of the Voyages and Plunders of the most notorious Pyrates.* London: Olive Payne, 1736.

Karlsen, Carol F., and Laurie Crumpacker, eds. *The Journal of Esther Edwards Burr, 1754–1757.* New Haven: Yale University Press, 1984.

Kent, James. "Lecture XXIX: On the Right of Persons." *Commentaries on American Law.* 4 volumes. New York: Little Brown and Company, 1896, first edition 1826.

Kilby, John. "Narrative of John Kilby." *Scribner's Magazine* 38 (1905): 23–41.

King, George. *Two Tracts: a) Natural and Political Observations and Conclusions upon the State and Condition on England b) Of the naval Trade in England Anno 1688 and the National Profit Then Arising Thereby.* Edited by George E. Barnett. London, 1698; reprint, Baltimore: John Hopkins Press, 1936.

Kirk, Robert. *Memoirs and Adventures of Robert Kirk: Late of the Royal Highland Regiment.* Edited by Ian McCullough and Jim J. Todish. Limerick: 1775; reprint, London: Osprey, 2004.

Kirkwood, Captain Robert. "Journal and Order Book of the Delaware Regiment of the Continental Line." *Papers of the Historical Society of Delaware* 6 (1910): 4–277.

Lacey, John. "Memoirs of Brigadier-General John Lacey of Pennsylvania." *Pennsylvania Magazine of History and Biography* 25, 26 (1901–2): 1–13, 191–207, 341–54, 498–515, 101–11, 265–70.

Laurens, Henry. *The Papers of Henry Laurens.* 14 vols. Edited by George C. Rogers, et al. Columbia: University of South Carolina Press, 1985.

Lewis, General Andrew. *The Orderly Book of that Portion of the Army Stationed Near Williamsburg, Virginia, March 18, 1776–August 28, 1776.* Richmond: Privately published, 1860.

Lidenius, John Abraham. *The Lawfulness of Defensive War: A Sermon Preached before the Members of the Church at Chiechester in the County of Chester . . . , February 14, 1756.* Philadelphia: James Chattin, 1756.

Locke, John. *Some Thoughts concerning Education.* London: A. and J. Churchill, 1693.

Loring, James Spear. *The Hundred Boston Orators Appointed by the Municipal Authorities and other Public Bodies from 1770 to 1852.* Boston: John P. Jewett, 1858.

Madison, James. "Notes on the Constitutional Convention" (June 22, 1787), http://www.avalon.law.yale.edu. December 8, 2012.

Mather, Cotton. "Diary of Cotton Mather." *Massachusetts Historical Society Collections* 7 and 8 (1911 and 1912).

Markham, Gervase. "The Muster Master, ca. 1630." In *Camden Miscellany*, edited by Charles L. Hamilton, 4th Ser. 26 (1975).

Markham, Francis. *Five Decades of Epistles of Warre.* London: Augustine Matthews, 1622.

McGhee, Lucy Kate. *Abstracts of Pension Papers Pertaining to Soldiers of the Indian, Revolutionary and 1812 Wars, Who Settled the Counties of Whitley and Hart—KY*. Washington, DC: Privately published, undated, ca. 1957.

———. *Logan County Kentucky Abstracts of Revolutionary War, War of 1812 and Indian Wars—Russellville*. Washington, DC: Privately published, ca. 1956.

———. *Records of Abstracts of Pension Papers of Soldiers of the Revolutionary and 1812 War, and Indian Wars who settled in Allen and Adair County Kentucky*. Washington, DC: Privately published, ca 1957.

"Militia Act 1792." *Second Congress, Session 1*. http://www.constitution.org/mil/mil_act_1792.htm. December 8, 2012.

Muhlenberg, Henry Melchior. *The Journals of Henry Melchior Muhlenberg*. Edited by Theodore G. Tappert and John W. Doberstein. Camden: Picton Press, 1993.

"A New Liberty Song—To the tune of the 'British Grenadiers.'" Norwich, Conn: Green and Spooner, ca. 1775.

New England Primer. Boston: T. Green, 1727, original ca. 1690.

Nowell, Samuel. *Abraham in Arms, or the First Religious General with His Army Engaging in a War*. Boston: John Foster, 1678.

"Obituary Notices of Pennsylvania Soldiers." Edited by William Summers. *Pennsylvania Magazine of History and Biography* 38 (1914): 443–60.

Occum, Samson. "Short Narrative of My Life." Baker Library Special Collections: Dartmouth College. Reprinted in *The World Turned Upside Down: Indian Voices from Early America*, edited by Colin Calloway, 55–61. New York: Bedford Books, 1994.

Paine, Thomas. *Common Sense: Addressed to the Inhabitants of America*. Philadelphia: R. Bell, 1776.

Painter, Thomas. *Autobiography of Thomas Painter Relating His Experiences During the War of the Revolution*. Privately published, 1910.

Penrose, Maryly B. *Compendium of Early Mohawk Valley Families*. Baltimore: Genealogical Publishing Co., Inc., 1990.

———. *Mohawk Valley in the Revolution: Genealogical Papers and Genealogical Compendium*. Franklin Park: Liberty Bell Associates, 1978.

———. *Mohawk Valley Revolutionary War Pension Abstracts*. Bowie: Heritage Books, 1989.

Perkins, Nathan. *A Sermon Preached to the Soldiers, who went from West Hartford, in Defence of Their Country, delivered June 2, 1775*. Hartford: E. Watson, 1775

Perry, David. "Life of David Perry." *Magazine of History* 35 (1928): 7–137.

Pinckney, Eliza Lucas. *The Letterbook of Eliza Lucas Pinckney, 1739–1762*. Edited by Elise Pinckney. Chapel Hill: University of North Carolina Press, 1972.

Ramsey, David. *History of the Revolution in South Carolina*. Trenton: Isaac Collins, 1785.

Ramsay, Martha Laurens. *Memoirs of the Life of Martha Laurens Ramsay*. Charleston: Samuel Etheridge Jr., 1811.

Rathbun, Jonathan. "Narrative of Jonathan Rathbun." *Magazine of History* 13 (1911): 551–54.

Recruiting Broadsheet for the Continental Army, Philadelphia, s.n., 1776.

The Renowned History of Giles Gingerbread: A Little Boy Who Lived upon Learning. Providence: John Waterman, 1768.

Resolutions, Laws and Ordinances, Relating to the Pay, Half Pay, Commutation of Half Pay, Bounty Lands and Other Promises Made by Congress to the Officers and Soldiers of the American Revolution. Washington, D.C.: Thomas Allen, 1838.

Roberts, Kenneth L., ed. *March to Quebec: Journals of the Members of Arnold's Expedition.* New York: Doubleday, Doran & Company, Inc., 1938: 67–123.

Rousseau, Jean-Jacques. *Emile, or On Education.* Edited and translated by Allan Bloom. Paris, 1762. New York: Basic Books, 1979.

Ruggles, Thomas. *The Usefulness and Expedience of Souldiers as Discovered by Reason and Experience . . . a Sermon Preached to an Artillery Company at Guilford, May 25, 1736.* New London: T. Green, 1737.

Rush, Benjamin. *Letters of Benjamin Rush.* 2 vols. Edited by L. H. Butterfield. Princeton: Princeton University Press, 1951.

———. "Thoughts Upon Female Education, Accommodated to the Present State of Society, Manners, and Government in the United States of America." In *Essays on Education in the Early Republic*, edited by Frederick Rudolph. Cambridge: Belknap Press, 1965: 25–40

Sargent, Walter. "The Massachusetts Rank and File of 1777." In *War and Society in the American Revolution: Mobilization and Home Fronts*, edited by John Resch and Walter Sargent, 42–69. DeKalb: Northern Illinois University Press, 2007.

Seymour, George Dudley. *Documentary Life of Nathan Hale.* New Haven: Privately published, 1941.

Sewall, Samuel. *Diary of Samuel Sewall.* Edited by M. Halsey Thomas. New York: Farrar, Straus, and Giroux, 1973.

Sherman, Sylvia J. *Dubrose Times: Selected Depositions of Maine Revolutionary War Veterans.* Augusta: Maine State Archives, 1975.

Shurtleff, Nathaniel, ed. *The Records of the Governor and Company of the Massachusetts Bay in New England.* Boston: William White, 1853.

Smith, Samuel. *Memoirs of Samuel Smith, a Soldier of the Revolution, 1776–1786.* Stockbridge: Hard Press, 2012.

Smith, Venture. "A Narrative of the Life and Adventures of Venture, a Native of Africa, but Resident above Sixty Years in the United States of America." New London: Privately published, 1798. Reprinted in *Five Black Lives*, edited by Arna Bontemps. Middletown: Wesleyan University Press, 1971.

"Speech of Josiah Quincy, November 21, 1812, 12th Congress, 2nd Speech." *Annals of the Congress of the United States.* Washington: Gales and Seaton, 1853.

"Speech of Laban Wheaton, November 21, 1812, 12th Congress, 2nd Speech." *Annals of the Congress of the United States.* Washington: Gales and Seaton, 1853.

A True Tale of Robin Hood. London: unknown, ca. 1750.

Tileston, John. "Extracts from the Diary of Mr. John Tileston." *NEHGR* 20 (1866): 11.

Thwaites, Reuben Gold, ed. *The Jesuit Relations and Allied Documents.* Cleveland: Burrows Brothers Company, 1896–1901.

The New-Year Verses, of the Printers Lads, who carry about the Pennsylvania Gazette. Philadelphia, 1770.

Tuttle, Timothy. *Sermon Delivered at Fort Griswold, September 6th A.D. 1821.* New London: Clapp and Francis, Printers, 1821.

Walter, Thomas. *Grounds and Rules of Musick Explained, Or an Introduction to the Art of Singing by Note. Fitted to the Meanest Capacities.* Boston: J. Franklin, 1721.

Washington, George. *Papers of George Washington.* Edited by W. W. Abbot. Charlottesville: University of Virginia Press, 1983.

———. *Writings of George Washington.* Edited by Worthington Chauncey Ford. New York: G. P. Putnam's Sons, 1889–93.

Webster, Noah. "On the Education of Youth in America." In *Essays on Education in the Early Republic,* edited by Frederick Rudolph. Boston: I. Thomas and E. Andrews, 1790: 41–78.

Webster, Samuel. *Soldiers, and Others, directed and encouraged when going on a just and important, tho' Difficult Enterprize, against their Enemies, preached March 25, 1756.* Boston: Edes and Gill, 1756.

Weed, Thurlow. *The Autobiography of Thurlow Weed.* Boston: Houghton, Mifflin, 1884.

Weedon, George. *Valley Forge Orderly Book of General George Weedon.* New York: Dodd Mead & Company, 1902.

Welles, Roger. *The Revolutionary War Letters of Captain Roger Welles of Wethersfield and Newington Connecticut With Four Such Letters From Three Newington Soldiers.* Hartford: Privately, 1932.

Willard, Joseph. *The Duty of the Good and Faithful Soldier.* Boston: T. and J. Fleet, 1781.

Winslow, Anna Green. *Diary of Anna Green Winslow: A Boston School Girl of 1771.* Edited by Alice Morse Earle. Boston: Houghton Mifflin, 1900.

Wright, Albert H. *The Sullivan Expedition of 1779: The Regimental Rosters of Men.* Berwyn Heights, Md.: Heritage Books, 2009.

Wright, Andrew. *The American Musical Miscellany: Collections of the Newest and Most Approved Songs Set to Music.* Northampton: Daniel Wright and Co., 1798.

Younglove, Samuel, "Record of Samuel Younglove." In *Revolutionary War Experiences of the Sons of Isaiah Younglove.* Ed. Jacqueline Baker Humphrey. Privately published, 1988.

Zeisberger, David. *David Zeisberger's History of the North American Indians.* Edited by Arthur Butler Hulbert and William Nathaniel Schwarze. Cleveland: Ohio State Archaeological Society, 1910.

———. *The Moravian Mission Diaries of David Zeisberger, 1772–1781.* Edited by Herman Willenreuther and Carol Wessel. University Park: Pennsylvania State University Press, 2005.

Secondary Sources

Abram, Susan. "Real Men: Masculinity, Spirituality, and Community Life in Late Eighteenth-Century Cherokee Warfare." In *New Men: Manliness in Early America,* edited by Thomas A. Foster, 71–91. New York: New York University Press, 2011.

Alter, Robert. *The Pleasures of Reading in an Ideological Age*. New York: Simon and Schuster, 1989.

Amory, Hugh, and David Hall, eds. *A History of the Book in America: Volume 1, The Colonial Book in the Atlantic World*. New York: Cambridge University Press, 2000.

Anderson, Fred. *A People's Army: Massachusetts Soldiers and Society in the Seven Years' War*. Chapel Hill: University of North Carolina Press, 1996.

——. *Crucible of War: The Seven Years' War and the Fate of Empire in British North America, 1754–1766*. New York: Alfred A. Knopf, 2000.

Andrews, Dee. *The Methodists and Revolutionary America, 1760–1800*. Philadelphia: University of Pennsylvania Press, 2000.

——. "Religion in the American Revolution." In *Encyclopedia of the American Revolution: Library of Military History*, edited by Harold E. Selesky, 977–84. Farmington Hills: Gale, 2006.

Auwers, Linda. "Reading the Marks of the Past: Exploring Female Literacy in Colonial Windsor Connecticut." *Historical Methods* 13 (1980): 204–14.

Avery, Gillian. *Behold the Child: American Children and Their Books, 1621–1922*. Baltimore: Johns Hopkins University Press, 1994.

Bailyn, Bernard. *On the Teaching and Writing of History: Responses to a Series of Questions*. Hanover, N.H.: Dartmouth College, Montgomery Endowment, 1994.

Baldino, Thomas, and Kyle Kreider, eds. *Of the People, By the People, For the People: A Documentary Record of Voting Rights and Electoral Reform*. Santa Barbara, Calif.: Greenwood Press, 2010.

Barry, John. *The Great Influenza: The Story of the Deadliest Pandemic in History*. New York: Viking Press, 2004.

Beales, Ross W. "The Child in Seventeenth-Century America." In *American Childhood: A Research Guide and Historical Handbook*, edited by Joseph M. Hawes and N. Ray Hiner, 29. Westport: Greenwood Press, 1985.

——. "The Reverend Ebenezer Parkman's Farm Workers, Westborough, Massachusetts, 1726–82. *Proceedings of the American Antiquarian Society* 99 (1989): 121–49.

Beales, Ross W., and James N. Green. "Libraries and Their Users." In *A History of the Book in America: Volume 1, The Colonial Book in the Atlantic World*, edited by Hugh Amory and David Hall, 399–404. New York: Cambridge University Press, 2000.

Beales, Ross W., and E. Jennifer Monahan. "Literacy and Schoolbooks." In *A History of the Book in America Volume 1, The Colonial Book in the Atlantic World*, edited by Hugh Amory and David Hall, 380–86. New York: Cambridge University Press, 2000.

Bell, Adrian, and Anne Curry, eds. *War and the Soldier in the Fourteenth Century*. Woodbridge: The Boydell Press, 2010.

Bell, J. L. "From Saucy Boys to Sons of Liberty: Politicizing Youth in Pre-Revolutionary Boston." In *Children in Colonial America*, edited by James Marten, 207–16. New York: New York University Press, 2006.

———. "How to Play Tip-Cat." *Boston 1775*, (July 2007), http://boston1775. blogspot.com/2007/07/how-to-play-tip-cat.html. August 12, 2012.

Billings, William. *New Grove Dictionary of Music and Musicians*. New York: Macmillan Publishers, 1980.

Blades, James. *Percussion Instruments and their History*. Boston: Faber & Faber, 1984, orig. 1970.

Blum, Hester. *The View from the Masthead: Maritime Imagination and Antebellum American Sea Narratives*. Chapel Hill: University of North Carolina Press, 2008.

Boatner, Mark. *Encyclopedia of the American Revolution*. Mechanicsburg, Pa.: Stackpole Books, 1974.

Boulware, Tyler. "' We are MEN': Native American and Euroamerican Projections of Masculinity During the Seven Years' War." In *New Men: Manliness in Early America*, edited by Thomas A. Foster, 51–70. New York: New York University Press, 2011.

Bowen, H. V. *War and British Society, 1688–1815*. Cambridge: Cambridge University Press, 1998.

Brereton, J. M. *The British Soldier: A Social History from 1661 to the Present Day*. London: The Bodley Head, 1986.

Brewer, Holly. *By Birth or Consent: Children, Law & the Anglo-American Revolution in Authority*. Chapel Hill: University of North Carolina Press, 2005.

Brigham, William Tyler. *The Tyler Genealogy: The Descendants of Job Tyler of Andover, Massachusetts*. 2 volumes. Tylerville and Plainfield: Privately published, 1912.

"British Traditional Mole Catchers' Register." http://www.britishmolecatchers. co.uk. February 7, 2011.

Brown, Richard D. "Introduction: Farm Labor in Southern New England During the Agricultural-Industrial Transition." *Proceedings of the American Antiquarian Society*. 99 (1989): 113–19.

Brown, Kathleen. *Good Wives, Nasty Wenches, and Anxious Patriarchs: Gender, Race and Power in Colonial Virginia*. Chapel Hill: University of North Carolina Press, 1996.

Broyles, William. *Brothers in Arms: A Veteran Returns to Vietnam in Search of His Enemy and Himself*. New York: Knopf, 1986.

———. "Why Men Love War." *Esquire*, November 1984, 55–65.

Brumwell, Stephen. *Redcoats: The British Soldier and War in the Americas, 1755–1763*. Cambridge: Cambridge University Press, 2006.

Brundage, W. Fitzhugh. "No Deed But Memory." In *Where These Memories Grow: History, Memory, and Southern Identity*, edited by W. Fitzhugh Brundage, 1–28. Chapel Hill: University of North Carolina Press, 2000.

Buechner, Alan Clark. *Yankee Singing Schools and the Golden Age of Choral Music in New England, 1760–1800*. Boston: Boston University for the Dublin Seminar for New England Folklife, 2003.

Buel, Richard, Jr. *Dear Liberty: Connecticut's Mobilization in the Revolutionary War*. Middletown: Wesleyan University Press, 1980.

Burns, Robert. *Selected Poems of Robert Burns*. Edited by George Ogilvie. Edinburgh: W. and R. Chambers, 1962.

Calvert, Karin. *Children in the House: The Material Culture of Early Childhood, 1600–1900*. Boston: Northeastern University Press, 1992.

Camus, Raoul F. "Military Music of Colonial Boston." In *Music in Colonial Massachusetts, 1630–1820, v.1: Music in Public Places, A Conference Held by the Colonial Society of Massachusetts, May 17 and 18, 1973*, edited by Barbara Lambert, 75–104. Boston: Colonial Society of Massachusetts, 1980.

Carlton, Charles. *Going to the Wars: The Experience of the British Civil Wars, 1638–1651*. New York: Routledge, 1992.

Cartledge, Paul. *The Spartans: World of the Warrior—Heroes of Ancient Greece from Utopia to Crisis and Collapse*. New York: Overlook Press, 2003.

Cheney, C. R. *Medieval Texts and Studies*. Oxford: Clarendon Press, 1973.

Childs, John Charles Roger. *Armies and Warfare in Europe 1648–1789*. Teaneck: Holmes and Meier Publishers, 1983.

Chudacoff, Howard P. *Children at Play: An American History*. New York: New York University Press, 2007.

Clodfelter, Michael. *Warfare and Armed Conflicts: A Statistical Reference to Casualty and Other Figures, 1618–1991*. London: McFarland & Company, 1992.

Cline-Cohen, Patricia. "Reckoning with Commerce: Numeracy in Eighteenth-Century America. In *Consumption and the World of Goods*, edited by John Brewer and Roy Porter, 320–34. New York: Routledge, 1993.

Colesworthy, D. C. *John Tileston's School, Boston 1778–1789: 1761–1766, Also his Diary from 1761 to 1766*. Boston: Antiquarian Bookstore, 1887.

Corvisier, Andre. *L'Armée Française de la Fin du XVIIe Siècle au Ministère de Choiseul: Le Soldat*. Paris: Presses Universitaires de France, 1964.

Cox, Caroline. *A Proper Sense of Honor: Service and Sacrifice in George Washington's Army*. Chapel Hill: University of North Carolina Press, 2004.

Crain, Patricia. "Print and Everyday Life in the Eighteenth Century." In *Perspectives on American Book History*, edited by Scott E. Casper, Joanne D. Chaison, and Jeffrey D. Groves, 47–78. Amherst: University of Massachusetts Press, 2002.

Cremin, Lawrence. *American Education: The Colonial Experience, 1607–1783*. New York: Harper Torchbooks, 1970.

Cressy, David. *Literacy and the Social Order: Reading & Writing in Tudor & Stuart England*. New York: Cambridge University Press, 2006.

Curry, Anne. *Agincourt: A New History*. Stroud, England: Tempus Publishing Limited, 2005.

———. "English Armies in the Fifteenth Century." In *Arms, Armies and Fortifications in the Hundred Years War*. Edited By Anne Curry and Michael Hughes, 39–68. Rochester, N.Y.: Boydell Press, 1994.

Davidson, Cathy N. *Revolution and the Word: The Rise of the Novel in America*. New York: Oxford University Press, 1986.

———. *Reading in America: Literature and Social History*. Baltimore: Johns Hopkins University Press, 1989.

Davidson, Philip. *Propaganda and the American Revolution*. New York: W. W. Norton & Company Inc., 1941, reprint, 1969.

Davis, Natalie Zemon. "On the Lame." *American Historical Review* 93 (1988): 572–604.

———. *The Return of Martin Guerre*. Cambridge: Harvard University Press, 1983.

Davis, Richard Beale. *A Colonial Southern Bookshelf: Reading in the Eighteenth Century*. Athens: University of Georgia Press, 1979.

Demos, John. *The Unredeemed Captive: A Family Story From Early America*. New York: Vintage Books, 1994.

Denson, Andrew. "Diversity, Religion, and the North Carolina Regulators." *North Carolina Historical Review* 72 (1995): 30–53.

De Vries, Jan. *The Industrious Revolution: Consumer Behavior and the Household Economy 1650 to the Present*. New York: Cambridge University Press, 2008.

Diptee, Audra Abbe. "Imperial Ideas, Colonial Realities: Enslaved Children in Jamaica, 1775–1834." In *Children in Colonial America*, edited by James Marten, 48–60. New York: New York University Press, 2007.

Ditz, Toby. *Property and Kinship in Early Connecticut, 1750–1820*. Princeton: Princeton University Press, 1986.

"District of Columbia—Race and Hispanic Origin for Selected Large Cities and Other Places: Earliest Census to 1990." *U.S. Census 1830*, http://www. census. gov/population/www/documentation/twps0006/DCtab.pdf. June 17, 2010.

Donagan, Barbara. *War in England, 1642–1649*. Oxford, England: Oxford University Press, 2008.

Duffy, Christopher. *The Army of Frederick the Great*. London: David & Charles, 1974.

———. *The Military Experience in the Age of Reason*. New York: Routledge & Kegan Paul, 1987.

Dye, Ira. "Early American Merchant Seafarers." *Proceedings of the American Philosophical Society* 120 (1976): 331–60.

Eltis, David, and Stanley B. Engerman. "Fluctuations in Sex and Age Ratios in the Transatlantic Slave Trade, 1663–1864." *Economic History Review* 46 (1993): 308–23.

Ervin, Samuel James, Jr. "A Colonial History of Rowan County, North Carolina." *North Carolina Historical Society* 16 (1917). http://www.rootsweb. ancestry.com/~ncrowan/rowanhis.txt. July 2, 2012.

Fann, Willerd R. "On the Infantryman's Age in Eighteenth Century Prussia." *Military Affairs* 41 (1977): 165–70.

Fass, Paula S. "Childhood and Memory." *Journal of the History of Childhood and Youth* 3 (2010): 155–64.

Fass, Paula S., and Mary Ann Mason, eds. *Childhood in America*. New York: New York University Press, 2000.

Fenn, Elizabeth. *Pox Americana: The Great Smallpox Epidemic of 1775–82*. New York: Hill & Wang, 2001.

Finlay, Robert. "The Refashioning of Martin Guerre." *American Historical Review*. 93 (1988): 552–71.

Fliegelman, Jay. *Prodigals and Pilgrims: The American Revolution against Patriarchal Authority, 1750–1800.* New York: Cambridge University Press, 1982.

Frey, Sylvia. *The British Soldier in America: A Social History of Military Life in the Revolutionary Period.* Austin: University of Texas Press, 1981.

———. *Water from the Rock: Black Resistance in a Revolutionary Age.* Princeton: Princeton University Press, 1991.

Furstenberg, François. *In the Name of the Father: Washington's Legacy, Slavery, and the Making of a Nation.* New York: Penguin Press, 2006.

Games, Alison. *Migration and the Origins of the English Atlantic World.* Cambridge: Harvard University Press, 1999.

Gilbert, Arthur N. "Changing Face of British Military Justice, 1757–1783." *Military Affairs* 49 (1985): 80–84.

Glasson, William Henry. *Federal Military Pensions in the United States.* New York: Oxford University Press, 1918.

Goldberg, P. J. P. "What Was a Servant." In *Concepts and Patterns of Service in the Later Middle Ages.* Edited by Anne Curry and Elizabeth Matthew, 1–20. Rochester, N.Y.: Boydell Press, 2000.

Gordon, Alexander, rev. Troy O. Bickham. "Gordon, William (1727/8–1807)." *Oxford Dictionary of National Biography.* New York: Oxford University Press (2004), http:oxforddnb.com/view/article/11088. March 24, 2011.

Graff, Harvey. *Growing Up in America.* Cambridge: Harvard University Press, 1995.

Greene, Evarts, and Virginia Harrington. *American Population before the Federal Census of 1790.* New York: Columbia University Press, 1932.

Greenwood, John. *A Young Patriot in the American Revolution, 1775–1783.* Edited by Isaac J. Greenwood. Tyrone, Pa.: Westvaco, 1981.

Grenby, M. O. *The Child Reader, 1700–1840.* Cambridge: Cambridge University Press, 2011.

Greven, Philip J. *Four Generations: Population, Land, and Family in Colonial Andover, Massachusetts.* Ithaca: Cornell University Press, 1972.

———. "The Self Shaped and Misshaped: The Protestant Temperament Reconsidered." In *Through a Glass Darkly: Reflections on Personal Identity in Early America*, edited by Ronald Hoffman et al., 348–69. Chapel Hill: University of North Carolina Press, 1997.

Grossberg, Michael. *Governing the Hearth: Law and the Family in Nineteenth Century America.* Chapel Hill: University of North Carolina Press, 1985.

Grossman, Dan. *On Killing: The Psychological Cost of Learning to Kill in War and Society.* New York: Little Brown & Company, 1995.

Gunderson, Joan R. *To Be Useful to the World: Women in Revolutionary America, 1740–1790.* New York: Twayne Publishers, 1996.

Hadden, Sally E. *Slave Patrols: Law and Violence in Virginia and the Carolinas.* Cambridge: Harvard University Press, 2001.

Haines, Michael. "Fertility and Mortality in the United States." *Economic History Services*, https://eh.net/encyclopedia/fertility-and-mortality-in-the-united-states. October 24, 2010.

Hall, David D., and Elizabeth Carroll Reilly, "Practices of Reading." In *A History of the Book in America, Volume 1: The Colonial Book in the Atlantic World*, edited by Hugh Amory and David D. Hall, 377–410. New York: Cambridge University Press, 2000.

Hare, John S. "Military Punishments in the War of 1812." *Journal of the American Military Institute* 4 (1940): 225–39.

Hawes, Joseph M., and N. Ray Hiner, eds. *American Childhood: A Research Guide and Historical Handbook*. Westport: Greenwood Press, 1985.

Herndon, Ruth Wallis, and John E. Murray, eds. *Children Bound to Labor: The Pauper Apprentice System in Early America*. Ithaca: Cornell University Press, 2009.

Hemphill, C. Dallett. "Sibling Relations in Early American Childhoods: A Cross Cultural Analysis." In *Childhood in Colonial America*, edited by James Martin, 77–89. New York: New York University Press, 2006.

Hedges, Chris. *War Is a Force That Gives Us Meaning*. New York: Public Affairs, 2002.

Heywood, Colin. *A History of Childhood: Children and Childhood in the West from Medieval to Modern Times*. Walden: Blackwell Publishing, 2001.

Hick, Stephen. "Soldaten gegen Nordamerika: Lebenswelten Braunschweiger Subsidientruppen im amerikanischen Unabhängigkeitkrieg." Ph.D. diss.: Universität Postdam, 2009.

Hickey, Donald R. *The War of 1812: The Forgotten Conflict*. Urbana: University of Illinois, 1989.

Hildebrand, David, Kate Van Winkle Keller, and Robert Keller. "Music of the War of 1812" (November 19, 2012), http://www.1812music.org. December 8, 2012.

Hillard, Reverend E. B. *The Last Men of the Revolution*. Edited by Wendell D. Garrett. Hartford, 1864. Reprint Barre: Barre Publishers, 1968.

Hindle, Steve, and Ruth Wallis Herndon, "Recreating Proper Families in England and North America: Pauper Apprenticeship in Transatlantic Context." In *Children Bound to Labor: The Pauper Apprentice System in Early America*, edited by Ruth Wallis Herndon and John E. Murray: 19–36. Ithaca: Cornell University Press, 2009.

Hodkinson, Stephen. "Was Classical Sparta a Military Society?" In *Sparta & War*, edited by Stephen Hodkinson and Anton Powell, 4–162. Swansea, Wales: The Classical Press at Wales, 2006.

Horton, Gerald. "Exodus from the Mohawk Valley." *Mohawk Valley History* 2 (2005–2006): 73–82.

Houlbrooke, Ralph Anthony. *Death, Religion and the Family in England, 1480–1750*. Oxford: Oxford University Press, 1998.

Houlding, J. A. *Fit for Service: The Training of the British Army, 1715–1795*. Oxford: Clarendon Press, 1981.

Howard, Joshua B. "Things Here Wear a Melancholy Appearance: The American Defeat at Briar Creek." *Georgia Historical Quarterly* 88 (2004): 477–98.

Illick, Joseph. *American Childhoods*. Philadelphia: University of Pennsylvania Press, 2002.

Immel, Andrea, and Michael Witmore, eds. *Childhood and Children's Books in Early Modern Europe, 1550–1800*. New York: Routledge, 2006.

"Instruments of Colonial Williamsburg." http://www.history.org/history/fife&drum/instruments.cfm. February 3, 2011.

Isaac, Rhys. *The Transformation of Virginia, 1740–1790*. Chapel Hill: University of North Carolina Press, 1982.

Isaacman, Allen, and Derek Peterson, "Making the Chikunda: Military Slavery and Ethnicity in Southern Africa, 1750–1900." In *Arming Slaves from Classical Times to the Modern Age*, edited by Christopher R. Brown, and Philip D. Morgan, 95–119. New Haven: Yale University Press, 2006.

Johnson, Peter. *Toy Armies*. New York: Doubleday, 1981.

Joyner, Charles. *Down by the Riverside: A South Carolina Slave Community*. Urbana: University of Illinois Press, 1984.

Kaplan, Sidney, and Emma Nogrady Kaplan. *The Black Presence in the Era of the American Revolution*. Amherst: University of Massachusetts, 1989.

Kars, Marjoleine. *Breaking Loose Together: The Regulator Rebellion in Pre-Revolutionary North Carolina*. Chapel Hill: University of North Carolina Press, 2002.

Kennell, Nigel M. *The Gymnasium of Virtue: Education and Culture in Ancient Sparta*. Chapel Hill: University of North Carolina Press, 1995.

Kett, Joseph. *Rites of Passage: Adolescence in Colonial America, 1790 to the Present*. New York: Basic Books, 1977.

Kettner, James H. *The Development of American Citizenship, 1608–1870*. Chapel Hill: University of North Carolina Press, 1978.

Keyssar, Alexander. *The Right to Vote: The Contested History of the United States*. New York: Basic Books, 2000.

Kiebowicz, Richard B. *News in the Mail: The Press, Post Office, and Public Information, 1700–1860*. New York: Greenwood Press, 1989.

King, Wilma. *Stolen Childhood: Slave Youth in Nineteenth-Century America*. Bloomington: Indiana University Press, 1995.

Krebs, Daniel. "Usable Enemies: German Prisoners of War During the American Revolution, 1776–1783." Unpublished manuscript.

Kropf, C. R. "The Availability of Literature to Eighteenth-Century Georgia Readers," *Georgia Historical Quarterly* 63 (1979): 353–63.

Laslett, Peter. *Family Life and Illicit Love in Earlier Generations: Essays in Historical Sociology*. New York: Cambridge University Press, 1977.

Le Bohec, Yann. *The Imperial Roman Army*. New York: Routledge, 1994.

Lee, Wayne. *Barbarians and Brothers: Anglo-American Warfare, 1500–1865*. New York: Oxford University Press, 2011.

———. *Crowds and Soldiers in Revolutionary North Carolina: The Culture of Violence in Riot and War*. Gainesville: University Press of Florida, 2001.

Lepore, Jill. *Book of Ages: The Life and Opinions of Jane Franklin*. New York: Knopf, 2013.

———. "Literacy and Reading in Puritan New England." In *Perspectives on American Book History: Artifacts and Commentary*, edited by Scott E. Casper, Joanne D. Chaison, and Jeffrey D. Groves, 17–46. Amherst: University of Massachusetts Press, 2002.

Lender, Mark E. "The Social Structure of the New Jersey Brigade: The Continental Line as an American Standing Army." In *The Military in America: From the Colonial Era to the Present*, edited by Peter Karsten, 65–78. New York: The Free Press, 1986.

Lewis, Jan. *The Pursuit of Happiness: Family and Values in Jefferson's Virginia*. New York: Cambridge University Press, 1983.

Levy, Barry. "'Tender Plants': Quaker Farmers and Children in the Delaware Valley, 1681–1735." *Journal of Family History* 3 (1978): 116–35.

———. *Town Born: The Political Economy of New England from its Founding to the Revolution*. Philadelphia: University of Pennsylvania Press, 2009.

Little, Ann. *Abraham in Arms: War and Gender in Colonial New England*. Philadelphia: University of Pennsylvania Press, 2007.

Lockley, Timothy J. "To Train Them to Habits of Industry and Usefulness: Molding the Children of Antebellum Savannah." In *Children Bound to Labor: The Pauper Apprentice System in Early America*, edited by Ruth Wallis Herndon and John E. Murray, 133–48. Ithaca: Cornell University Press, 2009.

Lockridge, Kenneth. *Literacy in Colonial New England: An Enquiry into the Social Context of Literacy in the Early Modern West*. New York: W.W. Norton, 1974.

Lombard, Anne S. *Making Manhood: Growing Up Male in Colonial New England*. Cambridge: Harvard University Press, 2003.

Lynn, John. *Battle: A History of Combat and Culture*. Boulder: Westview Press, 2004.

———. *The Bayonets of the Republic: Motivation and Tactics in the Army of Revolutionary France, 1791–1794*. Urbana: University of Illinois Press, 1984.

MacWethy, Lou D. *The Book of Names Especially Relating to the Early Palatines and the First Settlers in the Mohawk Valley*. Baltimore: Clearfield Company Inc., 1985.

Malcolm, Joyce Lee. *Peter's War: A New England Slave Boy and the American Revolution*. New York: Yale University Press, 2009.

Main, Gloria. "An Inquiry into When and Why Women Learned to Write in Colonial New England." *Journal of Social History* 24 (1991): 579–90.

———. "Gender, Work, and Wages in Colonial New England." *William and Mary Quarterly* 51 (1994): 39–66.

Maldonado-Torres, Nelson. *Against War: Views from the Underside of Modernity*. Durham: Duke University Press, 2008.

Marten, James, ed. *Children in Colonial America*. New York: New York University Press, 2007.

Martin, Joseph Plumb. *Ordinary Courage: The Revolutionary War Adventures of Joseph Plumb Martin*. Edited by James Kirby Martin. St. James: Brandywine Press, 1993.

Martin, Russell L. "Publishing the American Revolution." In *Perspectives on American Book History*, edited by Scott E. Casper, Joanne D. Chaison, and Jeffrey D. Groves, 79–108. Amherst: University of Massachusetts Press, 2002.

Martin, James Kirby, and Mark Edward Lender. *A Respectable Army: The Military Origins of the Republic, 1763–1789.* New York: Harlan Davidson, Inc., 2006.

Mason, Mary Ann. *From Father's Property to Children's Rights: The History of Child Custody in the United States.* New York: Columbia University Press, 1994.

Mayer, Holly A. *Belonging to the Army: Camp Follower and Community during the American Revolution.* Columbia: University of South Carolina Press, 1999.

———. "Wives, Concubines, and Community: Following the Army." In *War and Society in the American Revolution: Mobilization and Home Fronts,* edited by John Resch and Walter Sargent. DeKalb: Northern Illinois University Press, 2007: 235–62.

McCarthy, Molly. "A Pocket Full of Days: Pocket Diaries, Daily Record Keeping Among Nineteenth-Century New England Women." *New England Quarterly* 73 (2000): 274–96.

McCurdy, John Gilbert. *Citizen Bachelors: Manhood and the Creation of the United States.* Ithaca: Cornell University Press, 2009.

Meyers, Augustus. *Ten Years in the Ranks of the U.S. Army.* New York: The Stirling Press, 1914, New York: Arno Press Reprint, 1979.

Miller, Marla. "Gender, Artisanry, and Craft Tradition in Early New England: The View through the Eye of a Needle." *William & Mary Quarterly* 60 (2003): 743–76.

———. "'My Part Alone': The World of Rebecca Dickinson, 1787–1802." *New England Quarterly* 71 (1998): 341–77.

———. *The Needle's Eye: Work and Woman in the Age of Revolution.* Amherst and Boston: University of Massachusetts Press, 2006.

Millett, Allan R., and Peter Maslowski. *For the Common Defense: A Military History of the United States of America,* Revised Edition. New York: The Free Press, 1994.

Mintz, Steven. *Huck's Raft: History of American Childhood.* Cambridge: Harvard University Press, 2004.

———. "Rise of Democratic Politics, 1820–1860." *Digital History* (2007), http://www.digitalhistory.uh.edu/disp_textbook.cfm?smtID=2&psid=3541. November 18, 2011.

Mintz, Steven, and Susan Kellogg. *Domestic Revolutions: A Social History of American Family Life.* New York: The Free Press, 1988.

"Molecatchers: A Brief History." http://www.the-mole-catcher.co.uk/molecatchers.html. February 7, 2011.

Monaghan, E. Jennifer. "Literacy Instruction and Gender in Colonial New England." In *Reading in America: Literature and Social History,* edited by Cathy N. Davidson, 53–80. Baltimore: Johns Hopkins University Press, 1989.

Monelle, Raymond. *The Musical Topic: Hunt, Military and Pastoral.* Bloomington: Indiana University Press, 2006.

Morgan, David. "The Household Retinue of Henry V and the Ethos of English Public Life." In *Concepts and Patterns of Service in the Later Middle Ages.* Edited by Anne Curry and Elizabeth Matthew, 64–79. Rochester, N.Y.: Boydell Press, 2000.

Morillo, Stephen, Jeremy Black, and Paul Lococo. *War in World History: Science, Technology, and War from Ancient Times to the Present.* New York: McGraw Hill, 2009.

Moss, Bobby Gilmer. *The Patriots at King's Mountain.* Blacksburg, South Carolina: Scotia-Hibernia Press, 1990.

Mott, Frank Luther. *Golden Multitudes: The Story of Best Sellers in the United States.* New York: The Macmillan Company, 1947.

Murray, John E. "Mothers and Children in the Charleston Orphan House." In *Children Bound to Labor: The Pauper Apprentice System in Early America,* edited by Ruth Wallis Herndon and John E. Murray, 102–18. Ithaca: Cornell University Press, 2009.

Neuberg, Victor. "Chapbooks in America: Reconstructing the Popular Reading of Early America." In *Reading in America: Literature and Social History,* edited by Cathy N. Davidson, 81–13. Baltimore: Johns Hopkins University Press, 1989.

Newman, Simon. "Reading the Bodies of Early American Seafarers." *William and Mary Quarterly* 55 (1998): 59–82.

Niemeyer, Charles Patrick. *America Goes to War: A Social History of the Continental Army.* New York: New York University Press, 1996.

Nicholson, Helen. *Medieval Warfare: Theory and Practice of War in Europe, 300–1500.* Gordonsville: Palgrave Macmillan, 2004.

Orme, Nicholas. *Medieval Children.* New Haven: Yale University Press, 2001.

Papenfuse, Edward C., and Gregory A. Stiverson. "General Smallwood's Recruits: The Peacetime Career of the Revolutionary War Private." *William & Mary Quarterly* 30 (1973): 117–32.

Peckham, Howard H. *The Toll of Independence: Engagements & Battle Casualties of the American Revolution.* Chicago: University of Chicago Press, 1974.

"Paul Revere: A Brief Biography." *The Paul Revere House,* http://paulreverehouse.org/bio/father.html. October 26, 2010.

Plumb, J. H. *The Death of the Past.* New York: Houghton Mifflin, 1970.

Purcell, Sarah J. *Sealed with Blood: War, Sacrifice, and Memory in Revolutionary America.* Philadelphia: University of Pennsylvania Press, 2010.

Quarles, Benjamin. *The Negro in the American Revolution.* Chapel Hill: University of North Carolina Press, 1961.

Rediker, Marcus. *Between the Devil and the Deep Blue Sea: Merchant Seamen, Pirates, and the Anglo-American Maritime World, 1700–1750.* New York: Cambridge University Press, 1987.

Rees, John U. "'The Music of the Army': An Abbreviated Study of the Ages of Musicians in the Continental Army." *The Brigade Dispatch* 24 (1993): 2–12.

Reinier, Jacqueline. *From Virtue to Character: American Childhood 1775–1850.* New York: Twayne Publishers, 1996.

Resch, John. "The Revolution as a People's War: Mobilization in New Hampshire." In *War and Society in the American Revolution,* edited by John Resch and Walter Sargent, 70–102. DeKalb: Northern Illinois University Press, 2007.

———. *Suffering Soldiers: Revolutionary War Veterans, Moral Sentiment, and Political Culture in the Early Republic.* Amherst: University of Massachusetts Press, 1999.

Richter, Daniel. *Ordeal of the Longhouse: The Peoples of the Iroquois League in the Era of European Colonization.* Chapel Hill: University of North Carolina Press, 1992.

Rockman, Seth. *Scraping By: Wage Labor, Slavery, and Survival in Early Baltimore.* Baltimore: Johns Hopkins University Press, 2009.

Rorabaugh, W. J. *The Craft Apprentice: From Franklin to the Machine Age in America.* New York: Oxford University Press, 1986.

Rosenbach, A. S. W. *Early American Children's Books, with Bibliographical Descriptions of the Books in his Private Collection.* Portland: The Southward Press, 1933.

Rothman, David J. *The Discovery of the Asylum: Social Order and Disorder in the New Republic.* Boston: Little Brown and Company, 1971.

Royster, Charles. *A Revolutionary People at War: The Continental Army and American Character, 1775–1783.* Chapel Hill: University of North Carolina Press, 1996.

Rudolph, Frederick, ed. *Essays on Education in the Early Republic.* Cambridge: Belknap Press, 1965.

Russo, Jean B., and J. Elliott Russo, "Responsive Justice: Court Treatment for Orphans and Illegitimate Children in Colonial Maryland." In *Children Bound to Labor: The Pauper Apprentice System in Early America,* edited by Ruth Wallis Herndon and John E. Murray, 151–65. Ithaca: Cornell University Press, 2009.

Sargent, Walter. "The Massachusetts Rank and File of 1777." In *War and Society in the American Revolution: Mobilization and Home Fronts,* edited by John Resch and Walter Sargent, 42–69. DeKalb: Northern Illinois University Press, 2006.

Schmidt, James D. *Industrial Violence and the Legal Origins of Child Labor.* New York: Cambridge University Press, 2010.

Schrader, Arthur F. "Songs to Cultivate the Sensations of Freedom." In *Music in Colonial Massachusetts, 1630–1820: A Conference held by the Colonial Society of Massachusetts,* 105–56. Boston: The Society, distributed by the University Press of Virginia, 1980.

Schulz, Constance B. "Children and Childhood in the Eighteenth Century." In *American Childhood: A Research Guide and Historical Handbook,* edited by Joseph M. Hawes and N. Ray Hiner, 57–110. Westport: Greenwood Press, 1985.

———. "Daughters of Liberty: The History of Women in the Revolutionary War Pension Records." *Prologue* 16 (1984): 139–53.

———. "The Revolutionary War Pension Applications: A Neglected Source for Social and Family History," *Prologue* v.15 (1983), 104–11.

Schwoerer, Lois G. *"No Standing Armies!" The Antiarmy Ideology in Seventeenth-Century England.* Baltimore: Johns Hopkins University Press, 1974.

Scott, Samuel F. *The Response of the Royal Army to the French Revolution: The Role and Development of the Line Army, 1787–1793.* Oxford: Clarendon Press, 1978.

Selesky, Harold E. *War and Society in Colonial Connecticut.* New Haven: Yale University Press, 1990.

———, ed. *Encyclopedia of the American Revolution: Library of Military History.* Detroit: Charles Scribner's Sons, 2006.

"Shaker Heritage Society of Albany, New York." http://www.shakerheritage.org. October 17, 2012.

Shammas, Carole. "Child Labor and Schooling in Late Eighteenth-Century New England: One Boy's Account." *William and Mary Quarterly* 3rd Ser. 70 (2013): 539–58.

Shoemaker, Nancy. "An Alliance between Men: Gender Metaphors in Eighteenth-Century American Indian Diplomacy East of the Mississippi." *Ethnohistory* 46 (1999): 239–63.

Shy, John. "New Look at Colonial Militia." *William and Mary Quarterly* 20 (1963): 175–85.

Skallerup, Harry R. *Books Afloat & Ashore: A History of Books, Libraries, and Reading among Seamen during the Age of Sail.* Hamden: Archon Books, 1974.

Smallwood, Stephanie E. *Saltwater Slavery: A Middle Passage From Africa to American Diaspora.* Cambridge: Harvard University Press, 2007.

Smith, Daniel Blake. *Inside the Great House, Planter Family Life in Eighteenth-Century Chesapeake Society.* Ithaca: Cornell University Press, 1980.

———. "Mortality and Family in the Colonial Chesapeake." *Journal of Interdisciplinary History* 8 (1978): 403–27.

Smith, Steven R. "Almost Revolutionaries: The London Apprentices during the Civil Wars." *Huntington Library Quarterly* 42 (1979): 313–28.

Southern, Pat. *The Roman Army: A Social and Institutional History.* Santa Barbara: ABC-Clio, 2006.

Spence, Jonathan. *The Death of Woman Wang.* New York: Penguin Books, 1978.

Stagg, J. C. A. "Enlisted Men in the United States Army, 1812–1815: A Preliminary Survey." *William and Mary Quarterly* 43 (1986): 615–45.

———. "Soldiers in Peace and War: Comparative Perspectives on the Recruitment of the U.S. Army, 1802–1815." *William and Mary Quarterly* 57 (2000): 79–120.

Stannard, David. "Death and the Puritan Child." *American Quarterly* 26 (1974): 456–76.

Sundue, Sharon Braslaw. "Class Stratification and Children's Work in Post-Revolutionary Urban America." In *Class Matters: Early North America and the Atlantic World,* edited by Billy G. Smith and Simon Middleton, 198–212. Philadelphia: University of Pennsylvania Press, 2008.

———. *Industrious in Their Stations: Young People at Work in Urban America, 1720–1810.* Charlottesville: University of Virginia Press, 2009.

Szasz, Margaret Connell. *Indian Education in the American Colonies, 1607–1783.* Albuquerque: University of New Mexico Press, 1988.

"The Instruments." *Colonial Williamsburg,* http://www.history.org/history/fife&drum/instruments.cfm. February 3, 2011.

Thelen, David. "Memory and American History." *Journal of American History* 75 (1989): 117–29.

Thornton, John. "Armed Slaves and Political Authority in Africa in the Era of the Slave Trade, 1450–1800." In *Arming Slaves from Classical Times to the Modern Age,* edited by Christopher R. Brown and Philip D. Morgan, 79–94. New Haven: Yale University Press, 2006.

Thornton, Tamara Plakins. *Handwriting in America: A Cultural History.* New Haven: Yale University Press, 1996.

Titus, James. *The Old Dominion at War: Society, Politics and Warfare in Late Colonial Virginia*. Columbia: University of Southern Carolina Press, 1991.

Trigger, Bruce. *Children of Aataentsic: A History of the Huron People to 1660*. Montreal: McGill University Press, 1987.

Tully, Alan. "Literacy Levels and Educational Development in Rural Pennsylvania, 1729–1775." *Pennsylvania History* 39 (1972): 301–12.

Ulrich, Laurel. *A Midwife's Tale: The Life of Martha Ballard Based on Her Diary, 1785–1812*. New York: Vintage Books, 1991.

Van Buskirk, Judith. "Claiming their Due: African Americans in the Revolutionary War and Its Aftermath." In *War and Society in the American Revolution: Mobilization and Home Fronts*, edited by John Resch and Walter Sargent, 132–60. DeKalb: Northern Illinois University Press, 2007.

Vickers, Daniel. *Farmers and Fishermen: Two Centuries of Work in Essex County, Massachusetts, 1630–1850*. Chapel Hill: University of North Carolina Press, 1994.

Volk, Anthony. "The Evolution of Childhood." *Journal of the History of Children and Youth* 4 (2011): 470–94.

Waldstreicher, David. *In the Midst of Perpetual Fetes: The Making of American Nationalism, 1776–1820*. Chapel Hill: University of North Carolina Press, 1997.

Walsh, Vince. "Young Men and the Sea: The Sociology of Seafaring in Eighteenth-Century Salem, Massachusetts." *Social History* 24 (1999): 17–38.

Way, Peter. "Rebellion of the Regulars: Working Soldiers and the Mutiny of 1763–1764," *William and Mary Quarterly* 57 (2000): 761–92.

Weikle-Mills, Courtney. *Imaginary Citizens: Child Readers and the Limits of American Independence, 1640–1868*. Baltimore: Johns Hopkins University Press, 2013.

Wells, Robert V. *The Population of the British Colonies in North America Before 1776: A Survey of Census Data*. Princeton: Princeton University Press, 1975.

Williams, Julie Hedgepeth. *The Significance of the Printed Word in Early America: Colonists' Thoughts on the Role of the Press*. Westport: Greenwood Press, 1999.

Wilson, Lisa. *Ye Heart of a Man: The Domestic Life of Men in Colonial New England*. New Haven: Yale University Press, 1999.

Winch, Julia. *A Gentleman of Color: The Life of James Forten*. New York: Oxford University Press, 2002.

Wonderley, Anthony. "The Burning of Oneida Castle (1780) and the Oneida Veterans Treaty (1795)." *Mohawk Valley History* 2 (2005): 7–23.

———. "1777: The Revolutionary War Comes to Oneida Country." *Mohawk Valley History* 1 (2004): 15–48.

Wrigley, E. A., and R. S. Schofield. *The Population History of England, 1541–1871: A Reconstruction*. London: Edward Arnold, 1981.

Young, Alfred F. *Masquerade: The Life and Times of Deborah Sampson, Continental Soldier*. New York: Alfred Knopf, 2004.

———. *The Shoemaker and the Tea Party: Memory and the American Revolution*. Boston: Beacon Press, 1999.

Index